Lean Mobile App Devel

Apply Lean startup methodologies to develop successful iOS and Android apps

Mike van Drongelen
Adam Dennis
Richard Garabedian
Alberto Gonzalez
Aravind Krishnaswamy

BIRMINGHAM - MUMBAI

Lean Mobile App Development

First published: November 2017

Production reference: 1241117

Published by Packt Publishing Ltd.
Livery Place
35 Livery Street
Birmingham
B3 2PB, UK.
ISBN 978-1-78646-704-1

www.packtpub.com

Credits

Authors
Mike van Drongelen
Adam Dennis
Richard Garabedian
Alberto Gonzalez
Aravind Krishnaswamy

Reviewer
Thiyagarajan Maruthavanan

Commissioning Editor
Wilson D'souza

Acquisition Editor
Rahul Nair

Content Development Editor
Trusha Shriyan

Technical Editor
Sneha Hanchate

Copy Editor
Laxmi Subramanian

Project Coordinator
Kinjal Bari

Proofreader
Safis Editing

Indexer
Aishwarya Gangawane

Graphics
Kirk D'Penha

Production Coordinator
Melwyn Dsa

About the Authors

Mike van Drongelen works as a mobile solution consultant in the Netherlands. He develops Android, iOS, and .NET solutions for various customers and has some start-up projects of his own. Creating successful software using less code is what he is aiming for. He thinks developing software is fun, but waste is not. Too often, the business guys do not fully understand the tech guys and the other way around. This, among other insights, explains why he is interested in the lean start-up methodology and why he thinks it is important to apply it to mobile application development too. When he is not developing apps, he likes to go on trips on his motorbike or with his 2 CV.

Adam Dennis is a seasoned unicorn who has run political campaigns, created tech training centers for at-risk youth, and founded and sold a successful SaaS. Adam, as VP of Product Development, now runs more than 10 software teams for Dominion Dealer Solutions, an enterprise SaaS serving US autodealers. Adam promotes team excellence, fact-driven decision-making, and failing fast. At Dominion, Adam integrated lean / agile methods and coding best practices into all his teams. Adam lives on the island of Antigua. When offline, Adam etches glass and enjoys life with his wife and daughters.

Richard Garabedian has spent more than 20 years developing software for businesses ranging from defense contractors to small internet start-ups. He currently works for Dominion Dealer Solutions as the Director of Development for mobile and two desktop applications. Rich loves the Java programming language and is an avid Android user. He also pulls his own espresso shots and, according to his wife, spends too many hours video gaming. Outside of work, Rich is either competitive cycling or chasing after his three amazing daughters.

Alberto Gonzalez has spent his career providing creative leadership and delivering premium digital design for a wide array of clients that span from small businesses / agencies to some of the largest digital media companies worldwide. He has over 20 years of experience leading teams in award winning digital product design and marketing efforts. He currently serves as the Director of User Experience for Dominion Dealer Solutions, an enterprise SaaS serving autodealers and OEMs in the US.

Aravind Krishnaswamy is an entrepreneur and tech executive. He lives in Bangalore, India, with his wife, Monami, and his dog. He's passionate about all things cloud, mobile, and social. He cofounded Levitum and is fortunate to work with a wonderful set of friends. In the past, he lived and worked in Silicon Valley, where he was a part of one IPO and exit. He also holds a patent for work done during his MS research at Iowa State University. In his spare time, he enjoys playing tennis, writing, and travelling with his talented wife and dog. He's also a frequent public speaker at a number of product and tech conferences.

www.PacktPub.com

For support files and downloads related to your book, please visit www.PacktPub.com. Did you know that Packt offers eBook versions of every book published, with PDF and ePub files available? You can upgrade to the eBook version at www.PacktPub.comand as a print book customer, you are entitled to a discount on the eBook copy. Get in touch with us at service@packtpub.com for more details. At www.PacktPub.com, you can also read a collection of free technical articles, sign up for a range of free newsletters and receive exclusive discounts and offers on Packt books and eBooks.

https://www.packtpub.com/mapt

Get the most in-demand software skills with Mapt. Mapt gives you full access to all Packt books and video courses, as well as industry-leading tools to help you plan your personal development and advance your career.

Why subscribe?

- Fully searchable across every book published by Packt
- Copy and paste, print, and bookmark content
- On demand and accessible via a web browser

Customer Feedback

Thanks for purchasing this Packt book. At Packt, quality is at the heart of our editorial process. To help us improve, please leave us an honest review on this book's Amazon page at `https://www.amazon.com/dp/1786467046`. If you'd like to join our team of regular reviewers, you can email us at `customerreviews@packtpub.com`. We award our regular reviewers with free eBooks and videos in exchange for their valuable feedback. Help us be relentless in improving our products!

Table of Contents

Preface   1

Chapter 1: Yes, There Is an App for That   9

  The app ecosystem   10

    Not every app has a flappy ending   11

  An introduction to the Lean Startup methodology   11

  Getting your users hooked on your app   14

  Summary   18

Chapter 2: Lean Startup Primer   19

  The Business Model Canvas   19

    Key partners   21

    Key activities   21

    Value propositions   21

    Customer relationships   22

    Customer segments   22

    Channels   23

    Cost structure   23

    Revenue stream   24

  Example BMC - mobile marketplace app   24

    Summary of the BMC   25

  Lean Canvas   25

    One metric that matters   26

  Agile development and customer development   27

  The MVP   29

  Summary   30

Chapter 3: Challenges in Applying Lean to Building Mobile Apps   31

  Higher design bar   32

  Apple's App Store submission cycles   32

  Inability to dynamically load libraries   34

  Cross-platform releases   35

  Getting users to download an app   35

    Maintaining app ratings   36

  Summary   38

Chapter 4: An Agile Workflow in a Nutshell   39

An Agile workflow   40
   Kanban   41
   Scrum   41
Epic, Stories, and Tasks   42
   Scrum team   42
   The daily stand-up   44
   Backlog refinement   45
   Definition of Ready   46
   Sprint planning   47
   Definition of Done   47
   Sprint review, planning, and retrospective   47
Tools that you can use   48
Summary   51

Chapter 5: A Pragmatic Approach   53
Timeboxed programming   54
   Concierge service   55
   Is it crappy or perfect?   56
   Release early and often   56
How do you get started with nothing?   57
   The chicken and egg problem   57
   Fake it until you make it   58
   Become an expert   59
   Grab and adapt   59
   Offer an app or a service that does not yet exist   61
How to keep things well structured   62
   Design patterns   62
   Become independent   63
   Data layer   64
Are there any shortcuts?   65
Mash-up   66
Summary   66

Chapter 6: MVP is Always More Minimal Than You Think   67
What is MVP?   68
   Benefits of MVP   68
How to define your MVP   69
   Building MVP   69
   Bringing components together to form an MVP   70
   Applying MVP to enterprise   70

Fail fast – validate everything   72
    Apply agile prototyping - eliminate tech debt   72
       Lean UX cycles – the Build-Measure-Learn feedback loop   73
       Advantages of a feedback-focused development model   74
       Phases of the Build-Measure-Learn feedback loop   74
          Phase I - Build   74
          Phase II - Measure   74
          Phase III - Learn   75
10 essential UX testing methods   75
Iterate and evolve - from viable to lovable   76
    Five tips to go from viable to lovable   77
Summary   78

Chapter 7: Minimal Viable Product Case Studies   79
    Fun with Charades - Initial vision   79
       The big ifs   80
          Hypothesis 1   81
          Hypothesis 2   82
          Hypothesis 3   82
          Hypothesis 4   84
          Hypothesis 5   85
       The conundrum   85
          What we did well   86
          What we could have done better   86
       Summary   86

Chapter 8: Cloud Solutions for App Experiments   89
    Do you need to create a backend yourself?   89
       Leverage cloud solutions for app experiments   91
       Things to consider   91
    The story of Parse   92
       Strategic considerations   92
       What services are available as MBaaS?   93
       Technical considerations   95
    Canvapp - an Android MVP app using Firebase   95
    Sign up for Firebase   96
       Layout   99
       Dependencies   99
       Models   100
    Firebase dashboard   110
    Summary   112

Chapter 9: Native, Hybrid, or Cross-Platform   113

Who is your audience?   114
Measure - don't guess or use intuition   115
What are your technical requirements?   116
What are your technical capabilities?   116
Native versus hybrid - the strengths and weaknesses   117
Native apps   118
Hybrid apps   118
Pros and cons of going native   118
The biggest benefits of going native   119
Pros and cons of going hybrid   120
The ugly truth - a little hybrid doesn't hurt when you have clear goals   121
Making the final decision - factors to consider   122
Leveraging cross-platform development tools   123
Adobe PhoneGap   123
Xamarin   124
Appcelerator   124
How to choose the right tool   125
Summary   125
Chapter 10: There Is an API for That!   127
Succeed or fail fast   128
What is in a mash-up solution?   128
Publishing an API   129
Lego or Duplo?   130
APIs versus SDKs   130
Dependency management   130
Android   131
iOS   131
Available APIs   132
An iOS app proving our hypotheses, MoviUber   134
Hypothesis   134
Validating the idea through customer interviews   135
Let's build an app   135
Movie locations   135
Uber   136
IMDB   136
Displaying locations on a map   138
Uber integration   140
Enriching the data   143
Look! No code. Prove your hypotheses with IFTT   144
Recipes, channels, and triggers   145
Summary   149
Chapter 11: Onboarding and Registration   151

What is user onboarding all about? 152
Why does it matter? 153
Pirate metrics (AARRR) 154
Higher conversion 154
How to lower the barrier? 155
Single sign on using a social network like Twitter or Facebook 156
Show us what you have got 158
Phone number sign-up - a great alternative 158
Continuous onboarding - complete the user profile later 159
Tell a story - an example onboarding app 160
Onboarding sign-up when needed 161
Implementation 162
Summary 178

Chapter 12: Do Things That Do Not Scale 179
What we mean by "things that do not scale" 180
Three reasons to do things that do not scale 180
Improved testing and data collection 180
Failure that can be controlled 181
Development of products that are more lovable 181
How to acquire early adopters and establish a small-scale laboratory 182
Focusing on a narrow marketplace 182
Manually recruiting early adopters 183
Perfecting the user experience 183
How to transition from an unscalable MVP to scalable code 184
Focusing on learning with wireframes and prototypes 185
Zeplin 186
InVision 186
UserTesting.com 186
Focusing on scaling and sustainability 187
Writing perfect code versus getting the job done 187
Automation and optimization 188
How to handle technical debt 188
Summary 189

Chapter 13: Play Store and App Store Hacks 191
What is an experiment? 192
A/B testing as a technique for experimentation 192
Why perform split testing? 193
Store listing tests 193
App testing 194
Why do you care? 195

The competition is intense   195
Experiments work   195
Why running experiments with Google Play or App Store is hard   196
Obstacles to testing with store listings   196
Different app listing requirements   196
No standard way to measure results   197
Limited infrastructure for A/B testing   198
Why it is difficult to run parallel experiments   198
Hacks to workaround the challenges   199
Store listing hacks   199
How do users find apps in the first place?   199
Use microtesting to collect data   200
Running app tests   201
Summary   202

Chapter 14: A/B Testing Your App   203
Why do statistics matter?   204
About actionable metrics   205
Acquisition   205
Engagement   206
Conversions and pirate metrics   206
Get to know your audience   208
Split testing can help us to improve our apps   209
Keep the differences between variations subtle   211
Tools for split testing and getting actionable metrics   212
Using Firebase for split testing   213
Summary   222

Chapter 15: Growing Traction and Improving Retention   223
Traction   224
Freemium or premium only?   225
Improving retention   226
Notifications   228
Local notifications   228
Push notifications   229
In-app notifications   229
Services for push notifications   230
Implementation   233
Setup   234
Handling an incoming notification   238
Sending a notification   240

Summary	241
Chapter 16: Scaling Strategies	243
Make it scalable but do not scale it right away	244
A scalable backend	246
Cloud-based storage and processing	247
Seen from a client perspective	249
You should know when you need to scale up or to scale down	251
A real horror story about an app backend that did not scale	252
Captain hindsight to the rescue!	252
To scale up or to refactor? That is the question	253
Auto-scaling	254
Summary	256
Chapter 17: Monetization and Pricing Strategy	257
Monetization strategies	258
Selling or upselling your app	258
Selling a product or service in the real world	259
Offering your app for free and selling your service	260
Advertisements	261
Monetizing your data	263
Pricing strategy	264
Price perception	264
Android or iOS first?	266
In-app purchase product types	266
In-app billing	268
See how in-app purchases can be implemented	268
The case of the Empurror	269
Applying a pricing strategy to your store listing	275
Summary	278
Chapter 18: Continuous Deployment	279
Continuous Deployment = Continuous Integration and Delivery	280
Continuous Integration	280
Continuous Delivery	281
Repository and Git workflow	282
Automated tests	283
An example of a continuous workflow for an Android app	284
Building variants	284
The Gradle way	286
productFlavors	287

sourceSets 288
buildTypes 289
signingConfigs 290
Using TeamCity as build agent 291
Automated deploy and delivery 294
Self hosted 294
HockeyApp or Fabric beta 295
Fastlane, alpha/beta Play Store, and iTunes beta 295
DevOps 297
Summary 298

Chapter 19: Building an Unfair Advantage 299
Introduction - it's not just about your app 299
Digging your moat with intangible assets 300
Protecting your work with IP laws 300
Why you should care - Business-destroying patent trolls 301
How IP laws can protect your app and business 302
How to defend your intellectual property 302
Going on the legal offensive 303
The network effect and platforms 304
The network effect 305
The platform effect 305
Making use of vertical markets 306
Why target vertical markets? 307
How successful companies exploit vertical control 307
Switching costs 308
How to use switching costs to improve user retention 309
How to decrease competitors' switching costs 310
Good customer support 310
The right perspective on customer service 311
A recipe for great customer service 311
How successful companies use customer service to improve profits 312
A look at some great tools to help with customer support 313
The power of a well-developed brand name 315
Reasons to brand yourself 315
How to build your brand 316
Tools to monitor your brand via social media and app stores 316
Building a brand on a budget 317
Branding case studies 318
Summary 319

Chapter 20: The Flyng Case Study   321
That sounds awesome, but what is Flyng?   322
The team   323
   Mitchell Trulli   324
   Daniel Guthrie   324
   Mike van Drongelen   324
   The other contributors   324
The MVP   325
   A distributed team   325
   Flyng's USPs   326
   Growing a user base   326
   The business model   327
      Customer segments   327
      Value propositions   328
      Customer relationships   328
      Channels   328
      Revenue Streams   329
      Key resources   329
      Key activities   329
      Partners   330
      Cost structure   330
      Unfair advantage   331
   Getting feedback   334
      Unvalidated assumptions   334
      A zombie feature   335
      Feedback and actionable metrics   336
      Split testing   338
   Vision   338
   Technical considerations   339
      Parse server hosted at Back4App   340
      Real-time data   340
      The other dependencies   341
      Queries   342
      Complex operations   343
      Push notifications   344
      Crash reports   345
      Releases   346
Summary   347
Appendix: Appendix   349
Reading list and references   349
Index   351

Preface

The lean start-up methodology has become a well-known term in the start-up land. There are many books covering this (and related methodologies) such as The Lean Startup (Eric ries), Running Lean (Ash Maurya), The start-up owner manual (Steve Blank), and The Four steps to the epiphany (Steve Blank).

The lean start-up methodology is, among other things, about reducing waste by gathering feedback earlier. It makes no sense to develop a brilliant app for six months or longer only to find out later that nobody is interested in it.

Your start-up, or even an existing app, needs multiple but short iterations to find out what works and what does not. That raises questions such as: Does your app actually solve a problem worth solving it? And how does the lean start-up methodology come into this?

All the books are currently focused on business-oriented members of your start-up or company. However, a pragmatic approach for the technical-oriented members of a company, with a mobile first strategy, is missing in particular. Theory is cool but a practical approach could help developers to move faster.

This book tries to fill that gap. It explains the elements of the Lean Start Up methodology and elaborates on research and on implementation. In particular, the focus is on things that need to be done from a technical point of view. That makes this book a down-to-earth guide on how to apply the lean start-up methodology to real Android and iOS development. As such, it comes without any mumbo-jumbo. If you want real action and if you want to develop an app that people need and really want to use, then this guide is for you.

What this book covers

Chapter 1, *Yes, There Is an App for That*, contains some important questions to ask yourself, such as: Why are you building the app and for whom? The chapter explains how Lean startup can help.

Chapter 2, *Lean Startup Primer*, explains the business model canvas, what customer development is, and what a Minimum Viable Product (MVP) is.

Chapter 3, *Challenges in Applying Lean to Building Mobile Apps*, elaborates on the market place workflow and the discoverability of your app.

Chapter 4, *An Agile* Workflow *in a Nutshell*, talks about time-boxed programming, trusting on third-party solutions, and how you can make temporary shorts.

Chapter 5, *A Pragmatic Approach*, explains in a pragmatic way what an agile workflow, Kanban, and Scrum is and how you can implement it in your workflow.

Chapter 6, *MVP is Always More Minimal Than You Think*, investigates what features should go into a minimal viable product and how these features can help to prove your hypotheses.

Chapter 7, *Minimal Viable Product Case Studies*, contains some real-world examples of MVP implementations.

Chapter 8, *Cloud Solutions for App Experiments*, talks about your strategy for the backend of your app. What third-party services are available and do you need a backend developer at all?

Chapter 9, *Native, Hybrid, or Cross-Platform*, explains which platform (Android or iOS) to start with and what the possibilities are when you want to do both at once.

Chapter 10, *There Is an API for That!*, inspires you to combine existing data and services. It comes with an example combining movie information, maps and Uber integration. Finally, we will see how you can build an MVP and prove hypotheses using IFTT.

Chapter 11, *Onboarding and Registration*, talks about the onboarding and conversion of your users. It explains how you can lower the barrier and it comes with an Android example for signing up with Twitter or with a phone number.

Chapter 12, *Do Things That Do Not Scale*, instructs you to focus on proving hypotheses instead of focusing on automation. Try to find out what is working and what is not, with minimal amount of effort.

Chapter 13, *Play Store and App Store Hacks*, contains a first introduction to split testing and how you can apply it to the Play Store or App Store.

Chapter 14, *A/B Testing Your App*, tells you why split testing your app is important and how you can set up an A/B test for your app. It comes with an example using Android and the Firebase options Remote Config and Analytics.

Chapter 15, *Growing Traction and Improving Retention*, informs you what traction and retention is, why it matters and what you can do to gain more traction. It also discusses the importance of push notifications in order to increase retention (returning users).

Chapter 16, *Scaling Strategies*, inspires you to think about a scaling strategy. It may sound like a luxury problem, but if your app becomes a success your backend has to scale up. Cloud services have made this process a very easy one. Do not scale yet, but make your solution scalable.

Chapter 17, *Monetization and Pricing Strategy*, talks about the many monetization options for your app. If, for example, you choose for in-app purchases, you also need a good pricing strategy.

Chapter 18, *Continuous Deployment*, discusses a Git workflow and CI/CD tools, such as TeamCity and Jenkins. If you have a good testing strategy these tools can help you delivery often and fast.

Chapter 19, *Building an Unfair Advantage*, makes you think on how to build a 'moat' that makes your business defensible from new upstarts.

Chapter 20, *The* Flyng *Case Study*, talks about a case study of an existing social media app.

Appendix, *Reading List and Web References*, covers a list of a must-read books and websites worth visiting.

What you need for this book

In the first place, this book is to inspire technical-oriented cofounders of start-ups and existing business technical leaders seeking to integrate lead into their development operations. In addition, there are some Android and iOS code samples that we discuss to explain some of the concepts. Although the concept is more important than the code, you can try the sample for yourself. Where applicable, you can find a link to the Github repository, containing the code.

For the Android examples, you need to have **Android Studio 3** (or above) and the Android SDKs installed on your computer. **Android Studio** is available as a free download for Windows, OSX, and other operating systems. The Android examples are written in Kotlin and Java.

The samples for iOS requires **xCode 9** or above (xCode is available on OSX only and you need to have a paid Apple developer's account). The iOS examples are written in Swift 4.

Some examples require a (free) registration at Firebase, Facebook, Fabric, or other services.

Who this book is for

In particular, the audience of this book will be technical cofounders, developers, or CTO's working in a start-up environment. However, if you are a CTO, Development Director, or developer of an existing software company, then this is for you too. Lean, when applied well, helps start-ups and existing copanies equally.

Conventions

In this book, you will find a number of text styles that distinguish between different kinds of information. Here are some examples of these styles and an explanation of their meaning.

All Android and iOS examples and descriptions are based on Android Studio, xCode and various third party services, running on a OSX machine.

Console input is shown as:

```
$ gem install cocoapods
```

A block of code is set as follows:

```
func refresh (sender: AnyObject!) {
...
        let cngQuery = client.queryDataset ("wwmu-gmzc")
        cngQuery.orderAscending ("title").get { res in
            switch res {
            case .Dataset (let data):
                self.data = data
...
        }
    }
Data (XML, JSON or otherwise) is shown as:
<key>UberClientID</key>
    <string>your uber client id</string>
    <key>UberCallbackURI</key>
    <string></string>
    <key>LSApplicationQueriesSchemes</key>
    <array>
        <string>uber</string>
    </array>
```

Where you need to apply your own client ID, API key or API secret it, for example, reads as: your client_id within the code or the data.

New terms and **important words** are shown in bold. Words that you see on the screen, for example, in menus or dialog boxes, appear in the text like this: "Clicking the **Next** button moves you to the next screen."

 Warnings or important notes appear in a box like this.

 Tips and tricks appear like this.

Reader feedback

Feedback from our readers is always welcome. Let us know what you think about this book—what you liked or disliked. Reader feedback is important for us as it helps us develop titles that you will really get the most out of.

To send us general feedback, simply e-mail feedback@packtpub.com, and mention the book's title in the subject of your message.

If there is a topic that you have expertise in and you are interested in either writing or contributing to a book, see our author guide at www.packtpub.com/authors.

Customer support

Now that you are the proud owner of a Packt book, we have a number of things to help you to get the most from your purchase.

Downloading the example code

You can download the example code files for this book from your account at http://www.packtpub.com. If you purchased this book elsewhere, you can visit http://www.packtpub.com/support and register to have the files emailed directly to you. You can download the code files by following these steps:

1. Log in or register to our website using your email address and password.
2. Hover the mouse pointer on the **SUPPORT** tab at the top.
3. Click on **Code Downloads & Errata**.

4. Enter the name of the book in the **Search** box.
5. Select the book for which you're looking to download the code files.
6. Choose from the drop-down menu where you purchased this book from.
7. Click on **Code Download**.

Once the file is downloaded, please make sure that you unzip or extract the folder using the latest version of:

- WinRAR / 7-Zip for Windows
- Zipeg / iZip / UnRarX for Mac
- 7-Zip / PeaZip for Linux

The code bundle for the book is also hosted on GitHub at `https://github.com/PacktPublishing/Lean-Mobile-App-Development`. We also have other code bundles from our rich catalog of books and videos available at `https://github.com/PacktPublishing/`. Check them out!

Downloading the color images of this book

We also provide you with a PDF file that has color images of the screenshots/diagrams used in this book. The color images will help you better understand the changes in the output. You can download this file from `http://www.packtpub.com/sites/default/files/downloads/LeanMobileAppDevelopment_ColorImages.pdf`.

Errata

Although we have taken every care to ensure the accuracy of our content, mistakes do happen. If you find a mistake in one of our books—maybe a mistake in the text or the code—we would be grateful if you could report this to us. By doing so, you can save other readers from frustration and help us improve subsequent versions of this book. If you find any errata, please report them by visiting `http://www.packtpub.com/submit-errata`, selecting your book, clicking on the Errata Submission Form link, and entering the details of your errata. Once your errata are verified, your submission will be accepted and the errata will be uploaded to our website or added to any list of existing errata under the Errata section of that title.

To view the previously submitted errata, go to `https://www.packtpub.com/books/content/support` and enter the name of the book in the search field. The required information will appear under the **Errata** section.

Piracy

Piracy of copyrighted material on the Internet is an ongoing problem across all media. At Packt, we take the protection of our copyright and licenses very seriously. If you come across any illegal copies of our works in any form on the Internet, please provide us with the location address or website name immediately so that we can pursue a remedy.

Please contact us at copyright@packtpub.com with a link to the suspected pirated material.

We appreciate your help in protecting our authors and our ability to bring you valuable content.

Questions

If you have a problem with any aspect of this book, you can contact us at questions@packtpub.com, and we will do our best to address the problem.

1

Yes, There Is an App for That

There is an app for almost everything already, or so it seems. Creating a profitable app is not easy, but if you develop your app in a smart way, your company can be successful too!

This book aims to help you build a profitable business around your mobile app using the the Lean Startup methodology. Unlike many other books, this one is not only for the business-oriented members of your organization. Instead, it is a very practical guide, explaining what tools and techniques can be used to develop apps the Lean way. It is important that technical-oriented people also become enthusiastic about the Lean Startup methodology, which is the reason why this book is primarily aimed at technical co-owners and developers. They need to have the right tools in order to apply the methodology to their daily mobile app development. We will discuss how you can save time and reduce waste by using a number of techniques and tools.

On the other hand, the book will be of interest for nontechnical people too. It would be ideal if they could obtain a better understanding of the underlying technical processes involved in app development. We need the business folks to find and clearly define the problems, so that the technical folks can deliver the right solutions for them. Everyone needs to collaborate closely. If you have a good understanding of each other's perspectives, you can achieve much better results.

 If your startup is missing a technical cofounder, then now is the time to find one. Do not outsource the development (yet). That often does not work well when your startup is at an early stage.

In this chapter of the book, we will first look at the Lean Startup methodology, and learn why it matters to all members of your startup company.

This chapter is about the following topics:

- The app ecosystem
- An introduction to the Lean Startup methodology
- Getting your users hooked on your app

The app ecosystem

We'll first dive into the paradox that the app ecosystem presents--the prospect of fame and fortune, but the obscurity of being lost amongst the millions. We'll also cover critical questions that every intrapreneur or entrepreneur needs to think about before they venture into building a new app. The same principles apply also for new ideas for an existing app. The first things you should ask yourself are:

- Why would users want to use my app?
- For what purpose or when would they actually need it?
- Why would they keep coming back to use it?

Creating a profitable app is hard, but not impossible. There are many well-known examples. One of them is Flappy Bird. In May 2013, an obscure solo app developer living in Vietnam named Nguyen Ha Dong released a game in the iOS App Store. The initial response to the app was muted, with just a few downloads. Several months later in early 2014, the game revived with a surge in popularity, and became the most downloaded game in the App Store at that time.

At the height of its popularity in January 2014, the game was earning $50,000 a day, from in-app advertisements as well as sales. A month later in February 2014, Dong famously pulled the game from the stores. This led to a short, frenzied period when phones with the app installed were being sold at a premium online.

The app is now a much-storied example of a rags-to-riches overnight success story. But whether by serendipity or by design, Dong's success is far from typical. Few solo app developers have succeeded in monetizing their apps.

For every intrapreneur or entrepreneur with shiny, bright, new ideas, the odds are stacked against them. When Steve Jobs famously quipped *There's an app for that*, he really did mean it. There's an app for just about everything! So, why does your bright new idea matter?

Not every app has a flappy ending

If you build it, they will come. Well, that obviously is not true. Just publishing your app in the App Store or Play Store will not be sufficient. On both Google Play and the Apple App Store, 9 out of 10 apps that are published by developers see fewer than 5,000 downloads, ever. There are so many apps already available. How will people ever notice your app?

No matter how good your app is, it will drown in an ocean of apps without a good plan. To succeed, you first need to ask yourself some important questions:

- Who needs your app?
- How will people find out about your app?
- Why would someone download your app?
- Why would they keep coming back to use it?
- How would others hear about the app?
- What stops others from copying your app once it is successful?

Apps that make it to the top of the charts dwarf apps that don't by a large order of magnitude. There's a case to be made about long-tail characteristics in a marketplace. Amazon is known for having said that they make more money selling books that were never stocked earlier than the ones that are. Their marketplace has strong, long-tail characteristics, with several niche books finding an audience.

However, the App Store dynamics don't work well in favor of niche segments. The discoverability of an app continues to be a challenge, making it hard for publishers to succeed in niche categories. Apart from discoverability itself, there's just a little more friction involved in someone having to download an app over just visiting a mobile website.

An introduction to the Lean Startup methodology

Today's mobile world is well past the gold rush frenzy of the late 2000s. Google Play has 1.9 million apps with over 50 billion downloads. Apple's App Store has 1.4 million apps with 100 billion downloads. Most app categories are fairly saturated, and there are free apps for most things. The design of the marketplace incentivizes app developers to drop their prices in order to hit the top of the charts, giving them wide distribution.

Should you be dissuaded by all this? Does this mean that the chances of success are so low, and the field so daunting, that we might as well give up? Far from it! As time has shown, there are always new opportunities. Famously, today's leading companies, such as Google and Facebook, emerged from the dust of the dot com bust of the early 2000s.

But instead of the big bang approach that companies took to building products earlier, we are now equipped with more scientific approaches for taking new ideas to market. And here's where the Lean Startup methodology outlined by Eric Ries has radically changed how several start-ups and large companies develop software.

Lean start-up principles help realize your vision through rapid experimentation. They provide an approach for taking a bright new idea, and first identifying key high-risk assumptions that you are making. These are assumptions whose failure would mean that your idea would fail. The next step is to craft small market experiments to test these assumptions in the field. A successful experiment would validate an assumption, which lets you move on to your next assumption and craft the next experiment. Failure of an experiment would invalidate an assumption, which means that your idea in its current form would fail.

If you are a developer, you may wonder if the Lean Startup methodology is just a bunch of business management speak reserved for stuffy types in dark suits. That would be an unfortunate misconception. Eric Ries attempted to develop an easily understood management principle for entrepreneurship, which was otherwise seen as a mysterious dark art form.

However, Eric's own roots are closer to the developer community than to the busniess community. It was his experiences building software at IMVU that inspired his Lean Startup ideas. He was one of the early pioneers in endorsing continuous development and continuous integration in the software development process. It was an attempt to strip out all the wasteful cycles that developers spend time on, and help them focus on building things that mattered most to their customers.

Experienced developers care about efficiency and writing code that actually has an impact. Compared to other industries, the software industry has numerous examples where millions of lines of code are discarded because they go into building features no one wants. That's a waste of endless hours of developer effort that could be better used building useful software.

The Lean Startup approach is also closely associated with agile software development. Agile development outlines an important cycle for how software is built. This cycle is typically inward, and happens within a software development team between managers, developers, and testers. Lean Startup adds the concept of customer development. Customer development is an outward cycle that happens between the software development team and the customer. The cycle involves working with the customer by running interviews, observing customer behavior, testing with market experiments, and collating the results.

If you are a developer in an organization with a top-down culture, where suits with hand-waving skills and mastery with PowerPoint hold sway, Lean Startup can help. Decisions in many organizations still happen based on who has the best PowerPoint presentation and the power of key lobbies to influence decisions. Few things can hurt ground-up innovation in an enterprise more.

Lean Startup provides developers with a framework to influence decisions with real data from customer experiments. If a decision needs to be made, push others at the table to either bring data to justify it, or to run an experiment to collect it. This is critical.

Agile development has been embraced by most organizations over the last decade, with Scrum and extreme programming becoming commonplace. In the coming years, knowledge of Lean Startup will be a valuable asset for developers looking to enhance their skills.

Lean Startup isn't a defined hard and fast process set in stone. It's a set of principles to help chart your way through unknown territory. In the wild, a compass and a map are tools that enable hikers to navigate and avoid dangerous pitfalls that potentially be fatal. Much like a compass and a map, Lean provides a framework to navigate through new discoveries. These discoveries enable you to make crucial decisions about what steps to take next and in which direction.

A Lean approach is no guarantee of a next Flappy Bird. But think about it this way: we're still in an age where taking new ideas from concept to market is still serendipitous. This is much like how fire was discovered and how the wheel was invented, likely as much by chance and gradual evolution than deliberate choices. It took us centuries before science got us to the point where we developed systematic ways of running laboratory experiments. Despite that, it took legendary inventor Thomas Alva Edison hundreds of failed experiments before he invented the light bulb.

"Genius is 99% perspiration and 1% inspiration."

- Edison

What science did do, though, was accelerate the process. Serendipity took centuries. The last century has seen the acceleration of new discoveries and significant scientific advancements. Experiments still fail, and research projects that are pursued for years are often abandoned. But today, the chances of a laboratory scientist's success are significantly higher than that of a caveman in the wild.

Lean Startup has changed how we understand customer needs, and how we build products to meet those needs. Our chances of success are so much higher than they were for a software developer even just a decade ago. How can this methodology help developers do things using the right tools at the right time? The answer is in this book. It is aimed at technical cofounders and other developers involved with a startup company. It can help you learn how to apply the Lean Startup methodology to mobile app development specifically. It will give you insights on how to balance between a pragmatic and hands-on approach while still doing things the right way.

One of the key elements is early validation. Whether you are a solution or problem-oriented person, you have certain assumptions. These assumptions may be right, but most likely they will be wrong. The only way to find the answer is by creating an app, or a simulated app, that you can build very quickly and that you can use to gather feedback. Such a solution is known as the **Minimal Viable Product** (**MVP**). An MVP contains only the functionality that you need to have to prove your hypotheses. Everything else in the app that cannot contribute to gathering feedback is waste and should not be there.

For a business guy, the idea of an MVP may sound odd. You only have one chance for a first impression, right? Also, as a developer you do not want to write a bunch of code only to throw it away later. So what exactly should be in an MVP? A more in-depth explanation of an MVP will follow in `Chapter 5`, *A Pragmatic Approach*.

Getting your users hooked on your app

Not only do 9 out of 10 apps see fewer than 5,000 downloads, also 9 out of 10 apps are not launched more than once. You can do the math. Right there, you can see that the chances of having an app that's regularly used by more than 5,000 people dropped to 0.01, or 1 in a 100.

There are a number of reasons why this happens. Some users install an app they hear about, but don't like it and may choose to uninstall it right away. If they've liked the app, they may keep it. While this may sound like a win, it's not always the case. Often, users just forget about the app and may not think about launching it again, even if it fulfils a need that they have.

You may have built a fabulous app that helps the user save money through budgeting, but unless the user remembers to launch the app regularly and track her finances, it will not help her. In `Chapter 15`, *Growing Traction and Improving Retention,* which discusses traction and retention, we will see some practical implementations to get the attention of the user. For example, sending (relevant) push notifications is often an effective method to draw the user's attention back to the app.

Frequent usage creates more opportunities to encourage people to invite their friends, broadcast content, and share through word of mouth.

Let's take one step back and focus on the question, *How will people find out about the app?* Unless it gets featured (by Apple, for example), or unless it gets discovered by accident (as happened to Flappy Bird), you need to promote it actively. You can consider Google ads, flyers, and commercials. That can become pretty expensive. However, if you can let it grow organically, the results will probably be way better, and it will cost you less. For example, people might hear on Twitter and other social media platforms how great your app is. To make that happen, people first need to become enthusiastic and regular users of your app before they share it with their friends or business colleagues.

Users who continuously find value in a product are more likely to tell their friends about it.

Some products capture widespread attention. Nir Eyal describes in his book *Hooked* what makes us engage with certain products out of sheer habit. For example, Pokémon Go!, Facebook, or Instagram are all very addictive apps. People hear about the app, download it, and keep using it, on a daily basis even. Why is that? It seems there is an underlying pattern to the way technology hooks us. Nir Eyal provides answers to this and other questions by introducing the Hook Model. It is a four-step process that is embedded into the products of many successful companies to subtly encourage customer behavior.

Hooked users become brand evangelists-megaphones for your company.

Nir Eyal's classic Hooked Model contains four steps:

- Trigger
- Action
- Reward
- Investment

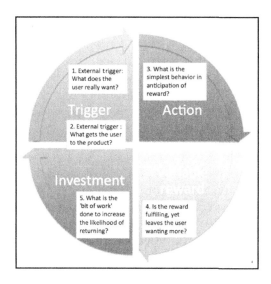

In a nutshell, this is what you see in this model: The trigger is what brings the user to a product to take an action that results in a reward that's followed by further investment.

At the action step, the user will be asked to perform a simple action that will boost the user's motivation. This phase of the hook draws upon the art and science of usability design, to ensure that the user acts the way the designer intends.

Offering variable and unpredicatable rewards are important tools to hook users. There are many feedback loops already, but they are all predictable. Predictable loops do not create any desire. We should surprise the user and create a desire in the user. Gamification is an example of a tool to accomplish this. We can reward the user with a badge or other digital (or non digital) incentive.

The last phase of the hook is where we will ask the user to do something in return. We do not just want to increase the odds that the user will make another pass through the hook. Besides encouraging the user to continue (unlock a new level and get another badge!), we can ask the user for a rating of the app in the App Store or we can ask the user to share content of the app on social media (challenge a friend!).

If we apply the model to another well-known game, Pokémon Go!, then the model will look like this: The user gets a notification and a pokemon is shown on the screen (Trigger). The user is bored or is looking for fun and wants to play (Action). The user is rewarded with a (special) Pokemon (Variable reward) and continues to play or is asked to share the recent achievement (Investment).

You can apply the model to your app too. What can or will be the addictive features of your app? What can you do to make your users return to your app more frequently? Not only can the process help your app grow, it will also increase the (perceived) value of your company—an investor will be more interested in the number of **monthly active users (MAU)** than in the number of users alone.

To accomplish this, you need to build an app that people really want to use. To find out what people want, you can ask them what they need. That sounds easier than it actually is. Make sure you ask the right questions, and avoid getting only socially desired answers. Also, make sure you listen carefully to what they tell you. Bear in mind that, sometimes, they will have no clue what they want, until they see it. Here's an example of a survey.

When we started to interact with real prospective users, one of the questions that we asked them were as follows:

"Do you like the app?"

Invariably, the answer would be polite:

"Yeah, it's a really cool idea."

"Wow, this karaoke idea is neat."

Initially, we didn't listen hard enough to comments from users:

"You don't have the songs or lessons that I want."

"My teacher's songs aren't on your app."

"How will this help me find a teacher?"

"Who will review my recording?"

If we'd only listened a little harder and asked the right questions, it would have become obvious to us, sooner rather than later, that we were looking at a marketplace that connected students and teachers, with the app as a tool that enabled this. We eventually went down this route and built a platform with several world-famous musicians and teachers. But we would have saved time and resources early on if we'd asked the right questions from the start.

Summary

In this chapter, we have seen that it is important that users become aware of your app. It would be even better if they get hooked to it, hence the introduction to the Hook Model that you have read about. Finally, we have learned how the Lean Startup methodology can help to make better apps.

In the following chapters, we will see what tools and methodologies you can use to shorten the development cycles, and how to reduce waste. In the next chapter, we will look at the business canvas model, where we can outline our assumptions for each element of our business. It can help us to determine our business ideas without the need to write a 100-page business plan that nobody is ever going to read. That sounds like you are going to save time already. How cool is that?

2

Lean Startup Primer

If you've picked up this book without extensive familiarity with concepts of the Lean startup methodology, this chapter will serve as a quick primer to get you started. If you are already familiar with Lean thinking, then this chapter may serve as a breezy refresher.

Here, we will cover a few key concepts that form the foundation of Lean Startup; namely, we will go over:

- The Business Model Canvas
- The Lean Canvas
- Agile development
- Customer development
- The Minimal Viable Product (MVP)

Knowing these concepts will be important for grasping and applying other lessons in this book, and we would encourage you to take the time to understand them thoroughly.

The Business Model Canvas

Every new intrapreneur or entrepreneur with an idea seeks to bring his creation to life and watch it grow over time. Successful growth over time needs sustainability, a key factor for enduring ideas. The most common way of communicating a sustainable proposition for a new idea is the business plan.

A business plan outlines a problem, the opportunity it presents, an approach for solving it, a model for generating revenues, ways for managing costs, and levers for growth over time.

There are two stages to writing a business plan. The first stage is actually writing the plan, and the second is keeping it up to date as your business evolves.

Business plans are often written for pitch or fundraising purposes, then promptly forgotten afterwards. Investor attention would tend to gravitate around targets and the company's performance in the direction of these targets, without paying attention to core aspects of the business. However, a business plan performs many functions throughout the life of your business. It should be treated as a living document, and it should be maintained and updated as your business evolves.

In 2008, Alexander Osterwalder proposed a new format called the **Business Model Canvas** (**BMC**). The BMC is a single-page document that lets you represent all aspects of a business plan:

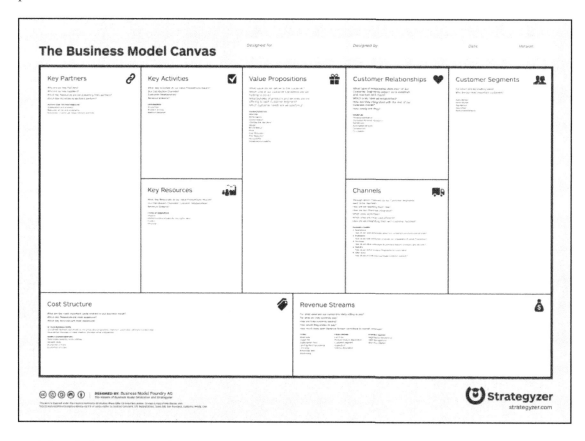

Let's break this down and go through each section of the canvas.

Key partners

Partners are other individuals or businesses that work with you as your business grows.

When filling out this section, consider the following questions:

- Who are our key partners?
- Who are our key suppliers?
- Which key resources are we acquiring from our partners?
- Which key activities do our partners perform?

Partners are important for co-creation and leveraging the scale and reach of others. For instance, a social discovery app may choose to partner with an e-commerce site that enables users to purchase products recommended by others in their social network.

Key activities

All broad activities that are essential for the business should be listed here.

Ask yourself the following questions:

- What key activities does our value proposition require?
- What key activities do our distribution channels require?
- What key activities do our customer relationships require?
- What key activities do our revenue streams require?

These activities may include the ones relevant for production of the mobile app, such as working with app stores, OEMs, and device manufacturers. Include other activities that come to mind, such as collaborating with app reviewers and bloggers, or tracking monetization through freemium, in-app purchases, or referral models.

Value propositions

It is important to clearly identify the problem your app solves, how customers benefit, and which specific emotional or physical needs are being met.

Ask yourself the following questions:

- What value do we deliver to the customer?
- Which one of the customers' problems are we looking to solve?
- Which bundles of products and services are we offering to each customer segment?
- Which customer needs are we satisfying?

To ensure that you develop a customer-centric product, it is critical to identify a unique value proposition for your venture. As we will see in following chapters, though, your initial value proposition--or your *value hypothesis*, as *Eric Ries* puts it--can evolve or even pivot later on, once you begin learning from your experiments.

Customer relationships

Understanding the nature of the interaction helps map out the customer's journey and their touchpoints with the app, so it is useful to think through the entire experience.

Ask yourself the following questions:

- What type of relationship does each of our customer segments expect us to maintain with them?
- Which ones have we established?
- How are they integrated into our business model?
- How costly are they?

Consider that the nature of most utilitarian apps involves a DIY self-service relationship. An app like Uber or Ola involves personal assistance through the taxi driver. Waze enables co-creation and a community aspect to the relationship. Knowing how users use your app will help you create an app that is more usable and more useful.

Customer segments

It's important to be specific about for whom you are making the app. You will need to answer questions such as:

- For whom are we creating value?
- How much do we know about them?
- Who are our most important customers?

Your definition of the target audience may broaden in the long term.

For instance, an Uber-like app may be looking to create value for all commuters seeking instant transportation. As we will explore in later chapters, however, being highly specific makes testing and growth much easier, which are two reasons why it is important to identify your most important customers. In Uber's case, these might be young working professionals (willingness to pay a premium for their time) in the financial district of New York (a city that already has a lot of people using taxis).

Channels

The importance of channels is often under appreciated. It is through channels that users come to know about your app, understand why they must install it, and develop habits that remind them to use it when they need it.

When filling out this section, ask yourself the following questions:

- Through which channels do our customer segments want to be reached?
- How are we reaching them now?
- How are our channels integrated?
- Which ones work best?
- Which ones are the most cost-effective?
- How are we integrating them with customer routines?

We'll discuss channels in further detail later in the book, but these questions will get you off on the right foot.

Cost structure

The cost structure refers to business expenses, such as salaries, resources, and infrastructure. Consider the following questions:

- What are the most important costs inherent in our business model?
- Which key resources are the most expensive?
- Which key activities are the most expensive?

For software companies, the primary driver of costs is employee salaries. In some cases, infrastructure costs can be high, and may be an important factor to consider. If your product involves hardware, like an IoT device, the cost structures are likely to be significantly more complex. Choosing between iOS, Android, and other mobile platforms may be a factor while considering costs of developers as well.

Revenue stream

Viability and sustainability are fundamental questions for every business, and your mobile app is no different. Figuring out what your revenue model is and understanding how you will monetize your hard work is often a tricky piece of the puzzle.

Ask yourself the following questions:

- For what value are our customers really willing to pay?
- For what do they currently pay?
- How are they currently paying?
- How would they prefer to pay?
- How much does each revenue stream contribute to overall revenues?

Some apps have succeeded to thrive just on advertising. Others have made it big through freemium models or in-app purchases. And finally, there are asset sales, which can be just as lucrative as other monetization methods.

Example BMC - mobile marketplace app

Here is a BMC for a mobile marketplace app that connects music students and music teachers:

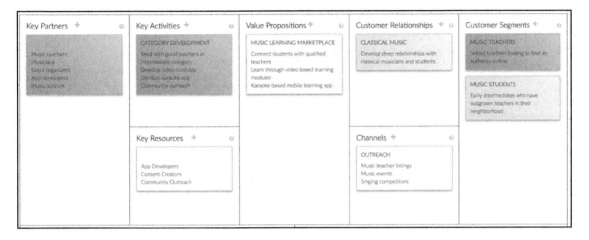

This graphic is just one example of how you can use the BMC to develop a business plan. Many more are available online.

Summary of the BMC

A business plan is an excellent way to clarify your ideas, present these ideas to potential investors or stakeholders, and establish business guidelines to help you on your journey.

However, some people have a polarized reaction to the BMC. They either love it and find it to be a vastly simpler version of a business plan, or they hate it and think of it as a complex theoretical abstraction that makes for a great workshop exercise, but not a practical tool.

It turns out that there's an interesting variant of the BMC that most people take to with greater ease. We will look at that variant next.

Lean Canvas

In 2009, Ash Maurya proposed the Lean Canvas. The Lean Canvas was inspired by the BMC, and by a variant by Robert Fitzpatrick that incorporated worksheets from Steve Blank's *The Four Steps to Epiphany*.

> *"Most startups fail, not because they fail to build what they set out to build, but because they waste time, money, and effort building the wrong product."*
> - Ash Maurya

Ash Maurya's *n* variant is tailored for entrepreneurs and intrapreneurs testing out a new idea. The Lean Canvas helps you test out the key hypothesis that needs to be validated in order for you to find the product/market fit:

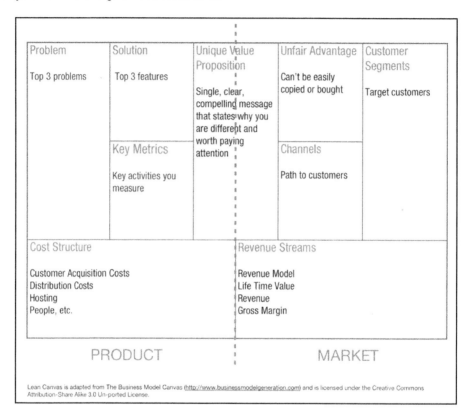

Lean Canvas is adapted from The Business Model Canvas (http://www.businessmodelgeneration.com) and is licensed under the Creative Commons Attribution-Share Alike 3.0 Un-ported License.

One metric that matters

Ben Yoskovitz and Alistair Croll detailed their concept of **One Metric That Matters** (**OMTM**) in their book *Lean Analytics*.

This concept--focusing on one important metric instead of a multitude of metrics--is designed to help entrepreneurs simplify and stay focused. According to the authors, this means that *at any given time, there's one metric you should care about above all else. Communicating this focus to your employees, investors, and even the media will really help you concentrate your efforts.*

This is a powerful metaphor that helps provide organizational clarity around what to focus on. Now, the hard part often is deciding which metric matters. Fortunately, their book covers various examples, depending on criteria such as the stage of the company and the nature of the business, to help serve as a guide for choosing the right metric.

The one change we've made to the preceding diagram is to switch key metrics in the Lean Canvas with OMTM:

BUSINESS PLAN CANVAS

PROBLEM (PH)	SOLUTION (SH)	UNIQUE VALUE PROPOSITION (UH)	DURABLE ADVANTAGE (DH)	CUSTOMER SEGMENTS (CSH)
Top 3 Problems Test Hypothesis: Intensity Frequency Density	Top 3 features + benefits Test Hypothesis Disappointment Survey	Why are you different? Why should people pay attention? Test Hypothesis: Product Fit Competitive Market Conditions	Cant be easily copied, bought or easily attained.	For who are we solving a problem or fulfilling a need? Who are the customers? Is this a single sided or multisided market? Test Hypothesis: Customer Problem Payer User
	ONE METRIC THAT MATTERS		**CHANNELS (CH)**	
	Activities you measure		Ways of finding customers Test Hypothesis: Acquisition channels	

COST STRUCTURE	REVENUE STREAMS
What are the most important costs in our business model? Test Hypothesis: Size of market/opportunity Validate business model	What is the revenue model? What are the pricing tactics? For what value are customers willing to pay? Test Hypothesis: - Pricing Model/Pricing

Agile development and customer development

The core DNA of Lean Startup is a beautiful helix. The two loops of this helix focus on two ideas that lie at the heart of the Lean methodology--agile development and customer development. Tied together, these two approaches enable developers to create products that are truly user-driven.

The outer loop of the helix involves working with the market to discover customer needs and the context in which they emerge, and to test whether possible solutions meet these needs. Originally coined by Steve Blank, this loop is known as **customer development**.

The inner loop involves a rapid iterative software development cycle of understanding needs identified by customer development and developing solutions that meet these needs:

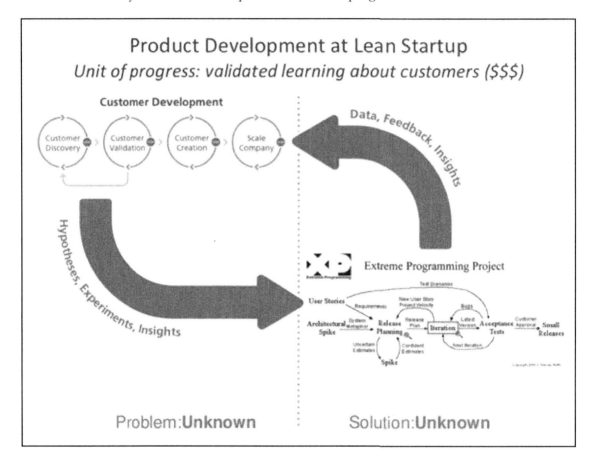

Agile development has matured over the last decade, and Scrum and XP are common today in many organizations. Agile radically changed organizations that were used to building software in large monolith waterfall releases by moving them to an iterative model. This enables teams to work more closely with customers to build software.

Where waterfall models usually expect that the problem definition was fixed, Agile practitioners went in with the assumption that the problem definition may be somewhat fluid. Note that in both cases, the solution is unknown. The engineering team works a close loop to iterate through solution definition, with the understanding that the problem definition may evolve along the way.

While waterfall and Agile both assume some level of definition of the problem, customer development is all about problem discovery. We start with exploring an unknown problem through customer discovery, an open-ended exercise to find unmet needs. This then leads to a rapid cycle of working early and often with customers to validate their needs and then to scale the model.

Applying these ideas in conjunction with one another will allow you to respond to customer feedback, adapt more quickly, and create useful products that customers love. Your very first step in that direction will be an experiment that tests hypotheses about your business plan, your customers, and your app idea.

The MVP

This experiment is called the **Minimum Viable Product** (**MVP**). The MVP is an important concept that is a departure from the traditional big bang approach of building out a polished product and then taking it to the market. It represents the minimal set of features and functionality that would need to be built in a product in order to test market viability and maximize validate learning.

The MVP and its subsequent iterations are initially designed to test two things: whether customers will value your product, and how easily your product will expand.

Of course, the hard part often is deciding how minimal you need to be. The initial tests can be simple landing pages, interactive wireframes, or functional prototypes. The key is to create an MVP that tests the validity of the hypotheses you created in your BMC.

For instance, a landing page that promotes a nonexistent product is an inexpensive way to dip your toe in the water. It can test whether your target audience is interested in the solution and value proposition you developed in your BMC. You can also measure word-of-mouth referrals on a prototype, for example, to see how scalable your solution is.

When asked how minimal is minimal, Eric Ries once responded, *More minimal than you think*. But this can be a challenge for many development teams who care about putting out polished work. If they feel that the product is incomplete, they will hesitate to put it out for review and testing.

The underlying fear is the fear of criticism or rejection, and is a natural human reaction. The important thing to recognize is that there will be criticism and rejection, and that is just part of the journey.

Understanding which criticism and feedback to act upon matters if you want to improve. Invariably, putting a minimal version of your product out in the market may lead to critical feedback about areas which you may have chosen not to pay attention to. This is where a balanced, pragmatic approach is important. You may choose to disregard feedback in these areas, since it was a deliberate choice that you made.

However, the MVP was released for a reason: to gain information about certain questions you had, and to see if you are on the right track towards developing a product your customers will want to, and be able to, use. It is important to focus on feedback in the areas you care about to surface surprises and data that will lead to the next round of tests.

As we will see in the future chapters, focusing on feedback is the key to effectively implementing the Build-Measure-Learn cycle. Each new iteration will provide you with more feedback, which can then be used to test and improve future releases.

Summary

In this chapter, we went through a quick primer on the key elements of Lean startup. First, we learned what the BMC is, how it is developed, and what its benefits are. Then we looked at a variation of the BMC in the form the Lean Canvas and discussed how Agile development and customer development work together.

In the next chapter, we will look at some of the challenges faced by Lean app developers.

3

Challenges in Applying Lean to Building Mobile Apps

In the last chapter, we covered a few core principles of the Lean startup. We discussed the business model canvas, agile development, customer development, and the MVP.

In this chapter, we'll delve into the underlying premise behind this book and explore some of the biggest challenges you will face as a Lean app developer. While there are a number of books about Lean in general, applying Lean to building mobile apps is relatively new territory. Next, we will introduce some of these core challenges, many of which will be revisited in detail later on in the book:

- The higher design bar that app developers face when developing mobile apps as opposed to web apps
- App Store submission cycles, which create delays between your completed iterations and the time they are made available to the public
- The challenges posed by developing multiple platforms
- Difficulties presented to early testers, and how that makes it difficult to grow an early user base
- App ratings, which have a direct impact on your ability to grow your user base and run certain types of experiments

Let's dive into a few of the main challenges and see why they are significant for a developer seeking to apply experimentation.

Higher design bar

From the humdrum of the mid-2000s web apps, Apple radically changed the mobile world with the iPhone, offering well-designed apps of their own and curating apps that were accepted into the App Store. Thanks to Apple's higher standards for design, consumers began expecting intuitive, well-designed apps. That influence has been far reaching, prompting Google to push their boundaries and develop material design, a design language that has become the distinctive hallmark of Android apps.

Compared to the web world where some popular apps could get away with mediocre design, mobile apps face a higher design bar.

A Lean developer is trying to validate an initial concept with a simple experiment. However, the underlying value of the app can be clouded by poor design and experience, resulting in false negatives.

On the other hand, fear of false negatives can lead the developer down the path of adding far more polish than necessary in order to test out their hypothesis.

As we will caution later, it is important to avoid analysis paralysis and early onset perfectionism. The goal is finding a sweet spot between a poorly-designed prototype, which could interfere with testing and data, and an over-polished app, which could cost you time and money.

Apple's App Store submission cycles

Apple's App Store review process-which is more strict than Google Play's-can cause major delays between the time an app iteration is ready for release and the time it actually goes live. This lag creates headaches that makes timing difficult and extends the time it takes to learn from your customers.

With web apps, developers have the luxury of being able to push an experiment over coffee at breakfast and then roll that back by the time they get into work. A range of tools that power continuous integration and continuous deployment enable significant agility in the web arena.

However, mobile app developers have often waited for weeks, and, at times, months in order to see their apps listed in the App Store. Apple's draconian review processes have left developers feeling like they would be better off talking to a wall.

During the early days of the App Store, companies fell over each other trying to build relationships with Apple to ensure that their submissions went through smoothly. I remember app submissions that took months, requiring several email exchanges between our team and the category leader at Apple:

Fortunately, times have changed, and today Apple is committed to prompt reviews.

However, when in doubt, check out `www.appreviewtimes.com` to see the average app store review times for the iOS and Mac App Stores. At the time of writing this book, the review times were in days, but that changes quickly around holidays and important Apple announcements.

App Store submission cycles must be taken into account by Lean developers, who focus on shortening the time it takes to complete a cycle of the Build-Measure-Learn loop. Progress can quickly grind to a halt when you are left waiting with uncertainty about when you can actually start testing with your users. The unpredictable nature of the App Store makes it hard to run an agile cycle with rhythm and velocity, and rapidly run through a closed loop with your customers.

Inability to dynamically load libraries

Native app development tool chains only permit static linking of libraries. What this means is that there is no straightforward way to dynamically load library components into your app, the way that a web developer may choose to pull different JavaScript modules over the web on the fly.

In the case of iOS, there are a few tricks through which libraries can be loaded. The default iOS Xcode settings don't permit you to create a dynamic library, but that can be worked around by copying over the MacOS settings. However, while this can be tested out locally, roadblocks appear during code signing, and the kernel kills app libraries that are not signed by Apple with the same certificate. That said, since the app review process bars dynamic loading, it's unlikely to make it through their checklist.

Workarounds such as this-or others that can be found online-can be tried and tested to see if they will make it through the submission process. However, in the event that they don't succeed, it may pay to develop a static-loading strategy for your app:

```
→ dashboard git:(master) ✗ otool -L /usr/local/bin/tig
/usr/local/bin/tig:
        /usr/local/opt/readline/lib/libreadline.6.dylib (compatibility version 6.0.0, current version 6.3.0)
        /usr/lib/libncurses.5.4.dylib (compatibility version 5.4.0, current version 5.4.0)
        /usr/lib/libiconv.2.dylib (compatibility version 7.0.0, current version 7.0.0)
        /usr/lib/libSystem.B.dylib (compatibility version 1.0.0, current version 1226.10.1)
```

In case of Android, there are similar tricks through which a `Dex` file may be loaded, extracted, and invoked. This is because the Dalvik VM permits some levels of custom class loading from alternate locations such as local storage or a remote network. However, this is not suitable for all apps and has a fair bit of complexity when it comes to properly dealing with all scenarios.

Whereas a web developer can easily flip a switch and change the components rendering on his dashboard, the app developer needs to perform a juggling act. If he would rather focus on the core problem of his app, he would need to push a new app build to the marketplaces and then wait for users to download the new version.

In real-world terms, this could translate into anything from weeks to months before an experiment starts to hit the target user base. Though such delays could be very problematic, in the later chapters we will discuss workflows and techniques that can help you workaround technical roadblocks such as these.

Cross-platform releases

If you are launching a new app, having to choose between iOS and Android quickly becomes an early decision point. If you are bootstrapped, you will likely end up choosing one or the other. While hybrid solutions exist, they can end up compromising some experiential aspects. We will cover hybrid versus native issues in Chapter 9, *Native, Hybrid, or Cross-Platform*.

Web developers about a decade back faced, in certain ways, similar issues with the browser wars. Building for IE, Mozilla, and Opera felt like three completely different browsers at times. Developers launching a new product often had to play it safe and focus on just one popular primary platform to start with.

For mobile app developers, choosing just one platform to start with works for a number of utilitarian apps. However, many apps, such as messenger apps, involve interacting with others in your community. This quickly becomes difficult in an experimentation context since it requires others to be on the same platform. This also gets slightly tricky while recruiting users for testing, since you need to focus on users who are on the same platform that you are targeting.

Later in the book, we will explore the benefits and drawbacks of cross-platform apps versus native apps, then discuss techniques for choosing the right approach for your initial business.

Getting users to download an app

As a web developer, getting someone to check out your app is as simple as dropping them a link and asking them to let you know what they think. You might even get onto a Skype call with them, get them to share their screen with you as they go through the app and observe their interactions.

A significant hurdle for mobile apps, on the other hand, is getting users to go to the store and download your app. You can send them the link, but they then have to follow it to the relevant store, go through the downloading process, and then access the app to test it out. And iOS makes the process even harder by requiring a password for you to be able to download the app.

Irrespective of how you recruit users for your experiments, making the series of steps as seamless as possible is important. In `Chapter 11`, *Onboarding and Registration*, we will discuss how to streamline the onboarding and testing processes in order to reduce such friction, using services such as TestFlight, HockeyApp, and the PlayStore's Alpha/Beta channels:

Preparing for TestFlight

Build and setup with Xcode and iTunes Connect

To get your app ready for testers, upload a beta build of your app from Xcode and add the names and email address of people that you'd like to test in iTunes Connect. For instructions on how to prepare your beta app and set up a list of testers, read the iTunes Connect Developer Guide or watch the TestFlight video tutorial.

- TestFlight Beta Testing Tutorial
- iTunes Connect Developer Guide: TestFlight Beta Testing
- TestFlight Release Notes
- Developer Forums: TestFlight

Inviting Testers

Internal Testing

Get feedback quickly by sharing your beta builds with your internal team. Each app can be tested by up to 25 members of your team who have been assigned the Developer or Admin role in iTunes Connect. Each member can test on up to 10 devices.

External Testing

Once you're ready, you can invite up to 2,000 users who do not need to be part of your development organization to beta test an app that you intend for public release on the App Store. Apps made available to external testers require a Beta App Review and must comply with the full App Store Review Guidelines before testing can begin. A

These tools will help simplify this process, but it's still not quite as smooth if your target audience isn't tech-savvy. Targeting early adopters, which will also be discussed later in the book, is one way to help you find users whose need for your app can be enough to push them past the onboarding friction.

Maintaining app ratings

If you've already got a significant user base on your app, you are likely pressured to maintain a 4+ rating on the app stores. App ratings determine the likelihood that your app may be featured prominently in listings and search results, which has a natural and direct correlation to your ability to expand your user base organically.

For instance, at a company like Intuit, despite the fact that there are a number of experiments that run during tax season, the pressure to keep ratings above 4.0-download rates decreases significantly as ratings drop:

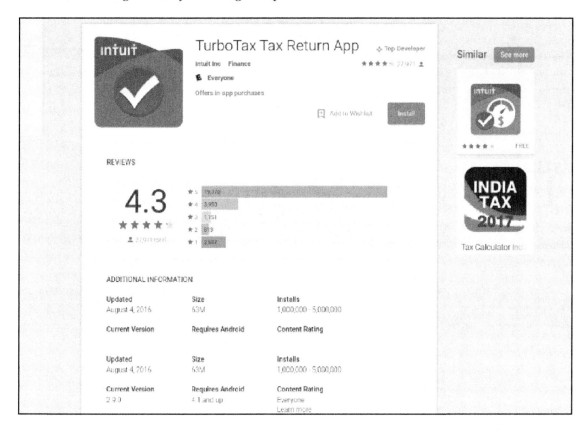

Running experiments, which are necessary to evolve your app, can have uncertain impacts on the ratings.

Healthy ratings and ongoing experimentation are both necessary when applying the Lean approach to app development. However, since reduced ratings negatively impact user acquisition, you will need to find a way to minimize such impacts. Finding a balance between potentially disruptive experimentation and good ratings is an ongoing challenge, especially as an app matures.

In the early stages, moving fast and breaking things works well. However, for an established app with healthy ratings and a healthy user base, it can be difficult to rationalize experiments that could cut ratings. After all, lower ratings decreases the likelihood that your app will be featured or receive an editorial listing, both of which can massively increase exposure and downloads.

Justifying experiments to other team leads may be challenging, but it can also be necessary, even after an app is well established. After all, the more an app becomes successful, the more likely it is to gain competition. Later, we will discuss ways to run split tests that provide useful data without causing too much disruption.

Summary

Applying Lean methods to mobile app development is not easy. There are certain unique challenges that get in the way of running a tight Build-Measure-Learn loop with customers and maximizing validated learning. In this chapter, we covered some of the biggest challenges, such as the ones presented by the platforms, the App Stores, and the users themselves.

In the next chapter, we will explore why you should take a pragmatic approach to app development, how to be pragmatic and structured at the same time, and we will look at a few real-world tools and techniques to help you stay focused and practical.

4

An Agile Workflow in a Nutshell

In this chapter, we will discuss Agile to find out what it is and how we can benefit from it.

Many companies have moved away from the waterfall methodology when developing software. They have switched to a more adaptive methodology such as agile, and for a reason. The waterfall methodology just follows the original plan and requirements and there is little to no room for change. It is obvious that such an approach is not going to work for your app. Unless you have a crystal ball, and you are right from the beginning, this approach most likely is going to lead to a lot of waste.

An agile workflow accommodates change through adaptive planning, promotes faster software development and delivery, and is rooted in a continuous improvement methodology. That is exactly what you need to validate your assumptions, and it is what you need to pivot when necessary.

There are a lot of implementations of agile software methodology. They all focus on the ability to adapt and to deliver releasable software as quickly as possible. Some of them focus on managing the workflow in particular. One of the most common is Agile Scrum. We will have a closer look in this methodology to see how well it works with Lean software development.

Specifically, in this chapter, we will learn more about the following topics:

- An Agile workflow
- Lean software development, Kanban, and Scrum
- Epic, stories, and tasks
- The Scrum team and the daily standup
- Backlog refinement and the definition of Ready
- The sprint planning
- The definition of Done

- The sprint review, planning, and retrospective
- Tools that you can use, such as Trello and Jira

An Agile workflow

Using an Agile workflow helps your team to be flexible and able to quickly respond to changes. It also means that your team is self-organizing, and that members of the team are able to deliver early and often.

Good communication is fundamental to Agile and the members of your team have to collaborate well with the product owner, stakeholders, and each other. The users of your app need to also be involved, right from the beginning. Their feedback is vital, and is critical for you to make the right decisions for your app development. Finally, at any time, you should be able to deliver a working version of the software. A good git workflow and being able to continuously deliver are key elements here. You will read more about this in `Chapter 19`, *Building an Unfair Advantage*.

What all agile methods have in common is that they promote the ability to change, continually learn as you go, and to delivery software as quickly as possible.

Some agile software development methodologies are as follows:

- Lean software development
- Kanban
- Scrum

There are many more approaches, but these are the most interesting ones. Of course, Lean software development has the focus of this book. The key elements for this methodology are:

- Delivering as early as possible
- Making decisions as late as possible
- Gathering early feedback through Continuous Delivery

We will learn more about all these elements in the next chapters. Unlike the other methodologies, Lean is more focused on avoiding waste.

But, let's start with the basics first. Lean software development, Kanban, and Scrum have a lot in common. In this chapter, we will have a closer look at Kanban and Scrum, and discuss Lean in the rest of the book.

Kanban

Kanban is a way to visualize the flow and the current state of each action. Every participant can see the progress from start to finish. Team members start working as capacity permits. Unlike Scrum, there is no need for forecasting as it is a continuous process.

Kanban is a methodology that uses visualization with a Kanban board. The method originates from Lean manufacturing (inspired by Toyota), but it is often used for software development as well. In its most basic shape, it contains three columns, reflecting the state of each item—**To do**, **Doing**, and **Done**. Note that it is important to keep the amount of items in the Doing lane to a minimum. People are, in fact, not really good in multitasking, although they think they are. Switching from contexts will increase waste and should be avoided.

All you need to create a Kanban board is an empty wall and a number of post-its, but you can also use a software service such as Trello. If you sign up at `www.trello.com`, you can set up your own project for free and define a number of lanes. In this example, set up with Trello, it is clear to everyone which state each item is in. You can define additional lanes where needed:

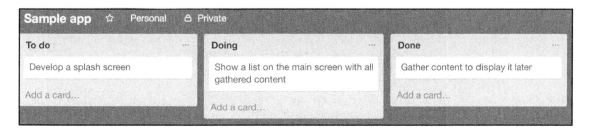

In Kanban, the flow of work is continuous, but in Scrum, work is divided into events that last for a specific amount of time. Scrum uses Kanban boards, but adds a forecasting element to it.

Scrum

Scrum is a way of software development management that is designed for small teams. The members of the team complete a number of actions during cycles of a fixed duration called **sprints**. The sprint is restricted to a specific duration. The duration is normally between one week and one month, with two weeks being the most common. The fixed length of a sprint is important because it allows the team to determine their velocity, or rate of speed at which they get work done, after a couple of sprints.

At the beginning of a sprint, the team decides which tasks can be accomplished in the given timeframe. After a number of sprints, it is easier to make appropriate estimations, since the team will have a better feel for the work they do. Knowing the velocity of a team will make it easier for the team to make estimations on the stories, and to make sure the team can truly commit to all stories defined for a given sprint (that it is doable).

The methodology places emphasis on a workable and potentially shippable product at the end of the sprint. This means that the software has not only been developed, but also that it has been tested and integrated. It should be possible to demonstrate the app, to perform an ad hoc distribution to beta testers, and even to publish the app or the update in the Play Store or App Store.

Epic, Stories, and Tasks

An **epic** is a large amount of work that is almost always delivered over a number of sprints. An epic often is a high-level description of functionality. It contains no specific details. Through customer feedback, the team can learn what is needed to complete the epic. An example of an epic may be: As a user of the app, I want to be able to set up and to review a Business Model Canvas in an app.

An epic is a high-level description of the feature or features. Since specific details are missing, the team needs to learn more about the epic, and often this will generate multiple **stories**. solve the problem that the epic defines, can become a story.

A user story should be as small as possible while it is still delivering business value. User stories are often written from the perspective of the users of the app, and they are described in a natural language. They describe a particular feature in only few sentences that outline the desired outcome. This can help the team to understand the objectives and the context of a specific desired feature.

A story may have one or more tasks. These tasks can describe in a very specific way which actions need to be taken in order to complete a story. An example of a task could be to develop an edit box where the user can edit text or add a **Save** button and persist the edited text. It is also important to specify the acceptance criteria. If you have clearly defined what the result of the implementation of a story or task should be, it will become easier for your testers to accept (or to decline) the new feature.

Scrum team

For the Scrum approach, you will typically find three main roles, although some organizations do define others in addition to the ones listed here:

- Scrum master
- Product owner
- Development team (and that includes the testers)

Scrum teams have one product owner. He or she is responsible to ensure that the team delivers business value that is required. To do so, the product owner is the connection between the stakeholders and the (technical) team. The product owner is primarily focused on the business side (problem definition). The product owner defines the user stories and adds them to the backlog.

The user stories describe the features that need to be implemented. You can think of a backlog as a to-do list. The team has to commit to these items, and each item needs some refinement to make clear what exactly is needed to implement a specific feature. It is the team, focused on finding a solution, that will give the feedback for this. The backlog also needs prioritization. This prioritization is often based on how important specific features are for the end user (the value).

The product owner demonstrates the app to stakeholders, and defines the milestones and releases of the app. He or she also informs stakeholders about the development of the app, and plays an important role at negotiation of funding, scope, and priorities. The product owner needs to be able to communicate effectively. He/she needs to find a balance between the stakeholders' (and end users') interests, and the collaboration with the members of the team to make sure they develop the right solution for the problems that stakeholders find or define:

This results in information on two totally different levels. Stakeholders are often only interested in obtaining a solution for the problem. However, the development team prefers to hear feedback with as much detail as possible, so they will know how a feature should be implemented.

The developers, testers, and others are all members of a self-organizing team. They will care for all tasks related to delivering or updating the app. Tasks that you can think of are:

- Design
- UX
- Analysis
- Technical research and development

- Code review
- Testing
- Documentation

The team commits to a sprint, and is responsible for delivering an updated and working app at the end of each sprint. It does not make a difference whether the update is a external or an internal one. It should always be possible to demonstrate the new features to the stakeholders.

Another role is that of the Scrum master. The Scrum master makes sure that the Scrum framework is followed. He coaches the team to make sure that the team delivers all the features for a sprint. He educates the team and the stakeholders about the Scrum principles. The scrum master helps the team to remove (or to avoid) internal or external impediments that might impede a sprint's success.

The Scrum master also maintains the backlog, and ensures the stories are clear and that they are defined in a nonambiguous way. It is important that the team understands the objectives of a story so it can actually make progress. Other important responsibilities of the Scrum master are helping the team to come up with the definition of Ready (when the development team can begin work on a story), and to come up with the definition of done (when can a new feature be rolled out). We will have a closer look at these definitions later.

The daily stand-up

The team holds a **stand-up** (also known as **Daily Scrum**) on each day of a sprint. It is a short meeting that is often limited to 15 minutes (timeboxed). It happens at the same time and place every day, even when some team members are missing. Anyone is welcome to join, although only team members should contribute.

During the stand-up, each member provides an answer to these three questions related to the context of the sprint:

- What did I do the last work day?
- What do I plan to complete today?
- What impediments do I see that prevent me or the team from meeting our sprint goal?

Since the meeting is timeboxed, it is important that each member focuses on these three questions alone and there should be no detailed discussions. The Scrum master will be notified about any impediment mentioned during the meeting.

Impediments are blockers, risks, dependencies on other teams or partner companies, and possible or expected delays. The Scrum master is responsible for removing impediments, or finding someone who is willing or able to find a resolution. A Scrum board displaying the actual impediments can be useful to note this, as finding a solution is something that needs to happen outside the stand-up.

Backlog refinement

Before a sprint can start, the sprint backlog needs to be defined. What stories need to go into the sprint? To provide an answer to that, the team needs to review the product backlog. The product backlog contains all actions (stories) that need to be taken to complete the product (the app). First, they need to be refined before the team can commit to them.

Each story needs an estimation of the amount of work involved. This estimation is usually expressed in story points, not hours. The story points relate to the expected complexity and amount of work. Typically, a specific and clear action such as **Edit a text on a button** will be defined as one story point. This creates an anchor for defining other more complex stories. All estimated stories will be derived from it.

To be able to assign story points, the story needs to be clear and well understood by the team. Planning poker is often used to let the team members make estimates. You can use cards for the estimates, or use one of the many apps that are available.

Here is an example of such an app, called Scrum Time. You can find it on the Play Store or App Store.

As a user of the app, you can pick a card with a number that you will show to the rest of the team. If the estimated points differ too much between the team members, then they need to discuss why they think the implementation and testing of a story will take more (or less) time. Perhaps a member of the team has knowledge that the rest do not have, or maybe he is looking at the story in a different way. New insights can contribute to a better estimation.

The numbers to pick from are typically derived from the Fibonacci sequence. In mathematics, the Fibonacci sequence is characterized by the fact that every number after the first two is the sum of the two preceding ones. The reason why these numbers are used here is that the larger a story becomes (having more story points), the more difficult it will be to make an exact estimation. If you have no clue, you can always play the question mark card, or if the action related to the story is infinite (think of delivering support), then there are cards for that as well. And yes, if you are thirsty, there is always the coffee/pause card that you can play.

The 1,2,3,5, and 8 cards are the ones that are played most often. Stories with more points very likely need to be split up into multiple smaller stories to reduce risk.

Definition of Ready

It is the responsibility of the product owner to add stories to the backlog. During the backlog refinement, the team has to provide feedback to get each story into an actionable condition. The stories at the top of the backlog, and that are candidates for the upcoming sprint, must be ready. Having a clear **Definition of Ready (DoR)** is important if you want to raise the productivity of your team.

The stories need to be immediately actionable. If they are not, how could one implement or test a feature? It must be clear what the objectives are, what needs to be done to make it happen, and what amount of work it takes. For example, the backlog may be filled with user feedback such as, "We want to able to create new invoices quicker." This statement clearly defines a problem, but if we want to work on it, we need more specific information. The team must be able to determine what needs to be done. If we could state that adding a button for creating new invoices to the main screen is the solution, then we can make an estimation for it and start working on it. A story that is ready is clear, concise, and actionable.

Sprint planning

The team selects the items that have the highest priority and that are ready for work to start. The team can only commit to stories that have clear objectives, and that are not blocked by anything else. Also, the team can commit only to a limited number of stories during a sprint. That means that the team needs to know how much work will be involved with these stories, and how much work can be done during a sprint.

To determine how much work can go into a sprint, we need to know the team's velocity, which is a number that expresses the total effort a team is capable of in a sprint. That number comes from evaluating and determining the average amount of work done (sum of story points) in previous sprints. Of course, seasonal influences (holidays) and other things that could determine the team's capacity need to be taken into account. No extra work should be added to a sprint once the team has committed to start.

Definition of Done

The Scrum framework determines that each story should be done at the end of every sprint. In an ideal world, the **Definition of Done (DoD)** means that each story has been developed, tested, and approved, and that your app's current state is in a potentially shippable state. We still need to define exactly what that means. The DoD may vary from one Scrum team to another, but must be consistent within one team. The DoD can help to ensure that features are implemented and tested and that their addition will truly contribute to a shippable app.

The definition could also contain a list of other actions, such as code reviews, running unit tests and UI tests, writing documentation, and ad hoc or public distribution. Each action should add a verifiable value to the product. This helps the team to focus on which features matter while avoiding activities that are wasteful.

Sprint review, planning, and retrospective

There are a couple of events at the end of each sprint: the sprint review and the sprint retrospective. There is also the sprint planning for the next sprint.

At the review, the team reviews all the completed work and demonstrates it to the stakeholders. They also review the work that has not been completed yet.

For the upcoming sprint, there is the sprint planning event. During this event, the team and stakeholders work together to determine which features can be delivered in the sprint, and how it can be achieved.

The retrospective is used to reflect on the past sprint so that a team can learn and improve over time. In general, the two main questions asked of each member are:

- What went well during the sprint?
- What needs to be improved in the next sprint?

The Scrum master facilitates the event and helps the team to determine what actions are needed in order to improve things. For the retrospective, you can use a tool such as Jira, but often using post-its works much better.

Anything that needs improvement will be prioritized, and actions will be defined for the top three issues.

By now, you have a basic understanding on what the Agile workflow and Scrum is about. To learn more about Scrum, you can visit `https://www.scrum.org`.

Tools that you can use

You can use a number of tools to support, automate, and visualize the process. Jira and Agilefant are well-known web-based solutions that can help you define epics, stories, estimates, and sprints. Most tools also have an option to add (sub) tasks to stories. Although a story should be the smallest amount of work possible, it can still be useful to divide them into multiple subtasks.

You can find more information about Jira at `https://www.atlassian.com/software/jira`. Agilefant can be found at `https://www.agilefant.com`.

The following is an example of Jira displaying a Kanban Board. Jira comes with good support for Agile and Scrum in particular, while Agilefant is more method agnostic:

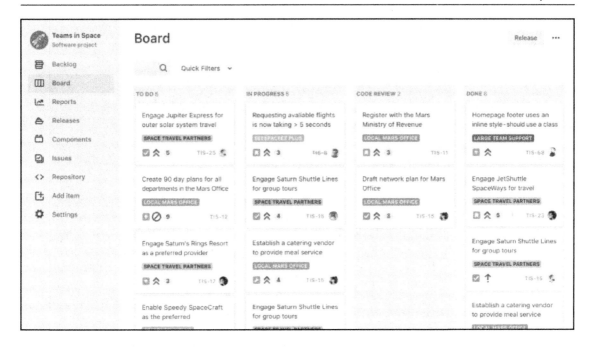

If you just got started, you might not need all these tools yet. In that case, a whiteboard and a number of post-its are sufficient to create your first Kanban board. This board comes in handy when all members of your team work in the same space. When you have a distributed team, Trello is a good choice. It is not as advanced as Jira, as it does not have support for Scrum, but it is a great way to get started in an organized way.

To start with Trello, sign up at `https://trello.com/`, create a new team and project, and you are ready to start. Just as is the case with Jira, you can create multiple lanes in Trello, each reflecting the actual state of a card/item. As said before, you can start with a **To do**, **Doing**, and a **Done** lane. However, you soon will find out that these states alone are not going to be sufficient.

If you configure the following lanes, you will have a decent start for an agile workflow in Trello:

- Backlog
- Ready (the story is clear, well understood, and has no impediments)
- In development (developing and testing)
- Test
- Done (it has been tested and approved)

It may look like the following example. You can also add more lanes to it, such as code review, or whatever suits your organization best:

All stories start as a card in the **Backlog** lane. Once you have clearly defined what the objectives are, the story is ready for development. You can then move the card to the **Ready** lane. When a developer picks up the story, he will move the card to the **Development** lane. At the moment, the implementation has been completed and the unit test(s) for the story succeed the card will be moved again, for example, to the **Test** lane or, optionally, to the **Code review** lane first:

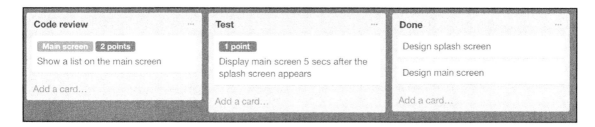

If a manual or automated UI test for the implemented feature succeeds, then the story can be considered as done, which correspond to the final lane.

This is, of course, just a simplified process, and tools such as Jira offer much better support for Agile and Scrum workflows, including epics and estimations. Nevertheless, Trello is still a good start for newbies. Trello comes with options to add labels and to define an expiration date and time. You can use it for multiple purposes, even to set epics and estimations, as shown in the preceding screenshot. The epics appear as green labels and the estimated story points appear in blue.

In the later chapters, you will read about other tools that can help you to organize an agile workflow. Think of Confluence. Just like Jira, it is a Jetbrains web-based solution that allows you to organize all of your documentation and discussions.

Summary

In this chapter, we saw a brief introduction to Agile and Scrum workflow and how you can benefit from them. We now know how you can use Kanban to visualize the state of each item of work, and what some possible implementations of the agile workflow are. In particular, we had a look at Scrum, the different roles that exist, and what planning and estimation a Scrum environment requires.

You might think that all of this makes sense, but it will be difficult to implement if you have limited resources and time. What can we do to keep waste to a minimum, but still act in a very pragmatic way? You will read all about that in the next chapter.

5

A Pragmatic Approach

You have made some awesome moves already! You know what you are passionate about and perhaps you have already created a very first **Minimum Viable Product** (**MVP**). This could be a website, a survey, or maybe even a very simple app. It does not really matter how it manifests itself. The only thing that is important here is that it is something that could prove your hypothesis and it is something that requires only minimal effort. Learn from the feedback that you get, and figure out if your earliest assumptions are correct. If so, it is time for the next step.

In this chapter, we will see how to move on and how to deal with one of the biggest challenges of a startup. Time and timing are essential. This is particularly true for a bootstrapped startup. We will look at how to get things done when nothing is there yet and when the most important resources (time and money) are very limited. What you need is the right mindset and a very pragmatic approach.

You do not need a huge office and all kinds of fancy stuff. Also, you do not need many rules, but most of the time things do not happen automatically. Anyhow, we need a few rules, no matter how cool your startup may be. A pragmatic approach is a nice balance between total chaos and bureaucracy. You will keep a clear focus on what you want to accomplish, and developing new features is not going to take you longer than strictly needed. Such an approach will result in developing exactly the required functionality during a particular stage of your app.

There are no shortcuts in startup land when searching for a product-solution or a product-market fit, but as a developer you often do not need to reinvent the wheel. Readymade solutions are widely available for most situations. For example, in Chapter 8, *Cloud Solutions for App Experiments*, we will investigate which parties are offering a **Mobile Backend as a Service** (**MBaaS**), and in Chapter 10, *There Is an API for That!*, we will look at various mash-up ideas. Such solutions are real-time savers irrespective of whether you are just using them to build an MVP or using them during the whole lifetime of your app.

Specifically, we will cover the following topics:

- Learn about the benefits of timeboxed programming
- See what options are available to get started with nothing
- Demonstrate how to keep things well structured
- Investigate whether there are any shortcuts

Timeboxed programming

For each iteration, you need to decide how long it will take and what features will come with it. As you have seen in Chapter 4, *An Agile Workflow in a Nutshell*, a typical sprint takes 2 to 3 weeks. Although this may be difficult at first, you will learn soon enough what you and your team members can accomplish during such a sprint. Sometimes you will have no clue how long the development of a feature will take. In that case, a timeboxed approach can help you as well. Before you start working on that feature, you allocate a particular amount of time. Afterwards, you can determine what you have accomplished and you can decide whether the feature can be released as it is. Even if it is not completely functional, as long as it contains no (severe) bugs, it can help you to get early feedback.

Keep things simple and develop only the features that you actually need for that particular iteration. You should ask yourself what it is that you want to prove and what feedback you need in order to proceed. Again, it is important to realize how relevant that feedback is when you look at your app's current phase. For example, you should not be focusing too much on the development of In-App Purchase functionality if the base functionality of your app has not been completed yet.

"You Aren't Gonna Need It", also known as the YAGNI acronym, is one of the ideas behind Agile development and extreme programming (XP), but it does apply here as well.

The goal should always be to achieve maximum learning with the least amount of effort. Also, keep it simple and solve one problem at a time for one product and for one type of customer. As a developer, you will often foresee scenarios that need to be supported, the so-called unhappy flows, but who cares about them if the happy flow is not ready yet?

Consider the scenario where the idea of timeboxing involves the focus more on the time spent instead of the tasks done. So, instead of thinking of features that should be done in a particular amount of time, think of a particular amount of time and what features you can implement given that amount of time. To maximize learning, the changes that come with each new release of your app should be as small as possible while still delivering relevant business value. Timeboxed programming is essential to make sure resources are delivered in a particular amount of time. Determine deliverables and a deadline for each timeboxed iteration. Using this methodology, your productivity will be improved and you can keep the promises to your customers.

In general, get to know your (potential) customers. Learn more about their problem. It is the problem your app needs to solve. This may sound like a job for your more business-oriented cofounder, but a better understanding of this also makes you a better developer. Ask questions and find out what the common problems are for all of your customers.

Concierge service

It is important to realize that some parts of the solution you are creating are essential, but may not necessarily be good candidates for automating processes right away. These parts can be offered manually as well. Such a solution is known as a **Concierge Service**, or as the **Concierge Minimum Viable Product** (CMVP). At first glance, that does not really seem to make much sense to a developer. You might be thinking that the lean startup methodology is about minimizing waste, and wonder why we should do things manually?

The truth is that doing things manually is indeed not very efficient, but that is fine for now. It is a short-term solution that can help you gain new insights and learn how to solve the user's or customer's problem. Once you fully understand the problem and know what the solution should be, it is time for automation.

What would happen if you worked on an awesome feature for 3 months and afterwards learned that your app does not seem to know your user's problem? It will probably be a huge disappointment for all stakeholders and you will wonder why this happened. You should always ask yourself whether you have all the required information to solve the issue and whether you understand your customer's needs. If that is not the case, your effort may lead to delivering a product that nobody wants. You might need to refactor a lot, or start all over again. Such activity would be a waste of your time (and if you are having bad luck, your credibility).

Is it crappy or perfect?

The fact that you focus on the features that are most important is because they contribute to the hypotheses that you want to prove. However, this does not mean that your product has to be crappy. Using a timeboxed approach will help you deliver often (daily or weekly) and on time.

The features that you will make available are unlikely to be perfect, but with each new iteration you can improve them. Of course, you will never have a second chance for a first impression, but aiming for perfection is not going to help you prove your hypotheses. Instead, it will prevent you from getting feedback early. Still, it is important that you choose your first users carefully. Early adopters are very different from mainstream users, having different expectations. Managing expectations is therefore very important when asking early adopters to test your solution. Be honest about the phase your startup is in and tell them that the solution has been built to maximize learning and that you would love to get their feedback. It may sound a bit harsh, but ultimate perfection does not exist anyway. The opinion of your early adopters is important and your opinion does not really matter.

Release early and often

Releasing early and often—for example, once a week or every 2 weeks—will maximize your learning. Timeboxed programming could help you deliver the features that matter.

The loop shown in the following figure is known as the **Build-Measure-Learn Feedback** cycle. It is easy to get feedback if you know your early adopters. That is not always possible if you are developing an app. There are great tools available to obtain analytical data. In Chapter 13, *Play Store and App Store Hacks* we will learn more about these tools and how to gather feedback through metrics:

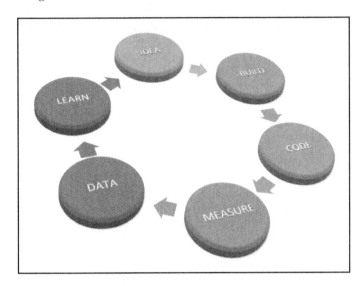

How do you get started with nothing?

A blank page, a basic idea, and an early MVP. That is how it starts, and it is not exactly nothing. But that does not make it a company, or an app, and it certainly does not come with customers, unless you have a really convincing MVP or a great production-solution fit.

The chicken and egg problem

Depending on the type of app you are developing, sooner or later you will face the famous chicken and egg problem. Simply put, an app that depends on user-generated content will have no content without users, but also no users without content. So, where do you start?

Any marketplace-based app has to deal with this challenge, whether it is an app for dating, job finding, or bringing companies together. But it does apply to other types of apps as well. There are many apps available in the App Store. They all are doing more or less the same thing, so why should your users (and later, your customers) use your app and not any of the other apps? Sooner or later you need to find an answer to the question, "What makes your app better?" Is your app better because it is cheaper, does it provide better services, or does your app appear to be more convincing simply because your app has a large user base? In short, you do not yet have a platform with many users or testimonials because you just got started. Oh, yes, you do have a chicken and egg challenge!

Fake it until you make it

To solve the chicken and egg challenge and to get your app started, there are some simple solutions. One of them is: Fake it until you make it. It sounds like cheating, or at least it sounds like something that is bad, while in fact it is not. It's a workaround for the chicken and egg problem. No, we are not going to lie, at most we will just pretend. If you are developing a dating app, ask all your relatives and friends to sign up with a nice profile photo. You can use this approach not only for user data, but for all types of content. If you are working on a B2B app, you could purchase some company data, enrich it, and present as if it is your own. Refer to `Chapter 10`, *There is an API For That!*, about mash-ups to read more information about that topic. Another option that would work well (for example, think of an app displaying job information) is to get data from various other sources and start as an app offering aggregated data. There are many ways to get started and they all are aimed at growing your app by developing content and your user base.

Become an expert

You too can become an expert, just by doing it. You can start to become a more significant player for some niche. Just be that expert while learning on the go. For example, when we began with our new startup built around a concept of narrow casting combined with social media, we really had no clue about what narrow casting was other than the television screens that you often see in stores or at train stations. By writing a blog about the topic of narrow casting, we have learned a lot and gradually we have become experts. And, even more important, it has helped us to shape our vision on the problem that we were trying to solve. In our case, this was about finding an answer to the question, how we could make narrow casting a more interactive process? Pretending will help you to set your targets, and once you have reached them, it is no longer fake, but real. You can build your reputation this way. How cool is that? Obviously, you have to keep things real. Do not fake things if you never can fulfil the expectations that come with them, but do it to buy more time, to get the job done, or to become an expert along the way. If you keep it real, your startup will become what you envision.

Grab and adapt

Almost all startup ideas derive from existing concepts. A little enhancement, different pricing, service, UX, or particular approach can be the **Unique Selling Points** (**USP**) that will lead to a unique product. The same service, but promoted with a different marketing approach, can result in a totally different product. It is a trend that you often see. For example, I have been working on a project for an enabler of **Mobile Virtual Network Operators** (**MVNO**). Their customers were all mobile service providers who did not own the infrastructure themselves. The biggest difference between all the virtual providers was just marketing strategy. Anyone can start their own network from scratch with little investment. All you need to do is grab and adapt. You have to be careful, though. You need to be aware of patents and copyright issues, but there are many (open source) projects that you can use as the foundation for your app, or just for a first MVP.

For very little money, you can also buy a concept, or even a complete app, that comes close to your startup idea. In that case, all you need to do is to enhance it and see if you can make a difference. To start something new, most apps just need a little twist. For example, have a look at http://codecanyon.net. You will find some great starting points here. There are apps for Android, iOS, web-based apps, and many more. You can find Flappy Bird clone apps, restaurant apps, and everything in between.

Let's say your startup is developing a travel app. You can search for these kinds of apps and buy one of them. You can quickly prove your hypothesis just by making some modifications to the app:

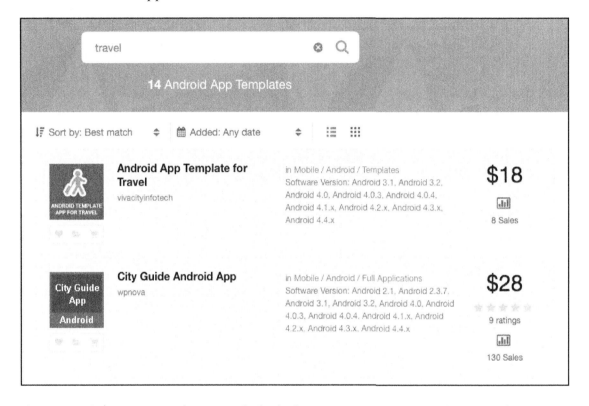

That is a real time-saver and it is worth the little investment. What you learn will help you define what the app should do and what it should look like at the early stage. Perhaps later you still want to develop your app more or less from scratch. However, if you think that a readymade base app will help you collect useful insights quickly, then it will not be a hard decision to follow this approach.

Offer an app or a service that does not yet exist

How can you offer or describe your app when it does not yet exist? A nonexisting app is pretty hard to demonstrate, so how will customers be made aware of it, and how will they know why they should get the app? They somehow have to find out that there is an (concept) app that solves the problems they are experiencing. Here, the funny thing is that your app itself is not really that important. Sorry, your app alone is not the product. It is just a vehicle for your users to get something done. Show a slideshow or a video that explains what your app does and why it can help solve their problem. This can be just as convincing. You will get their attention and if you are doing really well, you will get their pre-orders right away.

If you do not have the skills to create a great video, or if you are in need of a logo or any other design, then have a look at `https://www.fiverr.com/`. They have many freelance designers who can help you. Another website that you can look at is `https://99designs.com/`.

A video or presentation is not really that different from an MVP, right? Well, it is one, although in this example we are testing the product-market fit-related hypotheses, instead of the product-solution fit-related hypotheses. Every startup owner, regardless of his or her role, has to do sales and be able to sell stuff before it even exists. That is not lying and it is not even faking. It is a creative way of promising a solution for known problems.

However, don't ever fake testimonials or lie about the number of customers or make things ten times bigger than they are. Keep things real. Instead, work on a great reputation, become an expert, create a very convincing website and include a feature list, even when it has not been completed yet. To show that people can trust your company, also add a company policy link with terms and conditions. Add pricing tables to your website, even when you are not yet ready to sell. It is never too early to measure (revenue) traction. In `Chapter 15`, *Growing Traction and Improving Retention*, we will learn how we can measure traction and in `Chapter 17`, *Monetization and Pricing Strategy*, you will be able to read more about pricing strategies.

How to keep things well structured

If you start learning from the feedback you obtain through interviews or metrics, it is very likely that the flow or structure of your app will change. As business requirements change often, ad hoc changes need to be made. This requires you to refactor the code of your app. That is something that most developers consider to be important, but in reality it can be easily forgotten or it is never done, simply because there is not enough time for it. Sometimes, refactoring is considered to make the app unstable. However, do not let your technical debt become too large.

Technical debt or even spaghetti code can be the result if you understand underlying process insufficiently, or when you do not allocate enough time for development. In case a startup company has only business-oriented skills, it may have outsourced the development or it may have hired some third party to do the job. If that is the case, there is little to no insight into the technical structure of an app. I strongly recommend you to do most of the development yourself. If you do own a startup with no technical cofounder on-board, then stop reading and find one first! There are many meetups and websites where you can meet somebody (for a cofounder or another role) with the skills that you are looking for. Take a look at these websites: `https://angel.co/` and `https://cofounderslab.com/`.

It is important to keep things, and your code in particular, well structured. Design patterns and a number of disciplines could help you to achieve building apps for Android and for iOS. It is true that Android Studio is offering much more functionality for refactoring purposes, and that using Xcode refactoring requires some extra effort. Nevertheless, refactoring is equally important for both platforms.

Design patterns

There is no need to reinvent the wheel and there is no need for us to repeat ourselves. This is exactly what the **Don't Repeat Yourself** (**DRY**) software development principle dictates. A design pattern is a solution for a common problem, and such a pattern can be used in many places across your app. It is the methodology that we can trust, which will help us to speed up the development process. Patterns could help us develop high-quality software with minimal effort. They also can help us deal with the separation of concerns. Some well-known patterns are the **Model View Controller** (**MVC**) pattern, the somewhat similar **Model View Presenter** (**MVP**), and the **Model-View-ViewModel** (**MVVM**) approach.

There are some great books about design patterns and it is beyond the scope of this book to have a detailed look at all of them, but the MVC/MVP is of particular interest because it is used the most for mobile development. The idea behind the pattern is to separate the UI from the business logic and data from the logic. When you have a closer look on the structure of most Android or iOS apps in Android Studio or in Xcode, you will notice some parts of this pattern already. A controller gets data from another layer. This layer can be a client or a repository class. For example, it will get its data from an API or from a local source. The controller communicates the obtained data through a model (or view model) to the user interface:

Become independent

Ideally, it should not matter whether your app is getting its data from a local stub, a **Mobile Backend as a Service** (**MBaaS**), a third party API, or your own API. This is very easy to accomplish. You just need to realize that it is important to separate the different concerns and that implementing contracts matter.

Another lesson learned is that you cannot always trust third party services. You must have heard about Parse. It used to be of the most promising MBaaS and a lot of app developers were depending on it to store their app data in the cloud. Recently, they announced that they will shut down their business, which frustrated a lot of developers. Fortunately, Parse has created an open source version of Parse Server. Anyhow, it nicely illustrates what I am trying to say here. Make sure you do not go out of business even if one of your key partners does.

Data layer

Switching from one service provider to another (key partner) is easy if your app is well structured. Use a separate layer for accessing data and define contracts for the communication between your data layers and your controllers. Contracts are known as an **interface** (for Android) or as a **protocol** (for iOS). They contain no implementation and are nothing but appointments between one class and another. They define what methods are available, what parameters are required, and what the result type will be.

For example, let's say we are getting data from some kind of source. In the interface IRepository, we will define the names, results, and parameters for all methods that represent some operation. To be more precise, let's say we want to retrieve company news that we have stored somewhere in the cloud. It could be at Parse server (at Back4App or elsewhere), Amazon, Azure, or Firebase, it does not really matter where and how exactly we will get this data. Since it is an interface, we do not have to care about the actual implementation yet.

For Android, it could look like this:

```
public interface IRepository{

    public void getNews(OnRepositoryResult handler, GetNewsRequest
request);
```

For IOS, it looks like this (in Swift 2.x):

```
protocol RepositoryProtocol {
func getNews(handler: RepositoryResultDelegate, request: GetNewsRequest)
```

The data layer classes that implement this interface or protocol will perform the actual job. They will retrieve the data from a remote data source.

For example, the Android implementation begins like this:

```
public class RemoteRepository implements IRepository {

...
    @Override
    public void getNews(OnRepositoryResult handler, GetNewsRequest request)
{
        // Get data asynchronously  and return the result
    }
```

While the IOS implementation begins like this:

```
public class RemoteRepository: RepositoryProtocol  {
    ...
    func getNews(handler: RepositoryResultDelegate, request:
GetNewsRequest){
```

In `Chapter 8`, *Cloud Solutions for App Experiments*, we will see what an implementation with Firebase will look like.

 The data layer could also obtain the data from locally mocked or stubbed data. You can easily switch between the different sources. This makes it a great solution for testing purposes too.

Are there any shortcuts?

No there are not! Just kidding. There are some services and methodologies that are worthwhile to investigate. They could save you a lot of time and money. Think of an app that needs to communicate with a backend because it needs to support chat functionality, or to support the sharing of texts, pictures, audio, or video with other users. Such an app will have a lot of requirements, such as:

- Synchronizing data from the app to the backend
- Getting data from the backend to the app
- Data storage
- Data streaming
- Offline support
- Registration and login through email
- Registration and login with Facebook or Twitter

You probably can build the backend that supports all this yourself, but that is a lot of work and there is no need for that. There are many services available that will take care of all (or some) of the earlier mentioned requirements:

In Chapter 8, *Cloud Solutions for App Experiments*, we will have a closer look on Parse server. Later, we will also have a look at Windows Azure.

Mash-up

A mash-up can be seen as a composite app that is combining reusable data, presentation, and new logic. It is often seen as web solution, but this approach can be used for native app development as well. Data is everywhere. The government and various organizations have made their data publicly available through APIs. Mash-up solutions do not need to worry about the content in particular, but more about the presentation. They may occur as enterprise, data-oriented, or consumer mash-ups.

The app may gather data from multiple sources, combine and enrich them, and then present them in an app. An example of that could be as simple as producing infographics from the provided data. Another example is getting photos from Flickr and presenting them on a Google map. There are plenty of other and more sophisticated solutions that you can think of. A mash-up can be a great contribution to the development of an MVP or a **Proof of Concept (PoC)**. Often, when it turns out that a mash-up is a profitable solution, it mostly has the function of aggregator. An example is a website comparing insurance companies.

Keep in mind that you can develop a mash-up solution relatively fast, but the monetization of it could be more difficult. Again, the biggest downside of a mash-up is the dependency on third parties. If things start to become more serious, then do not just consume their data. You need to do more than that. Avoid a potential shutdown of your business in case the company, that is delivering the data, decides to discontinue its services. You can reduce that risk if you make that company a real key partner. Although there still is a dependency, it is no longer a problem because it has become a manageable one.

Summary

In this chapter, we have seen a few things that you could do to get started and keep going. We had a look at the chicken and egg problem and how to deal with it. We also had a look at patterns, and how they could help us to keep things well structured.

Finally, we had a short introduction to **Mobile Backend as a Service (MBaaS)** solutions and mash-ups. In Chapter 8, *Cloud Solutions for App Experiments*, and Chapter 11, *Onboarding and Registration*, respectively we will look at a hands-on implementation for both of them. But first, we will figure out how minimal an MVP actually should be.

6

MVP is Always More Minimal Than You Think

The M in MVP stands for Minimum, not Maximum. If your idea of MVP incorporates every potential use case, every potential mix of audience, all facets of available functionality, and creates a backlog that would take a development team longer than 90 days to complete, you don't have **Minimum Viable Product**. On the contrary, you have a different beast altogether that all too many times bring teams to their knees causing unnecessary rework, lost cycles, lost revenue, and all the other dysfunctional misery that comes with working on a product that isn't well defined and validated with its users.

In written context, the idea of defining MVP seems simple; the challenges surface when teams try to outline and define what minimal means in terms of their initial product release. "How Minimal is Minimal?", "Can I have multiple core functions?", "Are all my use cases covered and accounted for?", and "Can I have more than 12 buttons on a screen?" All these and many other questions make it difficult to know whether our proposed MVP is truly minimal and viable.

This guide is designed to act as a benchmarking tool, and will help ensure that you have successfully defined and validated an MVP that's ready for market release.

We're going to cover the following topics:

- What is MVP?
- How to define your MVP
- Fail fast/validate everything
- Iterate and evolve your MVP - from viable to lovable

What is MVP?

A **Minimum Viable Product** (**MVP**) is defined as:

"The version of a new product which allows a team to collect the maximum amount of validated learning about customers with the least effort"
- Eric Ries

Applications such as Instagram, Snapchat, and Tinder all share the same thing in common: when they were launched, they were a much more simplified version of what they are today. The same can be said about smartphones and iPods. At the time of their inception, they did one thing and did it well. Clearly, these products have matured and after years of capital investment and development, have become apps that deliver way beyond their core functionality. What's important to note is that they are great examples of products that were released to market with a minimal feature set, targeted at solving a core problem for an initial segment of users.

Benefits of MVP

Embracing a Lean MVP product design and development model within your organization helps keep costs at a minimum and allows you to test and validate your ideas much faster:

- **Keep it simple**: Focusing on core functionality that delivers immediate value/utility allows you to get your product into the market faster, rather than committing to endless cycles of development that are needed to deliver a full-blown multifeature product.
- **Save money**: Reveal the market validity of your product and justify a case for further investment and development. Have a working prototype that allows you to pivot or persevere with minimal costs or efforts.
- **Learn and evolve**: The iterative and evolutionary nature of the MVP model is meant to be fast and nimble. It allows you to mature and refine your product over time in short sprints, while simultaneously surfacing invaluable user feedback and insights that help inform and shape your future iterations.

How to define your MVP

There is a lot of controversy surrounding how to define an MVP, as it relates to answering the question of "How minimal is minimal?" It's a very subjective concept, and every product has its own set of nuances and requirements that make it a little different. It's not an all-or-nothing proposition, but there are techniques and best practices that can be applied to help you define your offering as a MVP. The market demands may require more than one core piece of functionality to define MVP.

In this section, we will discuss the following topics:

- How to build an MVP
- Bringing components together to form an MVP
- Applying MVP to enterprise

Building MVP

In the following first illustration, it's clear that the intended MVP was to build a vehicle that would allow its users to commute from point A to point B, not necessarily how fast, how far, or committing to a motorized vehicle versus self-powered, and so on:

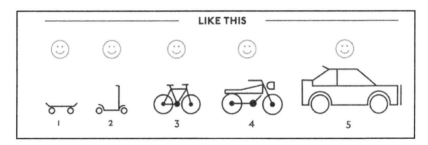

Clearly, in the second illustration, multiple use-cases and conditions were considered, and as a result this model won't allow for quick market validation and runs the risk of increasing costs and potentially missing the mark with its audience:

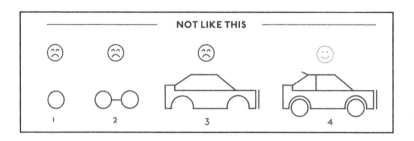

Bringing components together to form an MVP

In the first illustration, they brought together several components to create a skateboard. They needed a board, some wheels, and the truck mounts to connect the wheels to the board. All these things together made up the MVP for a commuter vehicle. Apply this metaphor and thought process to the MVP that you are defining. For example, if your MVP is a CRM software, at the most basic level, it will need to provide a central place where users can store customer and prospect contact information, share it with colleagues, and track sales progress. Multiple components or features will be combined in order to define the MVP. Bringing together the functionality for managing customers and the reporting functionality to track sales leads is what defines the MVP for our example CRM. Both of these components are mini MVPs in and of themselves, and as standalone components don't define the MVP for a competitive CRM in the market. Don't forget, the **V** stands for **Viable**, and that means having just enough features to start selling.

Applying MVP to enterprise

The traditional enterprise approach to software development is focused around delivering the perfect, full-blown and feature-rich product before it is released to customers. Neither of this is minimal or viable, as it relates to MVP guidelines and best practices. Enterprise teams struggle to define minimal (just the right amount of features that add value and utility) and balance it against viable (do I have enough features in my product that people are willing to pay for?).

There are different methods that can be applied to enterprise products that help redefine MVP in that space:

- **Data-driven design**: Place data at the center of product decisions. It's easier than ever to use the voice of customers, usage metrics, and existing performance reports to create a hierarchy of features that can be prioritized and paired down to minimum and viable.

- **Know your market**: You can't build everything for everyone. Make sure you have a clear target market segment and start there, even if that means your customer is an enterprise player. Clearly defining who it is you are building your product for will help you define a barrier of entry into market and solidify your MVP.

- **Minimum Sellable Product (MSP)**: Once you've defined your MVP, don't forget to make sure it's viable. Test it with your target market to ensure that it has the minimal amount of features that your users would be willing to pay for. And avoid the common mistake of relying solely on the product manager's intuition and internal assumptions to predict which features drive products. Validate!

- **Apply incremental UX**: Bring the concept of MVP down to the component or feature level, it's not an all-or-nothing proposition anymore. The basic idea is to have a planned progression (leaving room for improvements through testing) of a feature that adds functionality at each stage. This will allow you to get to the market faster (viability) and mature your product over time through validated learning that saves time and costs.

But don't think that everyone will understand this process immediately, especially in an enterprise where your colleagues and teams are spread out across the world. It requires relentless evangelism. In our company, *Dominion Dealer Solutions*, we have offices around the US supported by offshore teams in three different countries. To make things more challenging, many of the teams were former acquisitions that came with their own inherited cultures and biases. Getting everyone to understand and embrace the concept of developing MVPs took a lot of evangelizing by key people to develop buy-in. This took many months, but once the idea took hold, it spread like wildfire.

Fail fast – validate everything

The core fundamentals of MVP are to get user feedback, do user testing, and validate whether users are willing to use (and pay for) the product you are launching both before and throughout the entire product life cycle. Unfortunately, some teams get caught up with minimum/viable, and forget about validation altogether. Validated learning is the critical component that defines MVP, confirms market demand, and shapes future iterations and investment of time, revenue, and resources into your product. It is the best indicator of whether or not you should pivot and abandon a project before losing too much money and burning out resources, or persevere and keep forging ahead in the market. MVP is governed by a "fail fast and recover quickly" continuous validation model that ensures that teams remain hyperefficient in regards to time, resources, and operational capital.

Let's look at the three things that help us do a good job at failing fast:

- Apply agile prototyping - eliminate tech debt
- Adopt Lean UX cycles - the Build-Measure-Learn feedback loop
- Testing methods and best practices

Apply agile prototyping - eliminate tech debt

Prototypes allow you to explore design ideas, test assumptions, and gather feedback from users while minimizing technical debt. For the ones who might not know, technical debt refers to future work that builds up over time when a team codes quickly to get a product or prototype to market, rather than code well to create the best possible solution.

In many cases, given today's technology, you can create high-def prototypes that require no technical debt at all. Any time savings that might be potentially gained by bypassing prototyping is lost many times over in development if your MVP interfaces and functions need to be redesigned and recreated after they have been committed to code.

Here are some of the advantages and benefits that are gained if you apply agile prototyping to your product design and development process:

- **Ownership and collaboration**: Increase team consensus and ownership; discover potential usability issues and correct them in prototype before programming a line of code and potentially assuming tech debt.
- **Workflow efficiency**: Reduce and eliminate the need for extensive story writing and requirement documentation. It's much different when everyone can click and engage over an actual experience versus imagining and interpreting user interactions using wireframes or mockups.

- **Validate often**: Gather real-time feedback from users and rapidly evolve your MVP quickly, sprint by sprint.

Lean UX cycles – the Build-Measure-Learn feedback loop

A core component of Lean UX is the Build-Measure-Learn feedback loop. The concept is originally derived from the book entitled *"The Lean Startup"*, by Eric Ries. Its goal is to validate uncertainties, assumptions, and potential risks in order to guide future MVP iterations and product direction. The loop forms a cycle, and the cycle is applied to a sprint in agile development. This approach provides a methodology that quickly and effectively proves whether a product vision (MVP) will flounder or flourish:

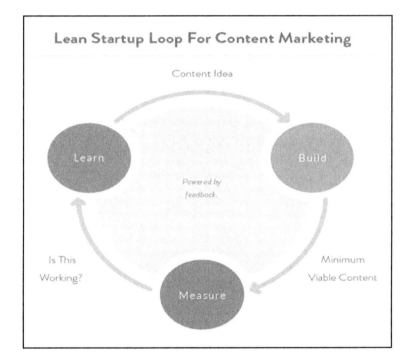

Advantages of a feedback-focused development model

Adopting a data-driven, feedback-focused development model allows organizations to manage development costs and resources much more efficiently. Development time and labor can immediately be reduced by creating a hi-fi prototype that can be used in validation cycles to inform the design process. It's a feast or famine digital marketplace out there—invalidated business assumptions are too risky and costly to produce in today's digital marketplace.

Phases of the Build-Measure-Learn feedback loop

There are three phases to this loop: Build, Measure, and Learn.

Phase I - Build

The first step is figuring out the problem that needs to be solved and then defining and developing an MVP to begin the process of learning as quickly as possible:

- **Ideate**: Develop your idea or concept. Identify what the problem that needs solving is in very clear terms.
- **Create your prototype**: Think simple and small. It's best to build the smallest possible increment that quickly brings back enough validation to inform next steps.
- **Define an experiment/test study to prove your hypothesis**: Create question sets, consider A/B tests, and task analysis.

Phase II - Measure

The next step is to gather as much validated learning as you can in an interactive cycle, and shape the patterns and insights derived from your testing to drive future investments and iterations of your MVP:

- **Initiate your test study**: Conduct interviews, distribute questionnaires, and validate your prototype.
- **Analyze**: Take a look at your data objectively. What surfaced? Are there any common patterns and behaviors?
- **Organize**: Cluster patterns and behaviors that overlap together start shaping and surfacing insights.
- **Compile**: Take your insights and translate them into actionable items and talking points that will help inform potential revisions, future iterations, and releases.

Phase III - Learn

This is where a decision will need to be made regarding whether to persevere or pivot with your MVP. Persevere, in this context, means forging ahead with the same goals, while pivot requires at the very least altering, and even potentially completely resetting your original MVP vision:

- Establish whether your MVP actually solves a problem for its users. Does my MVP meet the needs of my intended target user?
- Establish your MVP viability. Does my MVP provide a feature set that my users are willing to pay for?

10 essential UX testing methods

Validation is the cornerstone of MVP product development. It's the fuel that powers the MVP Build-Measure-Learn feedback loop. There are a number of different testing methods that can be used to help define MVP and continuously improve UX iteratively by applying Build-Measure-Learn cycles.

The following are 10 essential UX testing methods that can be used to help validate your MVP:

1. **Survey**: The most cost-effective way to find out who your users are, what they want, what they do, what they purchase, where they shop, and what they own is to survey them. You can find survey software that is free, so there's no excuse.
2. **Persona/market segmentation**: Use the survey data and identify meaningful patterns and behaviors among your user groups. Surface what functions certain segments demand as well as the pain points they experience. Find your MVP market sweet spot within your market segment.
3. **Contextual inquiry**: Sometimes it's difficult for users to communicate exactly what they want or what they are trying to achieve. It's always ideal to observe users in their environment performing the tasks and functions that are critical to their role. You can probe and survey them while they are performing their tasks to discover what works and what needs improving.
4. **SME/stakeholder interviews**: There's a lot of information that can be tapped internally within your own organization. Interview any SMEs, customer support, QA, development, marketing, or sales personnel to find out what needs to be built, for whom, and why.
5. **Task analysis**: Measure discoverability, usability, and performance by observing users engaged in specific tasks and workflows.

6. **Moderated in-person testing**: This is ideal for mobile device testing, or when it's tough to put prototypes up remotely, test users in a lab, conference room, or even a coffee shop to gather invaluable feedback and insight.

7. **Moderated remote testing**: This is the cheapest form of user testing available. Using services such as Zoom meetings, Google Forms, and InVision allow you to record and moderate user tests anywhere on the internet. Helps expands your recruitment base, and doesn't limit user pools.

8. **A/B testing**: This can be used in many conditions, remote, moderated, and so on. Comparatively test layouts, interface controls, buttons, CTAs, colors, tasks, performance... the sky's the limit.

9. **Comparative benchmark study**: Comparatively test the same tasks on competitive applications. Use core metrics such as completion rates, time and task difficulty as a basis for creating benchmarks. For example, is the checkout process at Zappos faster, more efficient, and easier to use than the checkout process at Amazon?

10. **Multivariate testing**: One-variable-at-a-time testing can take a long time, and you will quickly burn through your testers a lot faster than expected. If you need to test often, performing multivariate tests will allow you to not only maximize the returns you get from your testing pool, but also give you a great idea of how your experience works as a whole. For instance, changing the color of a button will glean some data, but nothing compares to the data you mine when you change the location, color, and label of the button and test all the variants together. You can do multivariate tests on both live and prototype environments. Products such as Optimizely helps you organize and launch multivariate tests in live environments with real users.

Iterate and evolve - from viable to lovable

Now that we have successfully launched our initial MVP into the market, and gathered some validated learning, what's next? How does it scale? Is it just more of the same? No, absolutely not. This whole process is all about evolving and maturing your product, your users, and your revenue. The goal has become about taking your product from viable to lovable, introducing **Minimum Loveable Product (MLP)**.

MLP is defined as the version of the product that brings back the maximum amount of love from its users with the least amount of effort. We all recognize products in our lives that we love and can't live without: cars, smartphones created by remarkable brands such as Apple, Audi, Samsung, and G-Star. We love these products because they evoke a positive emotional connection within us. In simple terms, they make us smile.

There are many different ways of making a positive emotional connection with your users, but the easiest is through good design.

Five tips to go from viable to lovable

Here are some great insights to help guide your product down a "Loveable" user experience path:

- **Focus on value**: Most often, teams are laser-focused on what they are building, not why. Users aren't motivated to buy the what (lawnmower); they buy the why (I need to cut my grass). Build stuff that matters.
- **Do one thing really well**: One solid function or feature is much better than three mediocre ones. Learn from success stories such as Dropbox and Instagram. They created masses of followers that love their products by simply focusing on doing one thing really well.
- **Validate and iterate often**: Working on moving targets with no end in sight equals lost vision, lost opportunity, lost motivation, and lost revenue. Validate your designs against short cycles. Timebox your MVP to 90-day increments (12-week cycles). 90 days is enough time to deliver on your vision, but not long enough to lose sight of it.
- **Make the user first**: Zoom in on problems that are real pain points for your customer. Have you validated these pain points, or are they your opinion? Remember, user-centered product design is an exercise in other-centeredness. It's about your audience's response to your products, not yours.
- **Talk the talk, walk the walk**: Commit to the objective and stay disciplined to the process. If design is important to you, demonstrate it through your actions: bring design in early to collaborate on MVP strategy/vision—start wireframes and protos early. Don't just say that your customer is important to you, show it through your actions: test and validate your MVP ideas.

Summary

In this chapter, we looked at the concept of MVP and why it's important. We covered techniques that will help you define and build your MVP. We outlined a Lean Agile UX process to follow, and demonstrated the advantages and benefits to validating your MVP. Lastly, we discussed evolving your MVP from viable to lovable, and how to evoke an emotional response from your users. Use these building blocks to save time and money, and begin building products that you know your users will love and need.

In the next chapter, we will review case studies that illustrate many of the ideas discussed here.

USER FIRST + GOOD DESIGN = LOVABLE PRODUCT

7

Minimal Viable Product Case Studies

In this final chapter, we explore different strategies for the construction of a **Minimal Viable Product (MVP)**.

These include the following:

- Concierge
- Landing page
- Fake-O-Backend
- Competitor apps
- Analog
- Dry-wallet
- Letter of intent

The preceding strategies provide a framework for running quick experiments at varying levels of fidelity, and leveraging the learnings to answer high-risk assumptions about your app's business model canvas.

In this chapter, we'll dive into an MVP case study to learn more about how they are applied across a series of experiment loops.

We'll discuss Fun with Charades, an app that my team and I built to help people around the world play charades through an online video chat room. We'll discuss the original vision, key high-risk assumptions we faced, how we developed a hypothesis-led approach to testing them, how we iterated based on learnings, and our final conclusions.

Fun with Charades - Initial vision

Here's the initial vision, target audience, and problem statement that we started with:

- **Vision**: To create a fun place where people make new friends online
- **Target**: Teens, college kids, yuppies, casual gamers
- **Problem**: To connect people online through dumb charades

As we thought about this, there were a number of questions:

- Do people care at all about charades? *Ellen's* charades game was wildly popular, and there was a lot of buzz around Heads Up Charades!, but that was not indicative of whether people would want to play online.
- Would charades be engaging enough that people would want to play regularly?
- If we set up a real-time game to mimic the mechanics of the game we are used to, that would require friends being present at the same time, which may be hard to schedule.
- If scheduling was hard, would people be comfortable playing with strangers in game rooms, like online poker?
- Wouldn't people freak out just a bit about using video online? Are there communities that are more open to using video online?
- If we built an async game with mobile apps so that people could play when they had time, that might work. But would it be practical for people to respond to a challenge by acting while simultaneously holding their smartphones in front of them?
- And then, there was the question of whether we had an interest and competencies in gaming.

The big ifs

We set out to break these down and tackle what we felt were the biggest doubts on our list:

- Are people interested in playing charades online?
- Are they comfortable using video online?
- Do they like the concept enough to invite friends or join a public game room?
- Do they enjoy the playing experience with others in the room?
- Do they enjoy this enough to keep coming back?
- Will they invite other people?

Next, we attempted to structure experiments around the major leap-of-faith assumptions being made, in order to seek validation.

Hypothesis 1

Of a sampling set of people searching for charades online, at least 25% will sign up to check out the game:

- **Audience**: Targets the people looking to play charades online.
- **Acquisition**: Uses Google Ads.
- **Validation**: This includes the percentage of sign-ups.
- **Execution**:
    - Build the signup page in a day.
    - Identify keywords and run ads for a week.
    - Track signups.
- **Result**: We ran ads targeting users who searched for "charades online", "charades games", and "charades words", and over 25% of the users signed up.
- **Learning**: There's an interest in playing charades online among those who search for it on Google:

Hypothesis 2

Of the users in the target demographic who are shown mockup flows of the game concept, at least 70% of them would be very interested in the game:

- **Audience**: Targets the young adults in India.
- **Acquisition**: Uses your friends network for recruitment.
- **Validation**: This includes the % of people who are very interested in the game.
- **Execution**:
    - Build rough mock-ups using MockFlow in a day.
    - Walk people through the mock-ups.
    - Collect feedback.

- **Result**: Overall, there was unanimous interest in the game concept, but a few mentioned that they may be uncomfortable being on video online.
- **Learning**: In general, charades is popular in India, and people are interested in trying out an online game:

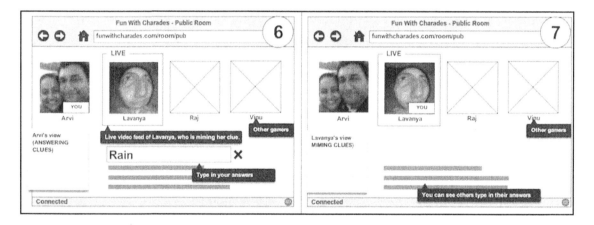

Hypothesis 3

Of the signed-up charades users invited to a game room, at least 25% will be willing to join a public room and use video online:

- **Audience**: This includes the signed-up users.
- **Acquisition**: N/A.
- **Validation**: Includes the % of users who used online video in a public room.

- **Execution**:
    - Invite users to the public room.
    - Provide an explanation on what the game is about.
    - Enable the user to turn the video on and start the game.
    - Track analytics.

- **Result**: 80% of the users visited the page, but < 5% turned the video on.
- **Learning**: This experiment invalidated our false hope that people in this era of FaceTime and Hangouts wouldn't hesitate to use video online. Therefore, we need to dig deeper, and talk to users to understand how they felt:

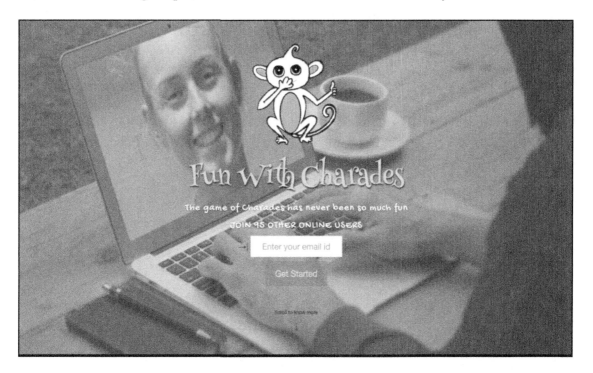

Hypothesis 4

Users are more likely to be comfortable using video online if they are playing with their friends, and 80% or more will then use video online:

- **Audience**: Targets friends of friends who are acquainted with each other, but don't know each other well.
- **Acquisition**: Uses your friends network for recruitment.
- **Validation**: This includes the % of users who use video online. % of users who like the game idea enough that they would be disappointed to not play.
- **Execution**:
    - Invite users to the public room.
    - Provide an explanation as to what the game is about.
    - Enable the user to turn the video on and start the game
    - Track analytics.

- **Result**: 100% of users turned the video on and were excited and ready to engage in the game, and they felt they would be very disappointed if they were unable to play.
- **Learning**: When asked if they would play with people they didn't know online, women said they would hesitate, while men in the group unanimously said they would be willing to try:

Hypothesis 5

Users from online communities who use video online with strangers are a lot more likley to be comfortable playing with each other, and at least 25% will use video online:

- **Audience**: Targets Chatroulette and Chatrandom communities.
- **Acquisition**: Uses Google Ads.
- **Validation**: This includes the % of users who turn the video on.
- **Execution**:
    - Run Google Ads for Chatroulette and Chatrandom, offering video-based charades online, and an opportunity to meet new people.
    - Invite users to the public room.
    - Provide an explanation on what the game is about.
    - Enable the user to turn the video on and start the game.
    - Track analytics.
    - Add a Qualroo-style prompt to find out why they don't turn the video on.
- **Result**: 50% of the users visited the page, but < 10% turned the video on. 5% answered the prompt indicating they didn't want to turn the video on, would try later, or weren't sure how to turn it on.
- **Learning**: Given the anonymity of these communities, it was hard to reach out directly and get feedback, and the sampling size of the responders to the prompt was too small to infer enough.

The conundrum

We spoke to a group of users and collated feedback. So, at this point, we were faced with this conundrum from our learnings:

- There's a certain level of interest in charades, but it's mostly seen as a family and friends game.
- For those who see their friends and family often enough, playing charades online wasn't appealing. (Playing live with them during Thanksgiving or Christmas was still appealing.)
- The average user isn't comfortable playing with random strangers online.
- Even communities that are comfortable dealing with nudity online, and have no reservations, didn't find the idea appealing

- Improvements in the visual design and explanatory information offered did not increase conversions.
- A game like this requires a fairly engaged community, and it didn't appear that charades would sustain that level of engagement.
- There's a community of people in the subcontinent that loves dumb charades, but the version that's played is fairly technical and geeky, and would not scale out.

What we did well

- Captured our thought process and assumptions, laying out the facts for us to succeed
- Identified small batches that could be proven (or disproven) with minimum cost, rapidly built, and iterated through the batches
- Stayed honest and objective, tracked metrics and cohorts well

What we could have done better

- Most early feedback was from subcontinent users, since reaching out to an international audience was not easy. Consequently feedback was not fully representative of the target audience.
- We built more than we should have before we understood the gaps in our understanding of the customer and their behavior.
- We included more online surveys early on enough to have better insights.

Summary

We still believed in the original vision, and it's possible that persevering and keeping this going out there in the wild may have yielded something. However, we were invalidated conclusively and decided to pivot away and explore other ideas. In hindsight, it was a good decision and likely saved us from the clutches of the sunken cost fallacy.

Many people have strong misgivings about wasting resources (loss aversion). The example we saw in this chapter involved a non-refundable sporting event ticket. Many people would feel obliged to go to the event despite not really wanting to, because doing otherwise would be wasting the ticket price; they feel they've passed the point of no return.

This is sometimes referred to as the sunk cost fallacy. Economists would label this behavior irrational: it is inefficient because it misallocates resources by depending on information that is irrelevant to the decision being made. (via Wikipedia).

The important takeaways from this case study are as follows:

- The rigor and discipline needed to run experiments
- The willingness to adapt based on new learnings and surprises
- The need to focus on the vision (although, in this case, our team did not stay committed to it long term)
- The leverage of proxy users and trade-offs involved

In the next chapter, you will learn more about using **Software as a Service (SaaS)** cloud-based services to enable you to rapidly run experiment loops.

8

Cloud Solutions for App Experiments

While an MVP could be something as minimal as a landing page, announcing your app, or a live mock up version of your app, there comes a time that your app should be a little more than that, whether it is to prove your next hypotheses or to see the actual thing in its most basic shape in action. It's about time to create a **Proof of Concept** (**PoC**).

Standalone apps are rare these days. Most apps have functionality to share content on Twitter or Facebook, have leaderboards (if it is a game), let the user post pictures or video, have a chat or otherwise communicate with each other, and so on. For this your app needs to have a backend.

You can of course create your own API or use the API of the many solutions that do exist for this purpose, the so-called **Mobile backend as a Service** (**MBaaS**). These solutions do work like any other **Software as a Service** (**SaaS**) but are specifically intended for this purpose.

In this chapter, we will have a look on MBaaS solutions and will see what it takes to build an Android PoC using Firebase, a popular cloud-based backend.

Specifically, in the chapter we will cover the following topics:

- Find out if we need to create a backend on our own
- Leverage cloud solutions for app experiments
- Determine what services are available as MBaaS
- Examine an Android PoC app using Firebase

Do you need to create a backend yourself?

It totally depends on your app's needs, but for most apps there is no reason at all to create a backend yourself, at least not for your **Minimum Viable Product** (**MVP**). There are plenty of readymade backend solutions available.

Most solutions support push notifications, data storage, social sign up and login (sign up or login using your Facebook or Twitter credentials for example) and data synchronization functionality, including offline support for your app.

If you have to program all these things for yourself, it could take up a lot of time and it will probably take even more time to make it error free.

Almost all solutions come as freemium service and most of the time the free options are good enough to build your MVP. Some of them, such as Firebase, come with real-time support, making it a great base for a chat app. Later, we will build a PoC with Firebase, but first let's see what solutions are currently available.

What a MBaaS can do for you is illustrated here. Most solutions offer a web-based **Content Management System** (**CMS**), an **Application Programming Interface** (**API**) and a **Software Development Kit** (**SDK**). Such a solution will take care of storing both remote and local data. In addition, it has support for the synchronization of data (it sends local persisting data to a remote location and vice versa) and for distributing push notifications:

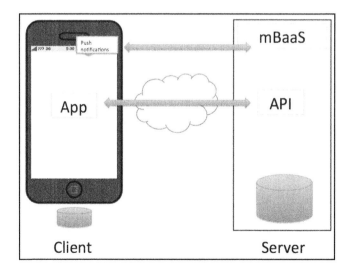

To be more precise, an API is a way for apps to communicate with the data stored at the remote server (cloud solution). Data can often be retrieved through a **Representational State Transfer (REST)** interface over http(s). The SDK is a piece of software that you can add to your own app. It will make the usage of the API more convenient. Often the API will take care of things such as obtaining data and data synchronization. The integration of the service will be simplified by using the API, but you can still use the REST interface, for example, to show the same data on the website.

Leverage cloud solutions for app experiments

MBaaS solutions are great for getting things going real quickly. Most solutions come with features that almost any app has in common, such as registration, login, retrieving, saving, and sharing data. Another big advantage of using an MBaaS is its scalability. Right now we are aiming for the development of an MVP and technical scaling issues are luxury problems. However, it is good to know upfront that these problems are easier to resolve using these kinds of third-party solutions. Your app has scalability but does not yet need to scale. If it needs to be scaled up, then you just switch to a bigger plan (from a technical perspective). You will read more about scaling strategies in `Chapter 15`, *Growing Traction and Improving Retention*.

Things to consider

There are some other things to look at, such as pricing. You can start with a free plan, but if you need to scale up your solution, it is important to know how fast the price will increase. Is the service still reasonably priced if you need to deal with high volumes. When that happens money may no longer be a big issue as your business already has grown significantly. It could also be that your strategy is to use the service only for a first MVP. It is all fine as long as you have a strategy and you keep these things in mind.

Another thing to think about is the fact that your user data resides on the server of a third party such as Facebook or Google. You should ask yourself if you should trust third parties to build a solution. Of course a lot depends on the nature of the solution. Anyhow there are things that you would like to know for sure such as "Is your data safe and what is going to happen if the service provider decides to discontinue its services?" Parse server and Firebase have some impressive names in their testimonials, so we can probably assume that in most cases your data is safe indeed.

The story of Parse

The second one is more relevant than you might think. A while ago Parse announced they were going to discontinue their services. That announcement made a lot of (independent) developers pretty angry. These developers were totally dependent on Parse services. The discontinuation of Parse made them fearful because they thought they had no other choice but to end their business. Developers had high expectations from the services, also because Parse had been acquired by Facebook. It seemed to be very solid. Apparently, that acquisition perhaps also led to that same announcement. For Facebook, the team was probably more interesting than the service itself.

Fortunately, this fairy tale has a happy end. Parse came with a nice migration plan, which nowadays is known as the open source solution Parse server. You can host it yourself but if you do not want to do that then there is no problem either. A lot of other parties jumped right on it and started to offer Parse server hosting. The server itself does not come with all the features that were available in Parse but parties such as Back4App did a great job adding them all back in.

In short, this story proves that you should not completely depend on services like these. Partners are important but when they become irreplaceable the future of your startup could possibly be uncertain. And while this story is about Parse, the same thing could happen to Firebase, for example. That is not very likely but Google has shut down some services before, so it also is not completely impossible.

Strategic considerations

If you need to make a decision whether to use a cloud-based service or not and if you need to make a choice from the various available services, then there are some strategic considerations that could be important. Using such a service comes with both advantages and disadvantages. A number of them are listed next.

The following are the advantages:

- The service shortens the development time
- Out of the box the service often comes with support for registration and login
- Most services can easily be scaled up or down, depending on the amount of traffic that you are expecting
- Almost all services support push notifications and media storage

The following are the disadvantages:

- A ready-to-use service is often more expensive. Pricing could be an issue.
- The privacy of your (user) data could be an issue. You have to trust that the company, that is offering the service, is taking the right precautions to ensure the security.
- There is always the risk that the service will be discontinued.
- There is a lock-in risk. It could be difficult to migrate to another service when all your data is residing with a particular provider.

What services are available as MBaaS?

There are a couple of services available that could act as a backend for your app. Given the strategic considerations from the previous paragraph and the specific needs of your app, one service might be more suitable than another.

Some offer real-time data, making it perfect for a chat application. Others are more about persisting data or come with building blocks, such as QuickBlox, allowing you to create your app even faster. Some are pretty dedicated solutions, pretty easy and fast to use but not very flexible. Others are very flexible but come with a steeper learning curve:

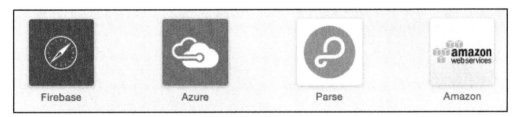

Most solutions store data in a document-related database, such as MongoDB. If you need to have a relational type of database for your app, then choosing Azure with SQL Server will probably be the best thing to do. Choose the service that matches most closely with your app needs and your current development skills:

- **Back4App**: The service offers hosted parse servers. The service has support for push notifications, data, and file storage and it supports Cloud code. Cloud code is code, often queries, that run on the Parse server. You can use the common Android and iOS Parse SDKs to communicate with the server.
- **SashiDo**: Just like Back4App, this is a service that offers a hosted parse server plus a couple of extra things.

- **Firebase**: It is a scalable real-time backend for web, Android, and iOS. It is perfect for chat and collaboration tools, but is also suitable for other needs. Storing media such as images or video is a bit more complicated when compared with Parse server or Azure, for example.
- **BaasBox**: This is an open source backend for your mobile app. It has SDKs for iOS, Android, and JavaScript.
- **QuickBlox**: This service provides building blocks for a backend infrastructure. It offers data storage, push notifications, text and video chat, and many other features. It allows developers to create apps quickly, but is a bit pricy. For this reason, it is most suitable for a PoC and less for a real app.
- **Azure**: Microsoft Azure comes with support for push notifications and other mobile services. It has become one of Microsoft's core businesses, so you can see Azure as one of the most trustworthy MBaaS solutions. The platform will stay for sure. It is also true that, compared to other MBaaS, the Azure services can sometimes be a little bit confusing. It is less dedicated to MBaaS alone. It can simply do way too many things and it can make the service a bit overwhelming if you just got started. It is very flexible and because of this it has a relatively steep learning curve. For your app needs, you can use table and blob storage (for images, documents, and so on), use the mobile services, the API services, or you can create your own API using .NET or another language. There are Azure client SDKs for Android, iOS, and Windows.
- **Backendless**: Backendless provides an instant mobile Backend as a Service and overall application development Platform.
- **remoteStorage**: `remoteStorage` offers an open protocol for per-user storage. Use a storage account with a provider you trust, or set up your own storage server.
- **CloudBoost.io**: This is a complete database service that comes with data storage, search, real-time and other stuff.
- **PubNub**: `PubNub` is a real-time network that enables software developers to rapidly build and scale real-time apps by providing the cloud infrastructure, connections, and key building.
- **Parse server**: The Parse server is an open source solution that you can download and host by yourself. You could also, for example, host it on Heroku or on Azure. The server uses a MongoDB database and utilizes Amazon S3 storage to store files, such as images, audio or video. The Parse SDKs for Android and iOS include all kinds of handy stuff, such as caching data and uploading data or files in the background.

Technical considerations

Besides strategic considerations, there are also a couple of technical aspects to consider. Before you choose a particular service, you should ask yourself the following questions:

- Does your app require real-time support?
- Does your app handle a lot of media (images, video, and audio)?
- How trustworthy should the service provider be?
- How good are your current skills that are required to use the chosen service?
- How much flexibility do you need and how much time do you have available?

In the next paragraph, we will examine an Android MVP that is using Firebase.

Canvapp - an Android MVP app using Firebase

Let's build an Android MVP app using Firebase. For this particular case, we will have an app that allows you to create and share your business model canvas, just by using your phone. Anyone can view or edit each other's canvases so you can gather feedback easily. If you do not remember what the business model canvas looks like, you can have a look at Chapter 2, *Lean Startup Primer* again.

We will be using a wireframing tool, such as SwordSoft Layout as shown in the following example . Let's say that the app should look more or less like this:

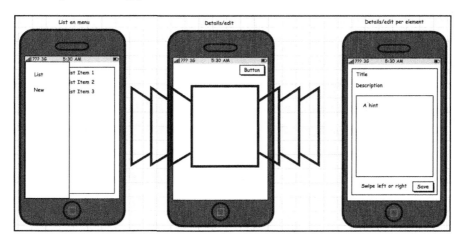

The first view displays a list of business model canvases and it has a sliding menu. The second view is the one that the user will see when he is creating a new canvas or when he chooses a canvas from the list. It displays a number of pages, each containing a title, description, and some hint. Users can swipe back and forward. It is a very basic app. It has only three views, but that will be sufficient to demonstrate how to use Firebase as a backend and we can use it to prove that this app concept does make sense.

For the sake of simplicity, we will just say, for this example, that you have already validated your earliest hypotheses. The hypotheses for this solution are:

- Startup entrepreneurs want to share their canvases to get feedback from other entrepreneurs.
- Startup entrepreneurs want to share their canvases using a smartphone or tablet. This will allow us to focus on the technical implementation of the app.

You can find the source for this project at:
`https://github.com/mikerworks/packt-lean-saas-canvapp`.

Sign up for Firebase

If you want to see things in action, you will have to go to `www.firebase.com` and sign up. Once you have done that, you can create your first app. The only thing that matters is the endpoint that Firebase will create. You need this endpoint to configure your app. In the following example, the endpoint is **torrid-head-3108.firebaseIO.com**:

First, download the Android Firebase example from GitHub (`https://github.com/mikerworks/packt-lean-saas-canvapp`), so we can go through it and see what it is all about. If you prefer, and if you have some time left, you can also build this app from scratch, of course. For now, you can download the readymade app, examine it, and modify it as needed:

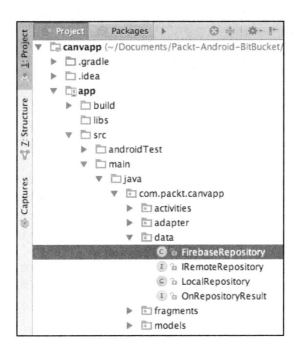

Open the app in Android Studio or another IDE if you prefer. One of the things that you need to modify is the Firebase endpoint in the application. Collapse the `data` package node within the app and open the `FirebaseRepository` class. Within the `FirebaseRepository` class, locate the constructor and adapt the firebase reference so that it matches yours:

```
public class FirebaseRepository implements IRemoteRepository {
    private Firebase reference;
    private Context context;
    public FirebaseRepository(Context context){
        Firebase.setAndroidContext(context);
        this.context = context;
        reference = new Firebase("https://<your endpoint here>/canvapp/");
    }
```

When you run the app and have added a couple of canvases it looks more or less like this. Yeah, it already contains some cool ideas:

When you run the app and have added a couple of canvases it looks more or less like this. Yeah, it already contains some cool ideas. The app will display a list of canvas models residing in Firebase. The title and description for each model will be shown. Anyone can view or edit it by clicking on a model. This will display the edit view, which will contain a swipeable collection of canvas elements. A new canvas can be created through the options in the menu.

For this app, we have created a new project in Android Studio and we chose the **Navigation Drawer** to be our first activity. This will give us a nice template with a readymade menu. It is here that the List and New canvas options are going to appear.

Layout

There are a few layout resources in the project (res/layout) that we will describe. These layouts are as follows:

- **The list layout**: This displays a list of canvases
- **The pager layout**: This shows a swipeable series of elements.
- **The element layout**: This layout will display a title, description, some hints, and edit box for each element of the Business Model Canvas.
- **The row layout**: This renders each row in the list of canvases.

The layout files are small and contain just some boilerplate code. It is nothing fancy but we need it anyway to create the Android Firebase PoC. You can examine them if you want, but for now let's proceed with the parts of the code that are most relevant.

Dependencies

To examine the list of dependencies for the app, open the `build.gradle` file within the `app` folder. Among other things, you will find the dependencies for Firebase and JSON deserialization here, as listed next:

```
dependencies {
    compile fileTree(dir: 'libs', include: ['*.jar'])
    testCompile 'junit:junit:4.12'
    compile 'com.android.support:appcompat-v7:23.3.0'
    compile 'com.android.support:design:23.3.0'
    compile 'com.android.support:cardview-v7:23.1.1'
    compile 'com.android.support:recyclerview-v7:23.3.0'
    compile 'com.squareup.retrofit:converter-gson:2.0.0-beta2'
    compile 'com.firebase:firebase-client-android:2.5.2+'
}
```

Within the `res` folder raw, you will find the `canvas.json` file. The JSON data in this file will be parsed using `Gson`. It will act as a template for each new canvas. All the user needs to do is to provide a value for each element.

The JSON object in the file looks like this. It will be processed by the `LocalRepository` class:

```
{
  "ELEMENTS": [
    ...
  {
```

```
  "ID": "PROPOSITIONS",
  "TITLE": "VALUE PROPOSITIONS",
  "DESCRIPTION": "what value do you deliver to the customer? Which of your
customer's problems are you helping to resolve? What bundles of services
are you offering? Which needs do you satisfy?",
  "HINT": "Enter your proposition here. What are the characteristics of it?
What does it make unique? Is it price? Cost or risk reduction? A better
design or performance? Is it more convenient? Why?..."
},
{
  "ID": "SEGMENTS",
  "TITLE": "CUSTOMER SEGMENTS",
  "DESCRIPTION": "For who are you creating value?\nWho are you most
important customers?",
  "HINT": "Describe your customer segments here. Be as specific as
possible. A niche market is much better as aiming for 'everybody'. If it is
a platform what customers do you want to bring together. Who are your most
important customers?..."
 },
{
  "ID": "CHANNELS",
  "TITLE": "CHANNELS",
  "DESCRIPTION": "Through which channels do your customer segments want to
be reached? How are you reaching them now? How are your channels
integrated?\nWhich ones work best?",
  "HINT": "Describe your channels. How do you raise awareness? How can you
help your customers to evaluate the value proposition? How can they
purchase your services and how are they delivered?..."
}
```

 This template implements a particular type of Business Model Canvas. There are some variants as well. Ash Maurya, for example, uses a different and, in my opinion, more suitable canvas. He calls it the Lean Canvas and it has been described in Chapter 2, *Lean Startup Primer*.

Feel free to modify the template or to create a totally different application, derived from this one, for example, for some kind of survey.

Models

A canvas typically has a collection of Canvas elements, each representing a section of the Business Model Canvas. For the sake of simplicity, these classes contain only the most basic information.

The most important models used in the app are the `Canvas` and the `CanvasElement` models. Both the `Canvas` and `CanvasElement` classes implement the `Parcelable` interface. This will make it easier to pass (complex) objects to each fragment:

```
public class Canvas implements Parcelable {
    private String id;
    public List<CanvasElement> ELEMENTS;
    public Canvas(){
        ELEMENTS = new ArrayList<>();
    }
    public void setId(String value){
        this.id= value;
    }
    public String getId(){
        return this.id;
    }
    ...
```

 The `CanvasElement` class and the JSON object found in the template file have similar fields. Each element of the canvas has an ID, title, description, and text for the placeholder. The user input will fill the `value` field:

```
public class CanvasElement implements Parcelable {
    public String ID;
    public String TITLE;
    public String DESCRIPTION;
    public String VALUE;
    public String HINT;

    @Override
    public int describeContents() {
        return 0;
    }
    @Override

    public void writeToParcel(Parcel dest, int flags) {
        dest.writeString(this.ID);
        dest.writeString(this.TITLE);
        dest.writeString(this.DESCRIPTION);
        dest.writeString(this.VALUE);
        dest.writeString(this.HINT);
    }
    ...
    protected CanvasElement(Parcel in) {
        this.ID = in.readString();
```

```
          this.TITLE = in.readString();
          this.DESCRIPTION = in.readString();
          this.VALUE = in.readString();
          this.HINT = in.readString();
      }

      public static final Parcelable.Creator<CanvasElement> CREATOR = new
  Parcelable.Creator<CanvasElement>() {
          @Override
          public CanvasElement createFromParcel(Parcel source) {
              return new CanvasElement(source);
          }
          @Override
          public CanvasElement[] newArray(int size) {
              return new CanvasElement[size];
          }
      };
  }
```

The local repository reads the raw JSON file, which contains the template. It will convert the data to a `CanvasElementsModel` class, which, in turn, is nothing but a wrapper around canvas elements:

```
public class LocalRepository {
    ...
    public static CanvasElementsModel getElements(Context context){
        Reader reader = getStreamReaderForRawAsset(context,R.raw.canvas);
        return new Gson().fromJson(reader, CanvasElementsModel.class);
    }
    private static InputStreamReader getStreamReaderForRawAsset(Context
context, int resId){
        InputStream stream = context.getResources().openRawResource(resId);
        return new InputStreamReader(stream);
    }
}
```

Now it is time for some Firebase stuff. The `IRemoteRepository` interface has been added to the app. This will avoid a vendor lock in. If you ever want to use another MBaaS or your own API, then all you need to do is change the implementation for the three methods found as follows:

```
public interface IRemoteRepository {
    Canvas createCanvas();
    void loadCanvasModels(OnRepositoryResult handler);
    void saveCanvasModel(Canvas model);
}
```

The `FirebaseRepository` class is the Firebase-specific implementation for the `IRemoteRepository` interface. The following code snippet shows you what is needed to store and to retrieve canvases. Let's have a look at the constructor first. Here, the reference to a Firebase endpoint is defined. You can modify the reference value to match the endpoint of your own Firebase app:

```
public class FirebaseRepository implements IRemoteRepository {
    private Firebase reference;
    private Context context;
    public FirebaseRepository(Context context){
        Firebase.setAndroidContext(context);
        this.context = context;
        reference = new
Firebase("https://torrid-heat-3108.firebaseio.com/canvapp/");
    }
```

In the `createCanvas` method, a new `Canvas` object will be created. It will be prefilled with the information we get from the template file through the `LocalRepository` class. We change the reference to a child node canvas and a canvas node is being added as a child node of that node. The `push` method obtains a unique identifier for the canvas. We will store that ID, created by Firebase, with the `Canvas` object. Finally, this method returns the new `Canvas` object:

```
    @Override
    public Canvas createCanvas() {
        Firebase ref = reference.child("canvases");
        Canvas canvas = new Canvas()
        CanvasElementsModel model= LocalRepository.getElements(context);
        canvas.ELEMENTS= model.ELEMENTS;
        Firebase postRef = ref.push();
        postRef.setValue(canvas);
        canvas.setId(postRef.getKey());
        return canvas;
    }
```

One of the cool things about Firebase is that developers do not need to worry too much about being online or offline. In case the device is offline, this method will succeed anyway. Firebase will take care of persisting the new `Canvas` object locally. Once there is an internet connection available again, Firebase will take care of synchronizing the data between your app and the remote repository.

Here is an example of what the app looks like when you start to create a new canvas:

The `saveCanvasModel` method implementation is even smaller. It will update the Firebase data in case the user has made some changes. All you need to do is to call the `setValue` method with a given `Canvas` object. The method retrieves a reference to the canvas data node. The unique ID we obtained earlier in the `createCanvas` method will be used to find the right node. Finally, we only need to call the `setValue` method to send the data to Firebase:

```
@Override
public void saveCanvasModel(Canvas model) {
    Firebase ref = reference.child("canvases").child(model.getId());
    ref.setValue(model);
}
```

In the `loadCanvasModels` method, we will retrieve all the stored canvases and we will add a listener to the canvases node. Every time data is inserted or when existing data changes, the `onDataChange` event will be fired. A snapshot will be provided with each event. It contains the (JSON) data for all child nodes under the canvas's node.

Each child node of the obtained snapshot will be deserialized to a `Canvas` object. The `CanvasList` fragment will be notified so that it can display or update the list:

```
@Override
public void loadCanvasModels(final OnRepositoryResult handler) {
    Firebase ref = reference.child("canvases");
    ref.addValueEventListener(new ValueEventListener() {
        @Override
        public void onDataChange(DataSnapshot snapshot) {
            CanvasListModel model = new CanvasListModel();
            for (DataSnapshot canvasSnapshot: snapshot.getChildren()) {
                Canvas canvas = canvasSnapshot.getValue(Canvas.class);
                canvas.setId(canvasSnapshot.getKey());
                model.canvases.add(canvas);
            }
            handler.onResult(model);
        }
        @Override
        public void onCancelled(FirebaseError firebaseError) {
            System.out.println("The read failed: " +
firebaseError.getMessage());
        }
    });
}
```

The `MainActivity` class is derived from the one that comes with the Navigation Drawer template. It has been slightly modified, so it can display the various fragments. It will also handle the clicks on any of the menu items. The `onList` method is triggered if the app starts for the first time or if the user chooses the list option from the menu. The `onEdit` method is triggered if the user chooses the **new canvas** option from the menu.

The onEdit method will also be called if the users click on any of the listed Business Model Canvases, as displayed in the CanvasList fragment. In the onEdit method, the canvas parameter will be passed. The getRepository method returns a class that implements the IRemoteRepository interface, which in our example is the FireBaseRepository class. If you want to switch from Firebase to Parse or another MBaaS, then all you need to do is return another repository here:

```
public void onList(){
    CanvasListFragment fragment = CanvasListFragment.newInstance();
    showFragment(fragment);
}
public void onEdit(Canvas canvas){
    CanvasEditFragment fragment =  CanvasEditFragment.newInstance(canvas);
    showFragment(fragment);
 }
public void onEdit(){
    Canvas canvas = getRepository().createCanvas();
    onEdit(canvas);
}
private void showFragment(Fragment fragment){
    FragmentTransaction ft = getFragmentManager().beginTransaction();
    ft.replace(R.id.main_layout_container, fragment,
fragment.getClass().toString());
    ft.commit();
}
...
public IRemoteRepository getRepository(){
    return new FirebaseRepository(this);
}
...
```

The app uses three fragments. There is one to display a list of canvases, another one to act as a container for a series of swipeable canvas elements, and there is one for the canvas elements themselves.

The CanvasListFragment has a loadData method, which calls the loadCanvasModels method from the repository:

```
public class CanvasListFragment extends Fragment
        implements OnCardViewClicked, OnRepositoryResult{
    private RecyclerView recyclerView;
    private CanvasListAdapter adapter;
    private CanvasListModel viewModel;

    ...

    @Override
    public View onCreateView(LayoutInflater inflater, ViewGroup container,
```

```
                            Bundle savedInstanceState) {
        final View view = inflater.inflate(R.layout.fragment_canvas_list,
container, false);
        recyclerView =
(RecyclerView)view.findViewById(R.id.canvas_recycle_view);
        loadData();
        return view;
    }

    private void loadData(){
        recyclerView.setLayoutManager(new
LinearLayoutManager(getActivity()));
        recyclerView.setItemAnimator(new DefaultItemAnimator());
((MainActivity)getActivity()).getRepository().loadCanvasModels(this);
        }

    @Override
    public void onCardClicked(View view, int position) {
((MainActivity)getActivity()).onEdit(viewModel.canvases.get(position));
        }
```

When the results are retrieved they will be handled in the onResult method, which will take the result and display list canvases:

```
    @Override
    public void onResult(CanvasListModel result) {
        viewModel = result;
        adapter = new CanvasListAdapter(viewModel,
R.layout.adapter_canvas_list, getActivity());
        adapter.setOnCardViewClicked(this);
        recyclerView.setAdapter(adapter);
    }
}
```

The CanvasPagerFragment is a container fragment. It can hold a number of canvas element fragments, each representing a particular element of the canvas. Users can swipe backward and forward:

```
public class CanvasPagerFragment extends Fragment
        implements OnRepositoryResult, View.OnClickListener {

    private static final String ARG_CANVAS = "ARG_CANVAS";
    private Canvas canvas;
    private ViewPager pager;
    private CanvasElementPageAdapter pagerAdapter;

    public static CanvasPagerFragment newInstance(Canvas canvas) {
        CanvasPagerFragment fragment = new CanvasPagerFragment();
```

```
        Bundle bundle = new Bundle();
        bundle.putParcelable(ARG_CANVAS, canvas);
        fragment.setArguments(bundle);
        return fragment;
    }

    @Override
    public void onCreate(Bundle savedInstanceState) {
        super.onCreate(savedInstanceState);
        canvas = getArguments().getParcelable(ARG_CANVAS);
    }

    @Override
    public View onCreateView(LayoutInflater inflater, ViewGroup container,
Bundle savedInstanceState) {
        final View view = inflater.inflate(R.layout.fragment_canvas_edit,
container, false);
        pager = (ViewPager) view.findViewById(R.id.canvas_edit_pager);
        view.findViewById(R.id.canvas_edit_save).setOnClickListener(this);
        loadData();
        return view;
    }
```

In the `loadData` method, we will create the `pagerAdapter` based on the provided `Canvas` object:

 The `setOffscreenPageLimit` method is set to 11 here (each canvas contains 11 elements, so we need 11 instances of the `CanvasElementFragment` class) to make sure we can access all element fragments. This is done for demonstration purposes only and it should be avoided in a real-world app. It may cause memory issues:

```
private void loadData(){
        MainActivity ma = (MainActivity)getActivity();
        pagerAdapter = new CanvasElementPageAdapter(
        ma.getSupportFragmentManager(),getActivity(),canvas);
        pager.setOffscreenPageLimit(11);
        pager.setAdapter(pagerAdapter);
    }

    @Override
    public void onClick(View v) {
        onSaveData();
    }
```

If the user clicks on the **Save** button, the `onSaveData` method will be triggered. There we call the `saveCanvasModel` method from the repository and pass the updated canvas object. Finally, we will navigate back to the list of canvases:

```
private void onSaveData(){
    Canvas canvas = pagerAdapter.getCanvas();
    MainActivity activity = (MainActivity)getActivity();
    activity.getRepository().saveCanvasModel(canvas);
    activity.onList();
}
...
}
}
```

The `CanvasElementFragment` represents an element of the Business Model Canvas. This, for example, could be the card where a user can enter ideas about the value proposition:

```
public class CanvasElementFragment extends Fragment {
    private static final String ARG_ELEMENT = "ARG_ELEMENT";
    public static CanvasElementFragment newInstance(CanvasElement element)
{
        CanvasElementFragment fragment = new CanvasElementFragment();
        Bundle bundle = new Bundle();
         bundle.putParcelable(ARG_ELEMENT, element);
        fragment.setArguments(bundle);
        return fragment;
    }
    private CanvasElement element;

    public CanvasElement getElement(){
        if (getView() != null) {
            EditText editValue = (EditText)
getView().findViewById(R.id.element_value);
            element.VALUE = editValue.getText().toString();
        }
        return element;
    }
    @Override
    public void onCreate(Bundle savedInstanceState) {
        super.onCreate(savedInstanceState);
        element = getArguments().getParcelable(ARG_ELEMENT);
    }
```

In the `OnCreateView` method, we will bind the element object to the view:

```
    @Override
    public View onCreateView(LayoutInflater inflater, ViewGroup container,
Bundle savedInstanceState) {
        final View view =
inflater.inflate(R.layout.fragment_canvas_element, container, false);
((TextView)view.findViewById(R.id.element_text_title)).setText(element.TITL
E);
((TextView)view.findViewById(R.id.element_text_description)).setText(elemen
t.DESCRIPTION);
        ((TextView)
view.findViewById(R.id.element_value)).setHint(element.HINT);
        if (element.VALUE != null){
            EditText editValue = (EditText)
view.findViewById(R.id.element_value);
            editValue.setText(element.VALUE);
        }
        return view;
    }
}
```

Firebase dashboard

If you have been playing with the app a little, have added some canvases and then gone to the Firebase dashboard, you will see all the canvases that you have just created appear here. All updates appear here instantly (of course, only if the device you are testing the app on is online).

This also makes Firebase very suitable for chat applications. It works the other way around as well. If you add a new canvas node here, it will appear instantly in the app. Just give it a try, add some nodes, play a bit and adapt the app a bit to test other Firebase functionality as well.

This is what the dashboard may look like.

To clarify this example, the title, description and hint fields, that already persist locally, are stored here as well. It makes sense to avoid data redundancy as much as possible and to store only the ID and VALUE properties of each element:

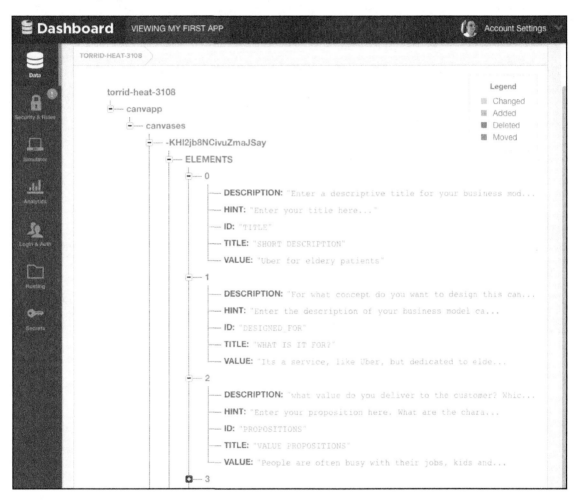

With only a little bit of code, you can persist your data in the cloud with Firebase. You do not need to worry about scalability issues, being online or offline and many other cases. Firebase has many more options such as user management (sign up, login), security, limitation, and paging options.

Summary

In this chapter, we have seen what services we can choose from if we do not want to create the backend for the app ourselves. We learned what could be important for making the right strategic and technical choices and also saw an example app, which is using Firebase as a mobile backend. You can use the app to learn from or you can enhance it and use it as a starter project for your own app idea.

The app that we examined is for Android only. What if you want to have this app built for iOS? Should you create it again, but this time using Swift and Xcode? Are there other options to develop an app just one time but for multiple (mobile) platforms? You can check out the next chapter to learn more about this.

9

Native, Hybrid, or Cross-Platform

Most developers are well aware of the fact that when it comes to market share, bigger isn't necessarily better. That is, Android's larger market size doesn't make it the better choice for app development. Likewise, iOS's greater developer payouts in and of themselves shouldn't turn you into a convert. So, what should you focus on when choosing your platform?

In this chapter, we'll take a pragmatic approach to answering this question. In short, we will explore the following:

- The real-world factors that could have a large influence on your platform choice, such as your audience's needs, your technical needs, and your technical capabilities
- The strengths and weaknesses of native apps and hybrid apps, and the pros and cons of each
- Cross-platform development tools that could allow you to develop on both platforms simultaneously

Let's start by looking at the most fundamental questions first.

Who is your audience?

Your target audience may prefer one platform over the other or they may be spread evenly across both. Knowing as much as possible about your audience will help you determine many things about your app, including whether to go native or hybrid. When performing research, look beyond pre-existing concepts and stereotypes.

For instance, most of us are probably already aware of the superficial differences between iOS users and Android users. That is, iOS users are more affluent, better educated, and younger, while Android users are the opposite.

A number of studies also suggest that, despite Android's market penetration, iOS users are more willing to dish out money for apps. Apple reported that `$20 billion` was paid out to developers in 2016 (refer to `https://www.apple.com/newsroom/2017/01/app-store-shatters-records-on-new-years-day.html`), and App Annie reported that although the Google Play Store has twice as many downloads as the App Store, iOS apps turn out twice as much profit (refer to `https://www.google.com/url?q=http://bgr.com/2016/07/20/ios-vs-android-developers-profits-app-store-google-play/sa=Dust=1501582800060000usg=AFQjCNFJYS1AAoGra88ceEN2y6y87UdA7g`).

Should these numbers make the decision for you? Maybe so, if your revenue model depends on earning money from your app. If not, then you need to focus on what matters to your audience. When exploring your potential audience, always look beneath the surface of such widespread reports. They are often too abstract to offer any real insight. Instead, do in-depth research using competitive intelligence tools, such as App Annie or Flurry, and work with market researchers to collect your own data.

Measure - don't guess or use intuition

The numbers for a given market segment may not reflect the industry average, so you should drill well below the "Apple users are more affluent" stereotype and find out specifically about your industry and your existing user base. You should use any and all analytics available to learn about your audience's platform preferences.

For instance, collect and analyze the following:

- Analytics services, such as Google Analytics for Mobile (`https://www.google.com/analytics/analytics/#?modal_active=none`), Yahoo's Flurry Pulse (`https://developer.yahoo.com/flurry-pulse/`), Localytics (`https://www.localytics.com`), and Adobe (`https://www.adobe.com/marketing-cloud/web-analytics/mobile-web-apps-analytics.html`)
- App store analytics
- Mobile website consumption
- Desktop website consumption

After evaluating these numbers, as well as any other available data you have on your audience, you can determine whether or not they have a bias toward any one platform.

Most people tend to fall into either the iOS camp or the Android camp, which then determines the devices they purchase, which app stores they use, and so on.

What are your technical requirements?

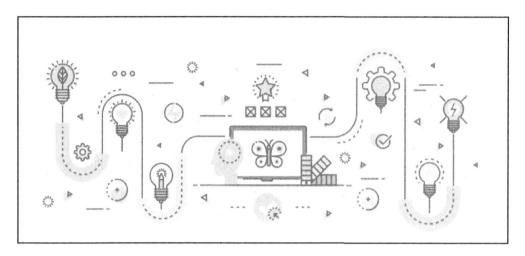

Not every app is an island. In some cases, apps are required to integrate with other platform-specific services or apps. In such cases, you are presented with firm restrictions that could limit your development options. At a minimum, it will help you get your development priorities straight.

As we'll see next, cross-platform toolkits exist that allow you to release across multiple platforms. Though these tools open up certain courses of action, they restrict others and may hinder compatibility with other native apps. Depending on your technical requirements and integration needs, this particular problem could trump all other issues completely.

What are your technical capabilities?

Sometimes, it's not critical to choose one operating system over the other. When your team's strengths lie in one platform, be practical and choose based on what you can do. After all, developing on an unfamiliar platform has risks, including:

- Increased time to market
- Higher technical costs
- Higher risks of rework through bugs or other errors

The impact of these problems can delay valid data collection and learning.

Developing on a platform that you already know has corresponding benefits:

- Lower technical costs
- Lower risks of mistakes
- Decreased time to market
- Decreased learning cycle time.

There are always exceptions to the rule, however. For example, if you have an energetic team with a track record of success, and they want to learn a specific platform, it may be wise to let them run with it. This is a judgment call. Only consider this if you have a team of veterans who know how to build according to best practices.

Native versus hybrid - the strengths and weaknesses

Now that we have covered the baseline requirements in terms of your audience, your technical requirements, and your technical capabilities, it's time to see how native and hybrid compare. Though most developers will be familiar with the basic differences between the two, it's important to examine the strengths and weaknesses of each. After that, we will be one step closer to determining the approach that best meets your needs. First, here is a brief overview:

Native apps

Native apps are developed specifically for one platform. In the mobile world, this usually means iOS or Android. The big selling point for native is that platform-specific apps make API calls directly to the OS, giving developers and designers much more flexibility and control over the user experience.

Going native gives you a full range of device features, but you have to pay the price. Native apps are more costly to create and require in-depth expertise... especially if you have to do native development on two different platforms.

Hybrid apps

Hybrid apps are part native and part web. HTML, CSS, and JavaScript are used to define the web portion of the app, which is executed via the device's rendering engine, usually Webkit. Mostly, these parts of the app are restricted to UI elements.

The advantage of hybrid apps over mobile web apps is that a hybrid app is still able to make native API calls. Hybrid apps fall on a spectrum between strictly web apps and native apps. They can be nothing more than web apps delivered in a native wrapper. Or they can also include native code in order to take advantage of OS-specific functions.

Pros and cons of going native

Purists maintain the "all native all the time" philosophy, though this attitude has softened in recent years. All businesses have limited resources, however, so it's impossible to ignore some of the downsides to going native:

- Native apps are more costly to build and maintain
- They take longer to create, which can be a problem if you need to launch soon
- Their development requires more expertise, which, again, can be more costly and time-consuming

- If you or your team doesn't have the requisite experience, you will have to get it

Another potential concern for going native is the possibility that an idea developed for one platform could be copied to the other. The threat of someone attempting to steal your ideas is always a risk, but bear in mind that novel ideas will always be copied. In `Chapter 19`, *Building an Unfair Advantage* we will look at ways to protect your IP from such possibilities.

Despite the downsides and potential risks, there are definite upsides to creating native apps:

- Native apps are platform and OS specific, so you will be able to directly take advantage of different levels of APIs, from the GUI toolkit to the filesystem
- Finer control over the app and its interface to the device gives you a better handle over app details that can impact the user experience, such as loading time or other subtle UI elements
- Integration with certain platform-specific apps or services is only possible when you build a native app

These considerations in and of themselves should demonstrate that the choice between native and hybrid is not always so clear cut.

Sometimes, you really have no choice and there is nothing to debate about. If integration requirements force you to develop a platform-specific solution, for instance, the question will never arise. When you can afford to debate, however, it's important to take a user-centric approach to the issue, which is where native apps really shine.

The biggest benefits of going native

Native apps offer finer control over the user experience. When viewing apps through the lens of Lean, it's vital to put the user experience front and center. Since smartphones have become ubiquitous, consumers have been demanding more and more of their mobile apps. Today, that experience often drives an app's success or failure. Since the early 2010s, study after study has shown that customers will quickly drop apps or sites that underperform:

- In late 2012, Equation Research surveyed over 3,000 mobile device users. 84% said that mobile app performance was at least somewhat important, and more than 50% felt that mobile apps should load in 2 seconds or less.
- According to a frequently cited pair of surveys performed by Gomez.com and Akamai in 2011, a 1-second delay in page loading time can cause a 7% decrease in sales. They also found that 40% abandon a web page that loads in 3 seconds or more.

- In July 2016, building on the results of the preceding pair of surveys, Think with Google assessed metrics from a large number of real-world e-commerce sites to create machine learning models that can analyze sites and predict conversion rates and bounce rates. The results were unsurprising: page complexity decreased conversion rates, and slow load times increased bounce rates.

Performance is only one factor that contributes to the overall user experience. It's possible to develop apps with attractive user interfaces, but the biggest complaint about cross-platform apps is that they don't have a truly native look and feel. However, hybrid apps have their own set of advantages that make them worth exploring.

Pros and cons of going hybrid

Hybrid apps fall on a spectrum between pure web app and pure native app, and bring advantages from each domain. As with native apps, there is no right or wrong--it's just a matter of determining which is appropriate for your situation. Hybrid apps may not have the same performance or graphics potential as native, but they offer benefits of a different sort:

- Write once, run anywhere. Cross-platform tools (which we'll cover next), translate code, such as JavaScript or C#, into native language for multiple platforms. Even a simple native shell wrapped around some web code will allow you to list your app in both stores and gain access to both audiences.
- Since you can develop a portion of the app as a single codebase, your overhead is much lower.
- Shorter development time not only results in lower development costs, it also means your app can be released more quickly.
- Hybrid apps, because they have a native component, can be listed in app stores, so you'll get the same exposure you would from developing a native app.

With all these upsides, it's easy to see why many developers are taking a softer approach to hybrid, but apps created with cross-platform development tools do have their own set of drawbacks:

- Since you won't have as much control over performance, hybrid apps can perform poorly, which can impact the user experience and user satisfaction.
- Certain interface elements are difficult or impossible to reproduce with a cross-platform development tool.
- Apps have a particular look and feel on each platform, and unless you take great care to mimic that, users will sense the difference.

- As mentioned, integration with other native apps or services can be difficult, or impossible.
- And, finally, as app complexity increases, it is likely that even a hybrid developer will need to have some degree of native-specific capabilities to effectively troubleshoot certain native issues when they arise.

All things considered, there are a few practical realities that convince some developers to choose hybrid.

The ugly truth - a little hybrid doesn't hurt when you have clear goals

Purists may not like this section, but the bottom line is that we're here to build great apps on whatever budget and timeframe we have. Though nativists may evangelize one platform or other, or both, that strategy doesn't cut it when you have deadlines and limited funds.

When it comes to creating an MVP, your most important constraint is the minimum, both in terms of viability and lovability. You need to meet a certain threshold in order to validate your hypothesis, win over your users, and learn from your experiences.

You can't do that if an impractical native or nothing mindset flushes your budget down the drain. This type of thinking actually opposes the Lean methodology. Perfectionism and purism can stall an app before launch, rack up costs, and even bomb it completely, all in the time it would take to put an MVP onto the market and start learning.

If you can get your app to market sooner by going hybrid, then you should. Downstream technical debt (which comes from converting your hybrid to pure native) is fine, as long as the debt is paid off before it burdens the app with problems.

If you want to build the best app you possibly can in the shortest amount of time possible, then you need to consider all possibilities, including hybrid. It is worth noting that hybrid apps can and do become successful. Twitter, EverNote, and TripCase are all well-known examples, demonstrating that hybrid can be a completely viable approach even in the long run.

Making the final decision - factors to consider

Earlier, you came up with answers to baseline questions about your audience, your technical needs, and your technical capabilities. Then, we examined the benefits, drawbacks, and capabilities of both native apps and hybrid apps. We also busted the *native or nothing* myth, demonstrating that hybrid can offer some very real advantages. Now, it's time to answer specific, practical questions that will help you decide which choice is right for you:

- **Technical needs of app impact**: Are native features critical to your app? If not, take a close look at the benefits you would gain from a hybrid approach, such as decreased time-to-market, savings, and access to multiple platforms.

- **Speed-to-market requirements**: Do you need to make it to the market in under 6 months? If so, then a native app may be out of the question.

- **Usability and functionality**: How much does customer experience of the app count? Usability enthusiasts and designers may disagree, but, again, practicality trumps ideology. Native certainly gives you an edge in what can be done, but if you can achieve 80% of the effort for 20% of the cost, keep your mind open.

- **Resource capabilities and budget**: This budget should include development as well as long-term maintenance and technical debt. Do you have the resources to do the work, and can you afford both iOS and Android developers?

- **Long-term goals**: Weigh your current needs and resources against your long-term goals. Will you need to go native in the future and rebuild your codebase from scratch? Map out possible courses of action and consider how these long-term and short-term overheads will impact your business goals.

Practical decision-making should win out every time. Stick with the facts of what you need to do without forgetting what you actually can do. It's critical to not fixate on how an app is developed. Instead, focus on what matters--or what would matter--to shareholders, namely, marketplace advantages such as market share, market opportunity, disruption potential, and IP. Concentrate on building great apps and following best practices for usability, design, performance, and security.

Leveraging cross-platform development tools

There are a variety of cross-platform development tools on the market. In this section, we will quickly scan a few of the most common, and discuss their strengths and weaknesses.

Adobe PhoneGap

Adobe PhoneGap is an open source distribution of Apache Cordova. It is not a framework for app development, but serves to package and release apps that have been built in web technologies such as HTML 5, CSS, and JavaScript. It is part of the Adobe Creative Cloud and offers similar benefits to other hybrid options:

- Write a core codebase in client-side web languages, and release it natively on some of the most popular platforms
- Developers with no native experience can turn a web app into a native app
- There is a wide selection of additional tools that make it easy to preview, build, and download test apps

PhoneGap's weaknesses are also in line with other cross-platform tools:

- Its performance is not on par with native apps.
- The graphics capabilities are wanting, and it doesn't deliver a native look or feel.
- As mentioned, PhoneGap is not a framework. Bear in mind that PhoneGap does not translate code into a native language, it just wraps up your app in a native package.

Xamarin

Xamarin is specifically designed for building C# apps on Android, iOS, Windows, and Mac. The company was acquired by Microsoft in early 2016 and leverages their existing services to make it one of the most competitive cross-development tools. Since a large portion of your app will be built from a common codebase, you will definitely save time and money. However, some code, such as UI and platform-specific features, will need to be written natively, so do not expect to quadruple your efficiency.

Apps can be developed in Visual Studio, Xamarin Studio (its own IDE), and Visual Studio for Mac. According to Microsoft, Xamarin completely supports Android and iOS SDKs--as well as third party controls or tools that are developed for native SDKs--and the platform will continue to stay current with new OS releases.

At the time of this writing, there is a free option for students, OSS, and independent developers, with pricier options available for professionals and enterprise clients.

Appcelerator

Appcelerator allows you to build an app in JavaScript and run it natively on any device. Its toolbox includes the following:

- A visual app designer
- A framework for building APIs
- Mobile analytics

As with the other tools mentioned here, it offers direct access to native APIs, but apps are still stuck with certain limitations in terms of performance and graphics. Though Appcelerator is reasonably priced, some developers don't feel that the bugs make it worth the effort.

How to choose the right tool

If you decide to try a tool similar to one of these, the first step is research. The best place to start is with the needs and priorities you have outlined in this chapter. Compare your needs and capabilities against the strengths and weaknesses of the tools available in the marketplace. Since the digital ecosystem changes so rapidly, don't be surprised if there are differences in price and quality.

These are just a few of the most popular cross-platform development tools on the market in early 2017. Here are a few others to explore:

- **Ionic**: This is an open source HTML5 app framework
- **Sencha Ext JS**: This is designed to build data-intensive HTML5 apps
- **Mobile Angular**: This is a mobile UI framework that uses Angular JS and Bootstrap
- **Progress Telerik platform**: This is a development platform for iOS, Android, and Windows phones
- **Unity**: This is a cross-platform game engine that includes mobile, but extends well beyond
- **Libgdx**: This is an open source platform for cross-platform game development

For more information about any of these tools, start with the documentation on their websites. GitHub contains code repositories for many of the tools listed here. Extensive tutorials, courses, and walkthroughs for the more popular tools, such as PhoneGap and Xamarin, can be found on online education sites, such as Pluralsight, Udemy, and Lynda.com.

Summary

In this chapter, we've looked at the debate over hybrid and native from a pragmatic perspective. We've outlined the most vital questions you need to ask in order to determine the best approach for you and your customers. Finally, we've glanced at a few of the most popular cross-platform tools on the market, which should point you in the right direction if you decide to use hybrid app development to jumpstart your testing.

In the upcoming chapters, we'll explore a few ways to speed up your experiments, including mash-ups, onboarding tactics, and app store hacks.

10
There Is an API for That!

In this chapter, we will see what we can do to prove our hypotheses by building a mash-up. It takes more effort than just a simple landing page but it takes less time than developing a full application. By combining apps or other resources, you can put a solution together for the problem that you are trying to solve with a minimum amount of effort. This is an interesting approach for at least a proof of concept. Once you have learned the lessons you wanted to learn you could always set up a more robust solution. On the other hand your strategy for your app can be just that- combining resources and launch it as your product or service itself. This applies in particular to apps that offer aggregated information. Alternatively, you can think of apps that require heavy integration with social networks, such as Facebook, Twitter, or YouTube. Social referring is always easier than building a user base completely by yourself, so integrating a social component into your app is always a smart thing to do, but it is particularly interesting if you create a mash-up solution with it.

You can combine various apps and services but there is also something else that could result in very interesting mash-up solutions. Data is available about almost everything and much of this data has been made publicly available through various API's. You can use that data, combine it with other data and visualize the outcome in a different way. For example, you can display the results on a Google map, instead of showing it in a list. The most popular mash-ups do exactly that. They visualize existing data in a different way.

In this chapter, we will cover the following topics:

- Investigate how mash-ups can help us to prove hypotheses
- Have a look at some popular mash-ups
- Investigate what APIs and mobile SDKs are available
- Prove our hypotheses by building a mobile mash-up solution
- Prove our hypotheses using an IFTT recipe

Succeed or fail fast

A mash-up allows you to succeed or to fail fast. If you fail you can rephrase your hypotheses at an early stage. Using the feedback you get you can build a better app and find out what it takes to build an app that people actually want.

It is also true that, by using APIs or SDKs of third parties you can rely on much larger platforms than yours and since it is proven technology it is less error prone. For example, if you want to integrate payments other than In App purchases you will of course use the existing solution of a payment provider.

You can take advantage of social networks, by providing a single sign on for your app. You could, for example, provide a way for the user to sign up or to login with his Facebook or login account. It lowers the registration barrier, resulting in higher sign up conversions. Not only does the user have to take fewer actions to get on board but you also have access to additional data such as a name and profile photo. Right after the sign up this results in a more personalized experience of the app. We will elaborate on this in `Chapter 11`, *Onboarding and Registration*, about the process of on boarding new users.

What is in a mash-up solution?

For now, let's have a closer look a mash-ups. What exactly are mash-ups and how does the phenomenon materialize? In general, mash-ups consume specific data from one or more sources, have an alternative presentation, and/or provide additional logic

A mash-up is typically a combination of consuming reusable data, specific complex functionality, presentation, and some new logic. It does not necessarily need to have all of these elements. A mash-up could be a solution that gathers and combines data from multiple sources. Through APIs anyone can consume various types of datasets. The added value of your app could just be the result of the fact that you aggregate data. For example, think of an app that displays all the available jobs for which otherwise you would have to visit over 10 different websites. Data mining and various other techniques can help you to further enrich data.

Mash-ups can also utilize APIs to perform complex functionality (data processing and payment handling) or they can be used to outsource various tasks in the nondigital world. This could be tasks such as 3D printing on demand, delivery of goods or the execution of small tasks performed by humans. Amazon's Mechanical Turk API is a good example of this. Through this API, you can dispatch small tasks to other people. You can think of writing reviews, validating or reviewing user input, or performing research. There are a huge amount of SaaS solutions available and most of them come with an **application-programming interface** (**API**). All this API can be tied together to create something new. They allow developers to test their hypotheses even faster.

Publishing an API

On the other hand, you can also offer an API yourself if you have got some (enriched) data to share. If that is data that others can utilize to build something new, you might want to think of an API as a service that you can charge some money for. If your API is providing some real value, then you can probably make a profitable business out of it. It could have an interesting, recurring revenue model.

 Since it may be hard to monetize your app the traditional way, it might be an interesting idea to think of publishing an API related to your app or your app eco system. Many companies, such as SalesForce or Expedia, already get most of their revenues from API subscriptions, so this is an interesting path to explore.

Lego or Duplo?

If you compare mash-up solutions with those that are created from scratch, it will be like comparing Duplo with Lego. If you use third-party solutions, then the development of your app will be faster, smarter, and probably cheaper. Small and reusable microservices can easily be assembled into a larger and more complex app. Obviously, playing with Lego is more fun, but you can build a tower much faster using Duplo.

Instead of diving deeply into all kinds of technical challenges, you can focus on what matters the most. The implementation of the functionality that will result in the **unique value proposition** (**UVP**) for your solution.

There are many different types of mash-ups. Think of consumer mash-ups, business mash-ups, data mash-ups, and logical mash-ups. Do you need specific data? Do you want to offer flights or holidays? Do you need a payment solution? Alternatively, do you need to send bulk SMS, dim the lights, or want to outsource tasks? Guess what? There is an API for that!

APIs versus SDKs

APIs are interfaces, often made available as a REST service. A **Software Development Kit** (**SDK**) is meant specially for implementing the API on a particular platform, such as iOS or Android. It will make the integration process more smooth. We have already seen an example of this in `Chapter 4`, *An Agile Workflow In A Nutshell*, where we looked at an Android app using Firebase. In that example, you might have noticed a Gradle dependency for Firebase. It is a reference to the Android SDK, which will take care of the communication with the Firebase API. The API itself allows you to perform all operations, but the SDK will save you a lot of time.

Dependency management

The nature of APIs and SDKs is that they will be updated often. For this reason, a smart dependency management plan is important. You do not want to update the modules or update the entire code everywhere in your app each time a new version of the SDK has been released.

Android

For Android, you should use external Gradle dependencies, rather than adding library modules to your project. If you are using Android Studio, then you can start using Gradle right away. You will find the listing of dependencies for your app in the `build.gradle` file within the app folder of your project. The dependency section would look like this:

```
dependencies {
...
    compile 'com.android.support:recyclerview-v7:23.1.1'
    compile 'com.android.support:cardview-v7:23.1.1'
    compile 'com.squareup.retrofit:retrofit:2.0.0-beta3'
    compile 'com.squareup.picasso:picasso:2.5.2'
    compile 'com.squareup.retrofit:converter-gson:2.0.0-beta2'
    compile 'com.squareup.okhttp:okhttp:2.4.0'
    compile 'net.hockeyapp.android:HockeySDK:3.6.2'
}
```

As you can see in this example, RetroFit, HockeyApp, and a couple of other dependencies are defined here. You might be familiar with them already. Retrofit and the Gson converter, for example, are solutions for consuming data over HTTP and deserializing the result into an object. While dependencies could also refer to local libraries, it is strongly recommended to use dependencies as illustrated earlier. For more information on Gradle, check the website at `http://gradle.org`.

iOS

For iOS (and many other languages and IDEs), you could use Gradle as well. This is particularly interesting and valuable if you work on both the Android and iOS platforms and if you wish to use the same tools for building your apps using build servers such as TeamCity or Jenkins. More on this in `Chapter 18`, *Continuous Integration, Delivery and Deployment*, about Continuous Delivery.

Another well-known solution, but available to iOS development only, is CocoaPods. It is a dependency manager for iOS projects (Objective C or Swift). It manages third-party libraries by creating a workspace that, besides your own projects will contain a CocoaPods project, where our dependencies will reside.

The `pod` file contains the list of dependencies and it looks like this:

```
platform :ios, '8.0'
use_frameworks!
target 'example-project' do
    pod 'ZXingObjC', '~>3.0'
    pod 'JSONJoy-Swift', '~> 1.0.0'
    pod 'SwiftHTTP', '~> 1.0.0'
end
```

As you can see in this example, the `pod` file is, among other pods, referring to the `Zxing` library. It is a perfect solution for creating and for scanning bar code images. Installing and configuring `cocoapods` is pretty easy. You just type `gem install cocoapods` in your terminal app to do so. The next thing to do is to define the `pod` file that will contain the references that your project will use. You need to do a `pod install` to actually get the dependency libraries. Running this command in your terminal app will add all the dependencies as listed in the `pod` file. We will have a closer look at this process in the paragraph where we build our MVP:

```
$ gem install cocoapods
$ pod install
```

 Also worth mentioning here is Carthage. It is an alternative solution to CocoaPods and it is the first dependency manager to work with Swift explicitly. CocoaPods is built with Ruby, where as Carthage is built with Swift. Carthage seems to be a bit more flexible but also more complex to use.

For more information on CocoaPods, you can look at `https://cocoapods.org`. If you would like to know more about Carthage and the differences between CocoaPods and Carthage, you can check out `https://github.com/Carthage/Carthage`.

Available APIs

Data about many different topics and from various sources can be gathered through (open) APIs. You will find them on the websites of many companies delivering SaaS or you can check them out on one of the sites that offers aggregated lists of almost all available APIs.

On `https://www.programmableweb.com/` or `http://mashable.com/`, you will find many APIs that you can use for inspiration. You will also find many mash-up solutions there. You can find many APIs that you can use for your app. Most of them are not explicitly intended for mobile apps but as long as the data can be consumed as JSON or as XML then that does not really have to be an issue. On the website, you can search for particular categories, particular data types, or just browse through the latest additions. As you can see, following the weather is always an interesting kind of data source and there are many apps using this data. One example is the app InstaWeather (See `http://instaweather.me/`). In a later paragraph, we will see how we can use these APIs for our MVP:

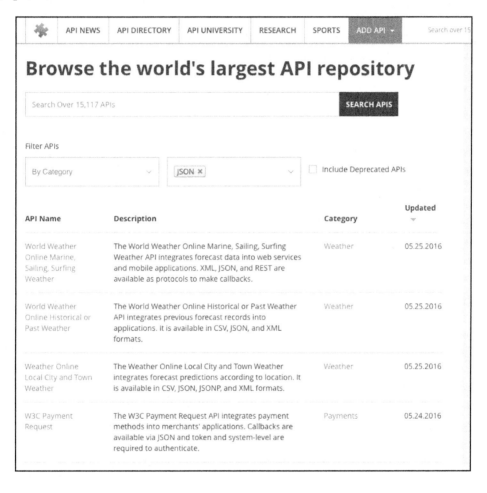

The other places to look for APIs and examples of mash-ups are:

- http://www.mashable.com
- https://www.data.gov
- http://www.opendatanetwork.com
- https://data.sfgov.org
- http://data.worldbank.org/developers
- https://dev.socrata.com
- http://developer.nytimes.com

If you know of a data source for which no API is available, then you can think of an alternative such as (site) scraping. It is an approach that many sites, offering aggregated content (jobs, real estate, and insurance), use. Site scraping can be tricky though. It could be very error prone, but sometimes it is the only way to get things done quickly or to obtain specific data. In particular for your first experiments (MVP) it is an interesting method to use.

An iOS app proving our hypotheses, MoviUber

So far for the theory. It is time to build our MVP. This MVP combines data from various sources to demonstrate how you can create a valuable app real quickly. In this section, we will build an app for iOS that can be used to explore locations of well-known movies. It will demonstrate the concept of using APIs and SDKs to prove our hypotheses.

Hypothesis

We cannot get started without defining our hypothesis first. All people like movies. Some people like them more than others. Let's assume that movie freaks love to travel to cities such as San Francisco to explore the city and visit the locations where well-known movies have been filmed. Many locations cannot easily be reached by public transport. To get there, they will have to use Uber.

So this app is about traveling in San Francisco and visiting movie hotspots using Uber. It consumes data, provides a new representation of the corresponding data (maybe on a map even), and connects a real-life service, such as Uber, to it. Maybe we can even enrich the data a little by looking up the movie title from the **Internet Movie DataBase (IMDB)**. Let's call this app MoviUber. For this app, we will not elaborate too much about the business model. We just want to figure out if we can connect the dots here. Would it not be cool if we can make this work? What do we need to do to make that happen?

Validating the idea through customer interviews

We need to know first if it makes sense creating this mash-up. And maybe you want to give your own twist to the concept first and then, as an exercise, try to validate the idea. See if you can find someone, who loves movies and who is already using Uber.

Tell him or her about the concept and ask what he or she thinks about it. Ask open questions only. If you ask a friend, "Do you think this will be a fantastic idea?", you will probably get a positive answer anyway. While this is nice to hear, it will not help you to get the idea validated.

Anyway, if he or she is very enthusiastic about the concept, then perhaps some new ideas or features will come up or maybe you get some great insights why this whole app idea is actually a very bad plan. You never know.

Since this chapter is specifically about creating a mash-up solution, we will assume the idea has been validated thoroughly. It is a brilliant plan and we have gathered positive feedback through customer interviews. Let's build an app.

Let's build an app

To get started, let's define the ingredients for our MVP. Here it is:

- Movie locations (duh), shown as a list to browse through all movies and locations.
- An Uber button, to call a driver to get us there.
- The IMDB is an optional ingredient but it would be nice to have. We can use this to display some additional information about a particular movie.
- A map will be a great feature that can be used for planning if the user wants to go from one site to another.

Movie locations

Using the San Francisco data API, powered by Socrata, we can get movie locations in San Francisco. To get an impression, you can browse through the dataset you will find at this location: `https://data.sfgov.org/Culture-and-Recreation/Film-Locations-in-San-Francisco/yitu-d5am`. You want to go where Sharon Stone went? You can look it up in this dataset.

But instead of downloading the dataset here, it would be more convenient to have access to the data through an API. That is something that can be found here: `https://dev.socrata. com/foundry/data.sfgov.org/wwmu-gmzc`. After doing some research, it turns out that there is even an SDK. That is even better. Soda-Swift is a native Swift library that can access Socrata open data servers. You will find it on GitHub at: `https://github.com/socrata/ soda-swift`.

Uber

Uber offers an API and SDKs for various platforms, including an iOS Swift library, available on GitHub. Check it out at `https://github.com/uber/rides-ios-sdk`. The API is described at `https://developer.uber.com/docs/tutorials-rides-api`.

IMDB

It seems there is no IMDb API yet, but there is the OMDb API. This API is a free web service for obtaining movie information. You can find it at `http://www.omdbapi.com`.

Finally, for the map we will be using Apple maps. All you need for that is the MapKit framework. Awesome. What do we need to do next?

For this, we will download the SDK. Also, we will download the Socrata sample app from `https://github.com/socrata/soda-swift`. We will use the sample app for our MVP. We will modify a few things such as the data token and dataset. To obtain a token, you need a developer's account at Socrata first. You can register for free at `https://dev.socrata.com`. Next you need to create an app on their website. Open the Socrata-Swift project in Xcode and from the SODASample project open the QueryViewController. Modify the domain and token for the client:

```
let client = SODAClient(domain: "data.sfgov.org", token: "<your token>")
```

In the `refesh` method, you need to modify the dataset for the query and change the order field to `title`:

```
func refresh (sender: AnyObject!) {
...
        let cngQuery = client.queryDataset("wwmu-gmzc")
        cngQuery.orderAscending("title").get { res in
            switch res {
            case .Dataset (let data):
                self.data = data
...
```

```
        }
    }
```

In the `cellForRowAtIndexPath` function, change the fields of the item to `title` and
`locations` as shown in the following code:

```
    override func tableView(tableView: UITableView, cellForRowAtIndexPath
    indexPath: NSIndexPath) ->
        UITableViewCell {

            let c = tableView.dequeueReusableCellWithIdentifier(cellId) as
    UITableViewCell!
            let item = data[indexPath.row]
            let name = item["title"]! as! String
            c.textLabel?.text = name

            if (item["locations"] != nil){
                let street = item["locations"]! as! String
                c.detailTextLabel?.text = street
            }
            return c
    }
```

Now, when you run the app, it will display a nice list of movies and locations on the first
tab. To display them as well on the map on the second tab, we need to do a little extra:

Displaying locations on a map

To display the locations on the map as pin points, we need values for longitude and latitude, but unfortunately we have only a (vague) address description. We need to convert the address to an actual location. To do so, you need to open the MapViewController and find the `updateWithData` function that we will modify by using the `CLGeocoder`. This class is very smart at converting addresses to actual locations with longitude and latitude values.

For each location, we will determine what the longitude and latitude values are for a particular address. Once we have found one of these or placemarks for a given location, we will create a pin point for it and add to the map. Finally, we will navigate the user to San Francisco on the map, so we can actually see the pinpoints.

The code will look like this:

```
func updateWithData(data: [[String: AnyObject]]!, animated: Bool) {
    self.data = data
      if (!isViewLoaded()) {
        return
      }
      if mapView.annotations.count > 0 {
        let ex = mapView.annotations
        mapView.removeAnnotations(ex)
      }
      var anns : [MKAnnotation] = []
      for item in data {
        var location = item["locations"]  as? String
        if (location != nil){
            location  = location! + " San Fransisco, CA"
            print(location)
            let geocoder:CLGeocoder = CLGeocoder();
            geocoder.geocodeAddressString(location!) { (placemarks:
              [CLPlacemark]?, error: NSError?) -> Void in
            print(placemarks?.count)
            if placemarks?.count > 0 {
            let topResult:CLPlacemark = placemarks![0];
            let placemark: MKPlacemark = MKPlacemark(placemark:
              topResult);
            let a = MKPointAnnotation()
            a.coordinate = placemark.coordinate;
            a.title = item["title"] as! NSString as String
            a.title = a.title! + " " + (item["locations"] as!
              NSString as String)
            anns.append(a);
            if (error == nil && a.coordinate.latitude != 0 &&
              a.coordinate.longitude != 0){
```

```
                    self.mapView.addAnnotation(a);
            }
        }
    }

        let w = 1.0
        let r = MKCoordinateRegionMakeWithDistance(
          CLLocationCoordinate2D(latitude: 37.79666680533*w,
            longitude: -122.39826411049*w), 40000, 40000)
        self.mapView.setRegion(r, animated: false)
    }
}
```

This is what the map will look like:

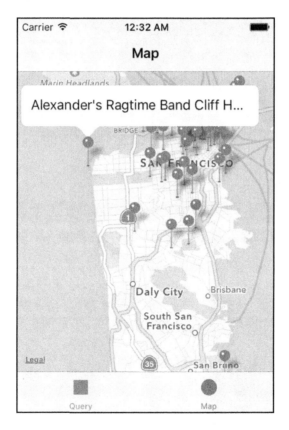

Uber integration

We have a map with pin points now. We can start with the integration of Uber functionality. We will keep it simple by just displaying an Uber ride request button in our app.

Create a new app at `https://developer.uber.com`. Log in or sign up for Uber first, if you have not done so yet:

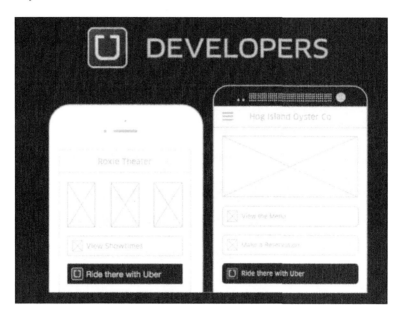

Give a name and a description for your app and save the changes. It will reveal a client ID that you need for implementing Uber functionality in your app. You can find the Uber Swift SDK on GitHub at `https://github.com/uber/rides-ios-sdk`, but you can also use CocoaPods to include it with your app, which is the recommended way of integrating the Uber functionality with your app.

If you have not done this before, install CocoaPods first:

```
$ gem install cocoapods
```

In the console app, go to the folder where the Soda Swift project is. To create a new `pod` file type the following:

```
$ pod init
```

Open the `pod` file that has been created and modified for you, so it will load the UberRides project for us into the workspace:

```
use_frameworks!
target 'SODAKit' do
end
target 'SODATests' do
end
target 'SODASample' do
    pod 'UberRides'
end
```

Next, install the dependency using this command:

```
$ pod install
```

Modify the `info.plist` content by right-clicking on the file and choosing **Open as**, **Source code**. Add these key-value pairs to the dictionary and add your Uber client ID, which you can find on the Uber developers site:

```
<key>UberClientID</key>
    <string>your uber client id</string>
    <key>UberCallbackURI</key>
    <string></string>
    <key>LSApplicationQueriesSchemes</key>
    <array>
        <string>uber</string>
    </array>
```

Modify the `AppDelegate` file in such a way that it will use the sandbox mode of Uber for testing. It probably will be somewhat inconvenient to be picked up at your location each time you test the app. Import `UberRides` and enable the sandbox mode in the `didFinishLaunchWithOptions` function:

```
import UIKit
import UberRides

@UIApplicationMain
class AppDelegate: UIResponder, UIApplicationDelegate {

  var window: UIWindow?
```

```
func application(application: UIApplication,
  didFinishLaunchingWithOptions launchOptions: [NSObject:
   AnyObject]?) -> Bool {
     // If true, all requests will hit the sandbox
     Configuration.setSandboxEnabled(true)
     return true
}
```

In QueryViewController, add new imports for `MapKit` and `UberRides`, just below the import of UIKit:

```
import MapKit
import UberRides
import CoreLocation
```

We need to modify the `didSelectRowAtIndexPath` function a bit. If the user clicks on any of the rows, a button will be shown that can be clicked to initiate a ride. Both the code and the UI require some beautification, but that is beyond the scope of the MVP. For that purpose, the selected item's longitude and latitude value will be retrieved, this time to tell Uber where the user wants to go to (the drop-off location). We do not specify a pick up location. By default, the Uber SDK will use the user's current location. That may not always be sufficiently accurate, but for an MVP it is just fine.

 The Uber Rides SDK checks the value of `locationServicesEnabled()` in `CLLocationManager`, which must be true to be able to retrieve the user's current location:

```
override func tableView(tableView: UITableView!,
  didSelectRowAtIndexPath indexPath: NSIndexPath!) {
  let item = data[indexPath.row]
  var location = item["locations"]  as? String;
  if (location != nil){

     location  = location! + " San Fransisco, CA"
     let geocoder:CLGeocoder = CLGeocoder();

     geocoder.geocodeAddressString(location!) { (placemarks:
       [CLPlacemark]?, error: NSError?) -> Void in

       if placemarks?.count > 0 {

         let topResult:CLPlacemark = placemarks![0];
         let placemark: MKPlacemark = MKPlacemark(placemark:
          topResult);
         if (error == nil && placemark.coordinate.latitude != 0 &&
          placemark.coordinate.longitude != 0){
```

```
        let behavior = RideRequestViewRequestingBehavior(
         presentingViewController: self)

        let dropOffLocationlocation = CLLocation(
         latitude: placemark.coordinate.latitude,
         longitude: placemark.coordinate.longitude)

        let parameters = RideParametersBuilder().
          setDropoffLocation( dropOffLocationlocation).build()

        let button = RideRequestButton(rideParameters:
          parameters, requestingBehavior: behavior)

        self.view.addSubview(button)
      }
    }
  }
}
```

In the end, the method shown adds an **Uber** button to the view. This is including the knowledge of where the user currently is and where he wants to go. This allows the user to click on a button in the app to order a ride and it contains all the knowledge Uber needs to know.

Enriching the data

Finally, as an optional exercise and if you want to enrich the movie location data, you can get some extra movie info and an image of the movie from the OMDb API. Since we know the title of the movie, we can perform a query on the API. The response, nicely formatted as JSON, teaches us something about the plot, actors and it even gives us the URL to an IMDB image. We can show this in the app to inform the user what the movie is all about.

To obtain an API key go to `http://www.omdbapi.com` and click on the **API key link**. You can get one for free if you register with your email address. You will receive an email with your own API-key and an activation link. After activation you can add your API key in the request.: `http://www.omdbapi.com/?t=Basic+instincty=plot=shortr=jsonapikey=<api key>`.

The response for this query looks like this:

```
"Title":"Basic Instinct","Year":"1992","Rated":"R","Released":"20 Mar
1992","Runtime":"127 min","Genre":"Drama, Mystery,
Thriller","Director":"Paul Verhoeven","Writer":"Joe
Eszterhas","Actors":"Michael Douglas, Sharon Stone, George Dzundza, Jeanne
Tripplehorn","Plot":"A violent, suspended police detective investigates a
```

```
brutal murder, in which a seductive woman could be
involved.","Language":"English","Country":"France, USA","Awards":"Nominated
for 2 Oscars. Another 5 wins & 18
nominations.","Poster":"http://ia.media-imdb.com/images/M/MV5BMTcxMjY2NzcyM
V5BM15BanBnXkFtZTYwMjAxNTQ5._V1_SX300.jpg","Metascore":"41","imdbRating":"6
.9","imdbVotes":"131,796","
```

By bundling data from multiple datasets, by displaying them in an alternative way (in a list and on a map on a mobile device), and by adding Uber functionality making traveling from one spot to another more convenient, we have created a really cool mash-up iOS app. To see where this could be going to, including the OMDb data integration, you can download and examine the full app code from Packt.

We had to do some coding to build this MVP. You might wonder if there is no way to get things proved without coding. And there is. We are not talking about user interviews or the analyzing metrics here. We can also use **If This Then That** (**IFTT**) to build an MVP. It allows us to automate simple but often interesting tasks.

Look! No code. Prove your hypotheses with IFTT

Services such as IFTT add a logical component to the possibilities of APIs. If something happens for a particular data feed (channel), then something else needs to be done. It works well for **Internet of Things** (**IoT**) related concepts in particular, but you can connect almost any service that you like. You can check it out for yourself at http://iftt.com/?reqp=1 reqr=.

Using IFTT requires little to no coding, making it the perfect environment to automate small tasks (the so-called recipes). It could also help you to validate your hypotheses, before you actually build the thing. Let's try this. If you have not signed up for IFTT yet, then do so before you continue. We want to prove our hypotheses, which for the sake of simplicity narrows down to the following:

Users want to be reminded to put a towel in their bag. That is particularly important on #towel day (May 25) but also when they go to the airport, where UFOs can easily land. Just wave to the UFOs using your towel, if you want them to pick you up.

Eh, what did you just read? If you think this is a lame example, or if it does not make sense to you, I suggest you read the Hitchhikers Guide to Galaxy first. You can also check it out on `http://www.towelday.org`. Anyway, let's examine what IFTT is about and how we can use it to prove this hypothesis:

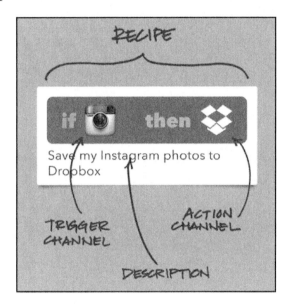

Recipes, channels, and triggers

Creating a new recipe is simple. For our MVP, the user location will be the trigger. In this example, we will be using the IFTT Android app.

We choose the Android location as the channel and we choose **You enter an area** as the trigger:

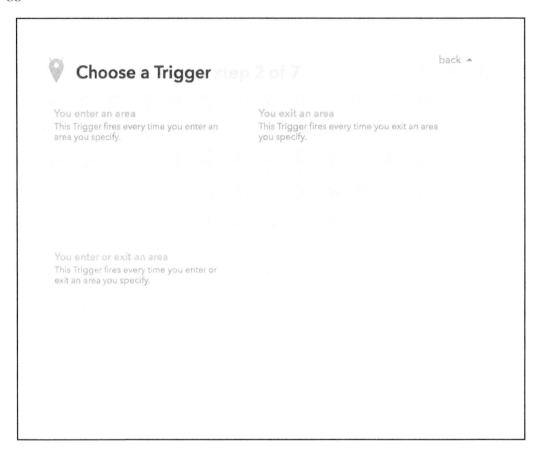

Next, you need to define the particular location, which is the nearest airport. In my case, it is Rotterdam Airport:

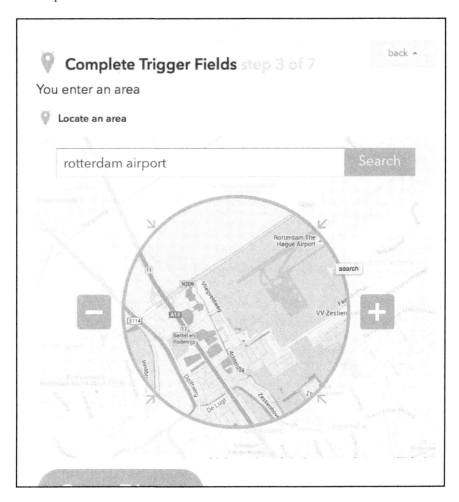

Whenever the user enters this area, we want to be notified. Let's use Twitter as the channel to send a message about the event. We will get a direct message from Twitter whenever this event happens:

And we are done. It technically works for yourself or for others, if you share the recipe. It is that easy to set something up that could help to prove your hypotheses. If you have completed the validation process, you can always build a real app that can perform the same task.

There are many other recipes that you can think of. For example, if you have a smart thermostat, you can lower the temperature, since you are at the airport anyway. Alternatively, you can have a look at this recipe; for example, "Send an email when you land" at https://ifttt.com/recipes/134835-send-an-email-when-you-land. Without any extra effort, your relatives will know that you are safe.

Summary

In this chapter, we saw how APIs and mash-ups can help us to prove our hypotheses. With a minimal amount of effort, we can create an MVP. Before we could use only APIs for consuming and combining data, but nowadays we can also use them to outsource tasks. You can think of image recognition, 3D printing, delivery or a task performed by humans.

We saw what mash-up solutions are and what types of mash-up exist. We created an iOS MVP app that demonstrates the idea of combining multiple API's.

Finally, we looked at the services provided by IFTT, which, depending on your needs, is probably the fastest way to prove your hypothesis first and then build the actual app later. There are plenty of recipes available at IFTT that you could use, or you can create your own. We also discussed the benefits from integrating the APIs and SDKs from social networks, such as Facebook and Twitter.

In the upcoming chapter, we will have a closer look at the integration of social networks and how this affects the on boarding process in particular. You will read more about this in the next chapter about the on boarding and registration process.

11

Onboarding and Registration

In this chapter, we will focus on the onboarding and registration part of your app. It starts with the people that have downloaded the app from the Play Store or App Store. That is an important conversion already. Now they need to be converted into regular users of the app. That is not as easy as it sounds. Studies show that on average 20% of apps are used only once. There are many competing apps in Google Play Store or the App Store. A perfect onboarding strategy for your app is therefore a must have and it could heavily contribute to a good conversion. The first impression your users get of your app should be a good one. To make the conversion as smooth as possible, it is important to show what is in it for them. You should ask yourself why they should have to continue to use the app. From the very start, you have to help them to understand the added value of your app.

There are many reasons why we want a user to sign-up. One of them is that a known user is more valuable than an anonymous one, but registration may be a barrier. This is the case, in particular, when users need to sign-up right away on one of the first screens of the app they see. Since they have no clue yet what the app is all about, you could already lose a part of your audience there. The more you ask, the more difficult the process will be. This is something you can avoid by using various techniques. In this chapter, we will see how to lower the barrier for the onboarding process and how a social sign-in process can contribute to it. Another thing we will look at is sign-up and verification through SMS.

To demonstrate this and other functionalities, we will create an app that uses the SDKs of Fabric and Firebase. We also will learn what we could do to improve app awareness and how a continuous onboarding flow could help you to get the best of both worlds. Such a flow will lower the barrier and it also will result in a rich user profile, as we will see later in this chapter.

In short, in this chapter, we will cover the following topics:

- See what user onboarding is all about and how we can improve conversions by lowering the barrier
- Learn about social sign-in using Facebook or Twitter
- See what the alternatives are, such as phone number sign-up, similar to what WhatsApp is doing
- Find out how we can get the best of both worlds (a low barrier and rich data) using continuous onboarding
- Investigate an app that demonstrates onboarding, including late onboarding
- Learn how sharing and friend finding can help to improve app awareness and help in the onboarding process

What is user onboarding all about?

Onboarding begins where a potential user, who has just downloaded your app, starts your app for the first time. You will have to convince that user and make sure that he instantly will notice the app's benefits. You want to convert your potential user into an engaged and active user, and this process starts with the first view that your app displays. To accomplish this, the first impression of your app should be interesting from a visual perspective and it should explain why the user should use this app. One of the ways of doing this is to create an introduction view with one or multiple slides. Remember that on a mobile device there is limited space, so you need to keep it short and simple. It should clearly explain the why and the what of the app. How things exactly work is something for later.

 Show your users the benefits (the why) of your app before talking about its features (the what).

Show a maximum of three or four benefits. For example, they could explain how the user can integrate the app into his life and what values are provided by the app. Present one benefit at a time using a page slider or other technique. Be clear in your communication and try not to confuse the user. Use a consistent style, vocabulary, and approach to explain concepts. At a first view, the onboarding flow may look pretty obvious, but it apparently is not. Many apps, even the well-known ones, require you to sign-up on the first page with little to no explanation what the app is about. That may work well for the Facebook app with which almost everybody is familiar. It probably is not going to work for your app.

A typical flow goes like this: After the user has downloaded an app, he sees what it is about in a short introduction and then he is required to sign-up. At that time, it is often not clear why one should enter his username, type in a password, confirm it, and enter a couple of required fields. In this phase, a number of potential users will be lost:

Why does it matter?

A great introduction story should point out what the core values of your app are and what is in it for the user. Onboarding matters because it has everything to do with successful conversion. With every step you will lose customers, which is something that cannot completely be avoided, but the number of losses can be limited if you have a great onboarding flow for your app. As an example, let's consider a scenario in which each day a 100 users download your app, of which 60 sign-up and the other 40 decide to do this later or maybe never. Of these 60 users, only 30 are still using the app the next month. Of these 30 users, only 15 invite a friend, share the content of the app, or make an in-app purchase. That is still a very optimistic story.

At this last point, we could consider to see the user as a customer, as he brings us revenue in some way (money or awareness). However, in the conversion from potential user to customer, we have lost 85 people. There must be some way to increase the conversion. To do so, we have to make some smart moves and we need to gather feedback on the process.

Onboarding is about the conversion, which is summarized as follows:

- From someone that becomes aware of the app in the App Store or Google Play Store to a potential user by downloading the app
- From a potential user that has downloaded the app to an actual user by signing up
- From a user that has signed up to a user that is regularly using the app
- From a regular user to an ambassador that is promoting the app by sharing it or by inviting a friend to it

Pirate metrics (AARRR)

We can make improvements only if we have insight into the optimization process. If we want to learn from the process, we need to measure it. The conversion is something that we are going to measure in another chapter. There we will take a closer look at actionable metrics that we can apply to mobile app development.

These so-called pirate metrics (AARRR, apparently that is what pirates say) perfectly describe why the onboarding flow is so important and what each phase represents in the conversion funnel. In short it goes like this:

- A for **Acquisition** or **Awareness,** so they find your app in the store and download it.
- A for **Activation**, when users sign-up.
- R for **Retention**, meaning that a user is using the app on a regular basis. How many of the users that have downloaded the app are still doing so 1 week, 1 month, or 1 year later?
- R for **Revenue**, as people make in-app purchases or other ways of monetization that we will review in another chapter.
- R for **Referral**, where users inform other users about your app by sharing content or by inviting friends. Can your app go viral via word of mouth or sharing?

Actionable metrics could help you to identify the friction points in the onboarding process. You will read more about this in `Chapter 13`, *Play Store and App Store Hacks* (Split testing) and `Chapter 15`, *Growing Traction and Improving Retention*.

Higher conversion

In general mobile apps do not focus very much on the onboarding flow. At least, that is the impression you could get if you review many of the apps in the App Store. You can make a difference for your app. If your onboarding story is more appealing and if the barrier for signing up is lower, your conversion from acquisition to activation will be better. If, in addition, you show your user how the app works and he becomes confident in the way things work, then you will increase your users retention rate. He will keep using your app on a frequent basis.

To get a head start, we need to think of a way to lower the barrier for the user. There are multiple known onboarding patterns that you can choose from and there is no reason why you cannot combine them. Some of these patterns are as follows:

- Introduction
- Tutorial (or tour)
- Joy ride
- Social sign-up
- Continuous onboarding

The **introduction** approach shows a couple of slides and often requires the user to sign-up, but some apps choose to show the content of the app right away. A tutorial or tour shows the real app, pointing out some example cases.

A **joy ride** approach is a little bit different as it lets the user use the app right away and highlights features, from time to time, that are new to the user. It is a great way of showing what the app is all about. But be careful. If your app is complex, this option may prove to be a little bit overwhelming for the user.

A **social sign-up** allows the user to perform a quick sign-up using his Twitter or Facebook account, for example. This may be required in order for the user to be able to continue using the app, but it will lower the barrier if you first show what the app is about and only ask to sign-up when needed to proceed.

Finally there is a **continuous onboarding** concept, which can be very powerful because it comes with benefits such as lowering the barrier and obtaining rich user profiles, by encouraging the user at a later stage to complete his profile.

How to lower the barrier?

Probably the best onboarding flow does not require a sign-up or login at all. Is it really needed to do so before your app can be used? On the other hand, it is also true that a known user is more valuable than an anonymous one. Known users can be converted into customers, which will result in a profitable app. An unknown user is nothing but a visitor. We have not much data available about such visitor and conversion probably will be tough:

To lower the barrier, you better make the sign-up process as smooth as possible. I have seen apps that require the user to fill in multiple fields on multiple pages at the registration process. That is not a fun thing to do on a mobile device and we can be sure the conversion loss will be huge. A typical old school onboarding and registration flow goes like this:

We can do better than that. So create a great and exciting introduction story and make sure the user can immediately see the app core values. A very clear call to action (think of a highlighted button with an explanation text) and a simplified sign-up form can help you with this. Describe the benefits that the user will have once signed up, or use gamification elements such as digital incentives to persuade the user.

A social sign-in option is a great solution to increase conversion and still get to know the user. It requires fewer steps, so the user is more likely to sign-up if the only thing he needs to do is to click on a Twitter or Facebook sign-up button.

To see some onboarding case studies, you should check `http://www.useronboard.com`. It has many onboarding flows of various well-known apps, including comments and suggestions for improvement. You can find onboarding flows for WhatsApp, Yo, Twitter, Foursquare, Snapchat, and many other apps here.

You probably also want to visit `http://uxarchive.com` to see more examples.

Single sign on using a social network like Twitter or Facebook

A social sign-up has multiple benefits, not just for the user but also for developers. Avoid a lengthy registration process with many fields. The likeliness that the user will sign-up increases and, with the appropriate permissions, you instantly access a range of information on that user, for example, an avatar and a name of the user, which is great for personalization options.

Offering a social login could be responsible for 50% more sign-ups compared to a form-based sign-up. Other information could be available as well, such as a contact list that you can use to invite friends to the app later. Depending on the nature of your app, you can allow your user to sign in with Twitter, Facebook, Pinterest, LinkedIn, or any other trusted social network. It may also depend on the nature of your user if your app is offering access to a platform (multi-sided market). For example, for an e-learning solution, there is a LinkedIn sign-up feature for teachers and professionals, but a Facebook sign-up flow for students:

The benefits of using a social login are as follows:

- Faster registration, thus higher conversion rates
- Instantly validated email addresses
- Increased chances that the obtained data is real
- Personalization, resulting in more loyal followers
- High engagement
- Less support (such as a reset password service) needed
- Increased number of repeated users
- Increased chance for referrals because of invites and sharing

There is no one solution that fits all. You need to decide which social networks you will support, and perhaps you choose to support multiple ones. This is of particular interest if you have international ambitions for your app. Facebook or LinkedIn sign-up features make perfect sense in the US and in large parts of Europe, but in other parts of the world (China or Russia for example) these networks may be less popular (or not accessible at all) and you may want to offer an alternative onboarding option for these particular regions. This could be another social network or you can provide a fall-back mechanism. You can still offer an onboarding flow in your app, based on forms. You can use that for the cases in which the user cannot or does not want to use a social sign-up. It is up to you if you decide to support it. You gain a little extra audience with it, but at a cost (development and conversion). For this reason, there are apps that choose only to support one or multiple social sign-up options.

Show us what you have got

An alternative approach is instantly showing the content of the app (if the nature of the app allows you to do so) and only asking for a social sign-up when needed.

This way no or little introduction is needed. Just as is the case with many e-commerce solutions (think of web shops), signing up is requested only when it matters. In the case of a web shop, this is required for check out. For a mobile app, it may be applicable, for example, when the user no longer just consumes but also wants to contribute to a stream. You can think of a news app that allows users to comment about the messages that appear:

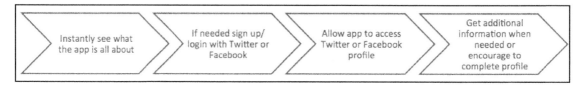

This lowers the barrier even more; however, the downside can be that a large number of users will never sign-up and for that reason will be less valuable to you. For example, anonymous users are not likely to share a lot on social media from your app and inviting their friends is impossible since we do not know who they are.

Phone number sign-up - a great alternative

WhatsApp and a couple of other apps are using the phone number of the device to identify a user for the registration. This is done through an SMS verification code. The user enters his phone number and receives an SMS with a verification code, which he needs to type into the app. This will ensure that the phone number is correct. There are even some implementations that intercept the receiving of the SMS verification code and then fill in the code automatically. This will take away another step from the onboarding flow:

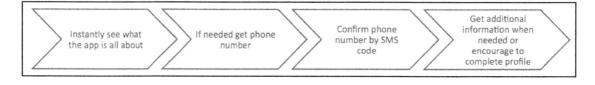

You have to make it clear to the user that his phone number is used for verification purposes only and that it will not be publicly available in the app. Using a phone number will also lead to more valuable contributions of the user. The reason for this is simple. He is aware that his phone number is attached to all the actions he performs in the app. There are services that will take away most of the hassle that comes with the implementation. In our sample app, which we will discuss later in this chapter, Fabric and Firebase will be used because it is the easiest solution to implement and because it is free to use.

Continuous onboarding - complete the user profile later

Obtaining the most minimal information from your user to get him on board is a smart way to keep the barrier low. Later you can encourage your user to add more details to his profile or by the user make particular choices from which your app can learn. The concept of continuous onboarding is exactly about that. The profile of the user will be enriched by the actions that the user will take. This will allow the app to offer a better and customized app experience that will become more dedicated over time.

LinkedIn is the perfect example, as everybody will recognize the reminders that LinkedIn displays. It asks you to complete your profile, to endorse connections (enriching the profiles of others), or to connect to people. You will often be reminded about that but it never will be mandatory to do these things.

The incentive here is not even that strong, but it works well. Who does not want have an All-Star profile? You can use this idea for your mobile app, as we will soon see in the sample app:

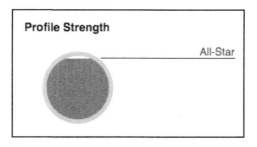

Tell a story - an example onboarding app

To demonstrate the various ideas related to onboarding, we will create an Android app that is using Fabric for Twitter authentication and Firebase SDK for phone authentication. You can use Firebase as well for Twitter authentication, but the one that Fabric is offering is more convenient to use.

We will name this app, Tell a Story. Using this app, users can write a story together. Anyone can read the stories that people create, but, if the user wants to contribute to the story, he needs to sign-up using Twitter or his phone number. Let's start simple with a couple of wire frames that will explain the exact flow of the app:

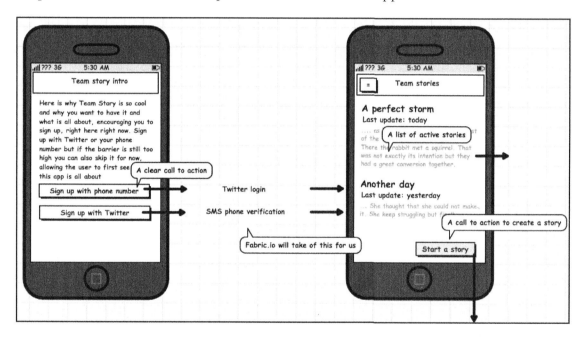

The user lands on the introduction view when he opens the app for the first time. This view contains a clear explanation of why he should want to use the app and what it is about. There are two very clear call to actions shown. One of them is the **Sign up with phone number** button, the other one is the **Sign up with Twitter** button.

After the sign-up, a list of existing team stories is shown. The user can browse through the list, and, if he clicks on any of the stories, the full story will be revealed in a detailed view. The user can also decide to start a story by himself. Here is another clear call to action, visualized as the **Start a story** button.

The detail view shows all lines for the story, including the names of the authors. The user can now read the full story or he can contribute to it by clicking on the **Contribute to story** button. Doing so will lead him to the **Contribute to...** view, where he can enter a new line of code. If the user chooses to start a new story by clicking on the **Start a story** button he will see the same view. In this case, the user will also be asked for a story title. Clicking on the **Add new line to story** button will add the new line to the story or will create a new story:

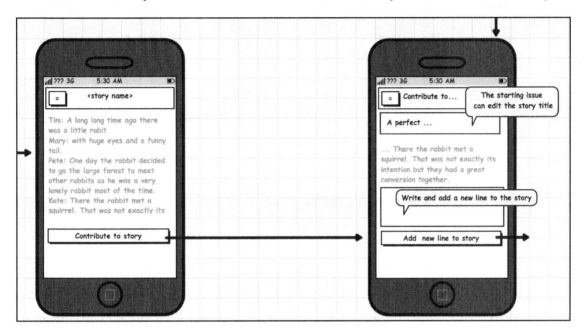

Onboarding sign-up when needed

We will also need to add a late onboarding option to the app. For this purpose, we will add a **Skip for now** button to the Introduction view. In Chapter 13, *Play Store and App Store Hacks*, about split testing, we will see how we can learn what approach will work best. We need to know which implementation will lead to the highest conversion. Based on this feedback, we can remove the **Skip for now** button, the sign-up buttons on the introduction view, or make the decision to keep all the three options in the introduction view.

Note that, although this button is highlighted next to demonstrate the late onboarding flow, this button should not be the primary call to action and therefore should not be marked as such. We want to lower the barrier, but we still want to encourage the user to sign-up early:

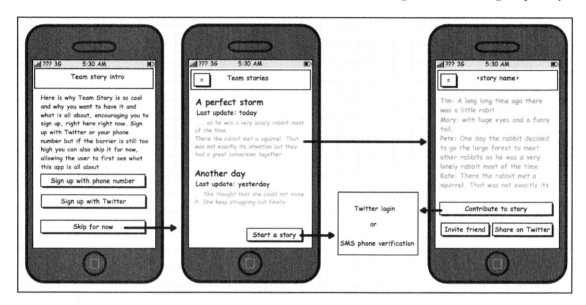

If the user chooses to click on the **Skip for now** button as he apparently is not quite convinced about the benefits of the app yet, he will see the story list right away. Only if he wants to start a new story, or if he wants to contribute to an existing one, he will be asked to sign-up via either Twitter or phone/SMS. For our app, we want to support both types of flow. Let's start with the implementation of what we just saw.

Implementation

You can find the sample project for this chapter here: `https://github.com/mikerworks/packt-lean-onboarding`.

The code sample has been updated, so it will use the latest and greatest (at the time of writing). Digits, the Fabric phone authentication service, has been replaced by the Firebase phone authentication service. The code sample is now using this service and, while I was busy anyway, I have converted the Android Java example to Kotlin.

You can have a look at the app first, or if you want to configure it for your own use you need to configure Fabric and Firebase first.

Visit `https://fabric.io` and create an account. Once you have done that and have confirmed it, you can proceed. Enter a team name (for example `packt-demo`) and choose a platform (**Android**). After that, a new page in the wizard will show a number of options. Pick the Twitter option first. The first piece of information tells you how to configure your Android project. Use the wizard (or do it manually) to create the first app in the Fabric environment and name it `onboarding`. You need to do this to obtain keys and IDs that allow you to use the Fabric SDK in your own app.

Next, we need to do a few things for the phone number authentication. The Digit service of the Fabric is doing exactly that but it has been replaced by FireBase phone authentication. So you need to set up a few things at Firebase as well. Go to `https://console.firebase.google.com` and create a new project, or if you have not signed up for Firebase yet, you need to do so first.

Follow the setup instructions at Firebase. In the authentication section, you can select which sign-up methods you wish to use for your application. If you click on the phone sign-up option and enable it, you can continue with the sample app.

Let's have a walk through the app. On the fly, you can modify the API key and the secret to match your own setup. Once opened in Android Studio, you should expand the app folder. Locate the build.gradle file in this folder and open it.

You will see that the file contains a couple of dependencies on Fabric and Firebase. We will use that later so we can login with Twitter or Firebase phone authentication. In addition, we can share stories on Twitter using the `TweetComposer` class. Note that you may need to update the version numbers to the latest versions. They appear as suffixes of the definitions of the various package names:

```
...
apply plugin: 'io.fabric'

repositories {
    maven { url 'https://maven.fabric.io/public' }
    maven {
        url 'https://maven.google.com'
    }
    mavenCentral()
}

dependencies {
    ...
    compile('com.twitter.sdk.android:twitter:1.13.3@aar') {
        transitive = true;
    }
```

```
    compile('com.twitter.sdk.android:tweet-composer:1.0.3@aar') {
        transitive = true;
    }

    ...
    implementation 'com.google.firebase:firebase-auth:11.4.2'
    implementation 'com.google.firebase:firebase-database:10.2.4'
}

apply plugin: 'com.google.gms.google-services'
```

Now, open the `AndroidManifest.xml` file in the `app/src/main/` folder. The metadata section contains the value for `ApiKey`. Modify it so it will have the value that corresponds with your own configuration at `Fabric.io`:

```
<meta-data
    android:name="io.fabric.ApiKey"
    android:value="fill in your api key" />
```

The layout associated with the onboarding activity displays a short introduction that explains to the user why they should want to use the app and how easy it is to get started. Both the phone number and the **Twitter sign up** button are clear calls to actions here:

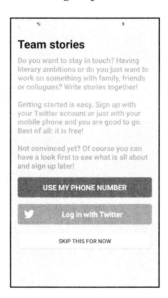

There is one additional button, which has been intentionally made smaller and less colorful. It is here to allow the user to skip the sign-up process for the time being, in case he wants to only see what the app is about.

Open the `strings.xml` value and update `twitter_key` and `twitter_secret`. Replace them with your own values. You will find them on the Fabric website:

```
<resources>
    <string name="twitter_key">fill with your own Twitter key</string>
    <string name="twitter_secret">fill your own Twitter secret</string>
```

Open the `OnboardingActivity` class. In the `onCreate` method, the `initFabric` method is called. This is where Fabric is initialized for Twitter authentication and sharing:

```
private fun initFabric(){
    val authConfig = TwitterAuthConfig(getString(R.string.twitter_key),
getString(R.string.twitter_secret))
    Fabric.with(this, Twitter(authConfig))
    Fabric.with(this, TwitterCore(authConfig), TweetComposer())
}
```

The click listener for the **Skip** button makes the app jump to the list immediately. If clicked on, the Twitter login button will display a Twitter dialog asking for permission. If this permission is given, the success method of the callback will be triggered. We will then store the `TwitterSession` object and show the list of stories to the user by calling the `onShowList` method:

For the sake of simplicity, `AuthenticationHelper` is not persisting the sessions other than during the lifetime of the application. In a production app, it would be more convenient to persist them as long as they are valid.

You can find the implementation of what we just saw in the `setupTwitterLoginButton` and the `signinWithTwitterAuthCredential` methods as follows:

```
private fun setupTwitterLoginButton(){
    twitter_login_button.setCallback(object : Callback<TwitterSession>() {
        override fun success(result: Result<TwitterSession>) {
            mTwitterSession = result.data
            Log.i(javaClass.simpleName, "Twitter login @" +
result.data.getUserName() + ")")
            val credential = TwitterAuthProvider.getCredential(
                    result.data.getAuthToken().token,
                    result.data.getAuthToken().secret)
            signinWithTwitterAuthCredential(credential)
        }

        override fun failure(exception: TwitterException) {
            Log.d(javaClass.simpleName, "Login with Twitter failure",
exception)
```

```
            }
        })
    }
```

The `signInWithPhoneAuthCredential` method registers the user with his Twitter name as a Firebase user. We will use this phone number later to identify the contributions of the user.

```
private fun signinWithTwitterAuthCredential (credential: AuthCredential){
    mAuth.signInWithCredential(credential)
        .addOnCompleteListener(this, OnCompleteListener<AuthResult> {
            if (it.isSuccessful) {
                AuthenticationHelper.user = it.result.user
                Log.i(javaClass.simpleName,
                    "User logged in or registered with twitter name
${AuthenticationHelper.user?.displayName}")
                continueFlow()
            } else {
                if (it.exception is FirebaseAuthInvalidCredentialsException)
{
                    onboarding_code_feedback_text.text = "Invalid code."
                }
            }
        })
}
```

To sign-up with a phone number, we need to tell Firebase to send a code by SMS to the user. We will do that in the `sendPhone` method:

```
private fun sendPhone(){
    val number = onboarding_phone.text.toString()
    PhoneAuthProvider.getInstance().verifyPhoneNumber(
        number, 60, TimeUnit.SECONDS,  this, getCallback());
}
```

The callback implemention is in the `getCallback` method. The `onCodeSent` is the most interesting event. If the code has been sent, we will store the returned verification ID. We will need it later to authenticate the user with the code:

```
private fun getCallback():
PhoneAuthProvider.OnVerificationStateChangedCallbacks {
    val callbacks = object :
PhoneAuthProvider.OnVerificationStateChangedCallbacks() {
        ...
        override fun onCodeSent(verificationId: String?, token:
PhoneAuthProvider.ForceResendingToken?) {
            mVerificationId = verificationId;
            mResendToken = token;
```

```
            . . .
        }
    }
    return callbacks
}
```

After sending the code to the user, he has to enter the code to ensure the provided phone number is indeed his phone number. This is done in the `sendCode` method:

```
private fun sendCode(){
    val verification = mVerificationId
    if (verification != null) {
        val code = onboarding_code.text.toString()
        val credential = PhoneAuthProvider.getCredential(verification, code)
        signInWithPhoneAuthCredential(credential)
    }
}
```

The `signInWithPhoneAuthCredential` method registers the user with his phone number as a Firebase user. We will use this phone number later to identify the contributions of the user:

```
private fun signInWithPhoneAuthCredential(credential: PhoneAuthCredential)
{
    mAuth.signInWithCredential(credential)
        .addOnCompleteListener(this, OnCompleteListener<AuthResult> {
            if (it.isSuccessful) {
                AuthenticationHelper.user = it.result.user
                Log.i(javaClass.simpleName,
                    "User logged in or registered with phone no
${AuthenticationHelper.user?.phoneNumber}")
                continueFlow()
```

Here is an example of both the users. The first one is registered using Twitter, while the other one has used his phone number to sign-up:

Now, open **MainActivity**. In the `onCreate` method, you will see that one of the first things that we do is call the `onList` method. The `onList` method creates a new `StoriesFragment`, and by calling the `showFragment` method a list of stories will be shown by default:

```
fun onList() {
    val fragment = StoriesFragment.newInstance()
    showFragment(fragment)
}

fun onCreateStory() {
    val newStory = Story()
    newStory.lastUpdate = "today"
    val fragment = StoryContributeFragment.newInstance(newStory)
    showFragment(fragment)
}

fun onContribute(story: Story) {
    val fragment = StoryContributeFragment.newInstance(story)
    showFragment(fragment)
}

fun onReadStory(story: Story) {
    val fragment = StoryDetailFragment.newInstance(story)
    showFragment(fragment)
}

fun onLateOnboarding(story: Story) {
    val intent = Intent(this, OnboardingActivity::class.java)
    intent.putExtra(OnboardingActivity.ARG_LATE, true)
    intent.putExtra(OnboardingActivity.ARG_STORY, story)
    startActivityForResult(intent, REQUEST_LATE_ONBOARDING)
}

private fun showFragment(fragment: Fragment) {
    val ft = fragmentManager.beginTransaction()
    ft.replace(R.id.main_fragment_container, fragment,
fragment.javaClass.toString())
    ft.commit()
}
```

The **MainActivity** is also responsible for showing other fragments, such as the StoryDetailFragment, which shows you the full story and the StoryContributeFragment. It also contains a call to the OnboardingActivity for late onboarding purposes. This will allow the user to sign-up if they have skipped the onboarding previously, but want to contribute to the app later. By adding content to a story or by creating a new story, they will be asked to sign-up once again:

```
val repository: Repository get() = Repository(this)
```

The getRepository method just returns a new instance of the Repository class that we are going to investigate next.

You will find the Repository class with the data package. As you can see, the getDummyContent method creates a list of dummy stories.

The repository class has already been prepared to be used with Firebase, but, since we do want to demonstrate the onboarding concept, the data is only persisting during the lifetime of the app. If you have read Chapter 9, *Native, Hybrid, or Cross Platform*, it will be pretty easy to set up Firebase and modify this class in order to be able to store stories in the cloud as well.

The class looks like this:

```
class Repository(private val context: Context) {

    fun getStories(handler: OnRepositoryResult) {
        val content = getDummyContent()
        handler.onResult(content)
    }

    fun updateContributions(story: Story) {
        if (story.id == null) {
            addStory(story)
        }

        dummyContentList.forEach {
            if (it.id.equals(story.id, ignoreCase = true)){
                it.contributions  = story.contributions
            }
        }
    }

    fun addStory(story: Story) {
        if (story.id == null) {
            story.id = UUID.randomUUID().toString()
```

```
        }
        dummyContentList.add(story)
    }

    companion object {
        private var dummyContentList = mutableListOf<Story>()
        private fun getDummyContent(): List<Story> {

            if (dummyContentList.isEmpty()) {
                val dummy = mutableListOf<Story>()
                val s1 = Story("A first story", "MikeR", "Today")
                s1.id = "1"
                s1.contributions.add(Contribution("Once upon a time",
"MikeR"))
                s1.contributions.add(Contribution("a giant rabbit did
exist", "Pete"))
                s1.contributions.add(Contribution("in a galaxy far far
away", "Floris"))

                val s2 = Story("A second story", "MikeR", "Yesterday")
                ...
                dummy.add(s1)
    ...

                dummyContentList = dummy
            }
            return dummyContentList
        }
    }
}
```

The getStories method returns all stories and the data asynchronously. The updateContributions method adds a new contribution to an existing story, or creates a new story with a first contribution if the story does not yet exist by calling the addStory method. The addStory method eventually creates a unique ID for the story and adds the story to the list.

In the models package, you will find the Story and Contribution class. A Story has a title and multiple contributions, and each contribution has an author and some content. The Parcelable implementation makes it more convenient to pass data from one fragment (or activity) to another, as we will see later:

```
class Story : Parcelable {
    var id: String? = null
    var title: String? = null
    var initiator: String? = null
    var lastUpdate: String? = null
    var contributions = mutableListOf<Contribution>()
...
    fun getFullStory(includeAuthors: Boolean): String { ... }

val summary: String
    get() {
        val builder = StringBuilder()
        if (contributions != null) {
            var start = contributions.size - 3
            if (start <= 0) { start = 0 }
            for (build in start..contributions.size - 1) {
                builder.append(contributions[build].paragraph.toString()
+ "\n")
            }
            return builder.toString()
        } else {
            return "This story has not started yet!"
        }
    }
...
```

The getSummary and the getFullStory methods make a Story object just a little bit smarter and it returns the last three lines or the full story, as text, respectively.

The Contribution class implements the Parcelable interface as well for the same reasons as for the Story class. Each Contribution instance has an author and a paragraph member.

The first thing a user will see, right after the onboarding view on see what the app is all about. For a more complex app it could be helpful to highlight specific features the first time the app is used. By showing them during the onboarding flow we can encourage the user to sign up for the app. For this app, things are pretty obvious:

Everybody likes stories, so the first action probably will be that the user clicks on a story of which the summary looks appealing. (Again this is a hypothesis that needs to be proven.) If the user clicks on the floating action button (the one with the plus sign on it), he will create a new story:

```
class StoriesFragment : Fragment(), OnCardViewClicked, OnRepositoryResult {
    private var recyclerView: RecyclerView? = null
    private var adapter: StoryAdapter? = null
    private var viewModel = mutableListOf<Story>()
...
```

If you take a look inside `StoriesFragment`, you will see that a `RecyclerView` widget and a `StoryAdapter` will be used to display the data shown here. In the `onCreateView` method, the `loadData` method will be called, which in turn calls the `getStories` method of the `Repository` class, passing the fragment itself as the handler of the results:

```
override fun onResult(result: List<Story>) {
    viewModel = result.toMutableList()
    adapter = StoryAdapter(viewModel)
    adapter?.setOnCardViewClicked(this)
    recyclerView?.adapter = adapter
}
```

When the results come in, an instance of the `StoryAdapter` class will be created and attached to the `RecyclerView` instance. The `StoryAdapter` binds the data for each story to a row in the list:

```
override fun onCardClicked(view: View, position: Int) {
    (activity as MainActivity).onReadStory(viewModel[position])
}
```

If the user clicks on any of the rows the `OnCardViewClick` event will be triggered, which will call the `onReadStory` method from `MainActivity`, passing the selected story as the parameter. This will bring us to the `StoryDetailFragment` implementation.

This fragment displays the full story to the user, including the name of the contributors. Here, the user can contribute to the story by clicking on the **CONTRIBUTE** (as shown in the example image):

```
class StoryDetailFragment : Fragment() {
    private var mStory: Story? = null
    override fun onCreate(savedInstanceState: Bundle?) {
        super.onCreate(savedInstanceState)
        mStory = getArguments().getParcelable(ARG_STORY)
    }
```

In the onCreate method, the selected story will receive through the bundle. It is here where the Parcelable implementation comes in handy. In the onCreateView method, the content of the story will be set as text for textView using the getFullStory method of the story object:

In the onClick method, you will find the handling for the various button clicks, such as the **CONTRIBUTE** button. This will call the onContribute method, which in turn calls the onContribute method of the **MainActivity**, including the currently selected story. It will result in displaying the layout associated with the StoryContributeFragment class.

In the onShare method of the StoryDetailFragment, you will find the lines that are needed to compose and share a tweet:

```
private fun onShare() {
    val builder = TweetComposer.Builder(getActivity())
            .text(String.format(getString(R.string.sharing_text),
mStory?.title))
    builder.show()
}
```

The `StoryContributeFragment` allows the users to contribute to a story or to start a new story. At that moment, the user changes from a passive to an active user. Also, the user will be converted to a known user as he is required to sign-up, which he may not have done yet. The fragment obtains the selected story as a bundle parameter. It may be an empty one, in case the user hit the plus button, as he wants to create a new story. If it is an existing story, a summary of the story (the last three contributions) will be shown.

If the user clicks on the **Contribute** button, the `onContribute` method will be called. Here a new `Contribution` object will be made and, optionally, a new story object will be made. The contribution will be added to the story and we will ask the `AuthenticationHelper` class whether the current user is already authenticated or not. If the user is authenticated, either by a Twitter sign-up or by a Firebase phone sign-up, we can proceed by filling in the contributor's name (Twitter name or phone number). Also, we call the `updateContributions` method of the `Repository` class, which will take care of storing stories:

If the user is not yet authenticated, we will call the `onLateOnboarding` method of the **MainActivity** instead. Here we will also pass the story (and with that the contributions) as a parameter:

```
fun onLateOnboarding(story: Story) {
    val intent = Intent(this, OnboardingActivity::class.java)
    intent.putExtra(OnboardingActivity.ARG_LATE, true)
    intent.putExtra(OnboardingActivity.ARG_STORY, story)
    startActivityForResult(intent, REQUEST_LATE_ONBOARDING)
}
```

The `OnboardingActivity` will also handle the onboarding on the fly. Better late than never is the idea here. If you want to contribute to a story, or want to create a story yourself, you have to sign-up first. Now, the activity will display a message that indicates this, and again it gives the user the choice to sign-up using his Twitter account or using his phone number:

```
private fun continueFlow(){
    if (mIsLateOnboarding){
        val returnIntent = Intent()
        returnIntent.putExtra(OnboardingActivity.ARG_STORY, mStory)
        setResult(Activity.RESULT_OK, returnIntent)
        this.finish()
...
```

If the late onboarding succeeds, the result will be returned to **MainActivity**, which will take care of adding the contribution to the story:

```
override fun onActivityResult(requestCode: Int, resultCode: Int, data:
Intent) {
    if (requestCode == REQUEST_LATE_ONBOARDING) {
        if (resultCode == Activity.RESULT_OK) {
            val story =
data.getParcelableExtra<Story>(OnboardingActivity.ARG_STORY)
            val lastContribution = story.contributions.last()
            lastContribution.contributor = AuthenticationHelper.userName
            repository.updateContributions(story)
            onList()
        }
    }
}
```

After that the list of stories is shown again by calling the `onList` method of the `MainActivity` class. This time the list will include the contribution, or the story of the user that is no longer an unknown one. Signed up at last!

So far, for the app, we have seen some cool implementations for signing up and late onboarding. If you like the concept, then feel free to do some further experimentation with the app. Think, for example, of two other great features for the app that we could add: An invite a friend option (to write the story with you) and a share option (to share the cool story on Twitter or another social media network). This will increase the awareness of your app. That will help you to grow the user base of your app. We will see more about this in Chapter 14, *A/B Testing Your App*, which is about traction and retention:

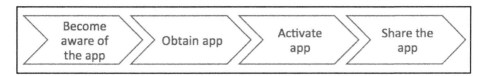

Growth hacking is, among other things, a continuous process that results in existing users inviting friends to join them and use the app as well. The reason that people start downloading your app is because they have become aware of it. You will see higher conversion numbers when implementing a friend referral flow.

Growth hacking:

Growth hacking (basically a modern word for marketing) is a topic that deserves some books on its own. You should consider building a growth engine before starting to build your app. Build an audience for the problem that you are going to solve with your app. It is a great way to test your app idea and to create awareness. The simplest way to do so is to create a regular blog about the topic.

The perfect conversion goes like this: Once the user has signed up and started a story or contributed to one (activation), and then decides to continue doing so (retention), he will become an ambassador of your app and he will start sharing stories or he will invite friends so they can write stories together (referrals).

Referrals are important, as word of mouth is one of the most effective types of marketing. More than 70% of potential app users download apps based on recommendations of friends, colleagues, or family. With that in mind, the goal should be to enable the app users to drive more awareness, which is exactly what the Team Stories app tries to do. Referrals are often the only way to promote an app. This is because of the fact that the cost of user acquisition (advertisements) for most mobile apps otherwise would be higher than the revenues.

Due to their nature, particular apps, such as social, or messaging ones, and of course game apps as well, are very suitable for inviting friends. Often they would not make much sense if collaboration in some way would not be possible. For a lot of other apps the reason for sharing or inviting might be less obvious. However, if you provide incentives, as, for example, Dropbox is doing by providing additional space for each new reference, you can still benefit from referrals.

Summary

In this chapter, we have seen that there are various ways for onboarding a user and to encourage a user to sign-up. We have seen that is important to keep the barrier as low as possible, and that you need to make it very clear from the beginning what the benefits of your app are and why the user wants to use it. Alternatively, just to quote Simon Sinek, "Start with why".

We have seen that the implementation for social sign-up using the Firebase or the Fabric SDK is fairly easy to implement and we have learned how we can offer multiple options to our users, including the option to initially skip registration. Although it lowers the barrier, the latter is not necessarily a good thing. An anonymous user has less value than a known one. Also, a known user is easier to convert into a paying one (customer). You need to find out what works best for your app. Maybe you just want to grow a large user base to begin with. In the next chapter, we will see how important it is to have a scalable solution.

12
Do Things That Do Not Scale

Your very first goal, once you have an MVP, is to push that experiment through its first iteration cycle in order to test your hypothesis. At this stage, the primary purpose is validated learning. Only after you have proved your hypothesis should you consider scaling and optimization.

In the Lean model, improvement happens over time as a result of user feedback. When you make that feedback loop the centerpiece of your initial experiments, a nontraditional set of business practices begins to emerge.

Look at the following points:

- How to acquire early adopters and establish a small-scale laboratory and why doing so can drastically improve your learning
- How to maximize learning with some of the most popular wireframing and prototyping tools
- How to balance the need for quality against speed-to-market requirements, budget requirements, or other limitations
- The best way to develop a technical debt management plan, which is vital for any app that does begin to scale

Before covering these topics, however, let's look at why you should do things that do not scale.

What we mean by "things that do not scale"

Your goal at this stage is to conduct an experiment, maximize learning, and minimize the time it takes to complete one turn of the build-measure-learn cycle. With the feedback loop as your bull's eye, you will find yourself engaging in activities that may seem superficially illogical, but which greatly accelerate your learning.

For instance, it probably seems extraordinarily inefficient for CEOs or founders to interact directly with customers. If a startup wants to shorten the feedback loop and understand its customers' needs on a deeper level, though, the purpose of this tactic becomes clearer.

Similarly, it may seem wasteful to hand users an interactive wireframe or to present a prototype made up of coding shortcuts and workarounds. When viewed as a stage in an MVP test, however, such an approach makes more sense.

The tools and techniques we explore next may not scale, but they will greatly accelerate early learning and prevent technical errors from overwhelming you as your MVP evolves.

Three reasons to do things that do not scale

Doing things that do not scale within a narrow market has significant benefits when it comes to experimentation, learning, and product development. Here are three of the biggest reasons to adopt a user-centric focus instead of a traditional production-oriented approach.

Improved testing and data collection

As we will see, the following are the direct interactions with early adopters, which will provide information that is much more valuable than downstream data collection. Additionally, this feedback will help you implement appropriate changes, features, and redesigns. The sooner you receive necessary feedback, the more money you will save.

Tapping into your customers' minds early on will help prevent costly errors. For instance, take a look at the following points:

- Up-front data helps you develop the features that customers actually need instead of the ones you think they need
- User testing, especially with some of the tools and methods mentioned as follows, will help you create a design that your customers like
- Early interactions with your MVP will also make you aware of usability issues sooner rather than later

Your first users will help you find the features, designs, and usability workflows that matter most, so you can focus on what's important before you start scaling.

Failure that can be controlled

Not every experiment will succeed. If your idea is going to fail, then it is better to fail early and fail fast, for several reasons:

- A low-budget experiment that fails inside a contained environment will have a smaller fallout than a full-featured product that fails in a large market
- The sooner you discover a mistake or disprove a hypothesis, the sooner you can cut your losses
- Failing early with a small audience will limit or eliminate any impact on you or your company's reputation

When the Lean methodology is correctly applied, failure becomes a mechanism for learning and adaptation, giving you the opportunity to pivot or start over.

Development of products that are more lovable

As mentioned previously, an MVP lets you create a product that is targeted, relevant, and useful. Functionality, however, is only half of the equation. People should use your products not just because they need to, but because they want to.

Lovable products have significant advantages over products that are merely usable:

- People who enjoy using a product will use it more often for longer periods of time
- A tribe of passionate users are more likely to talk about your products
- Customers who love your product will stay more loyal

A lean, learn-first approach should seek to understand not only what your customers want, but how they use apps. When you prioritize the user experience from the very start, you can create products that work with your users, their chosen platforms, and their lives.

Since early adopters are those who feel the strongest need for your product, they will also be your most valuable asset when it comes to improving the user experience.

How to acquire early adopters and establish a small-scale laboratory

When you conduct your first tests in a real-world laboratory, your strategies should aim to accelerate the build-measure-learn cycle. As mentioned, since the focus is on learning, not production, much of this early work will be impractical on a larger scale.

The exact nature of the unscalable work will vary from situation to situation. However, the following three strategies will help you accelerate the feedback loop:

- Working within a narrow marketplace facilitates expansion and provides a miniature laboratory within which to work
- Manual recruitment of—and interaction with—your users will give you immediate, detailed information about your audience and your ideas
- At this early stage, perfecting the user experience with early adopters is often more effective, more efficient, and more economical than doing it later in the process

Unscalable work could mean performing tasks manually, doing work outside your comfort zone, or working outside your area of expertise. User acquisition and customer service, for instance, may be arduous or tedious to a coder.

However, given the overwhelming benefits that these strategies offer the lean developer, their importance cannot be emphasized strongly enough. The following three strategies will help you establish a testing ground for your MVP, shorten the build-measure-learn cycle, and push your experiment closer toward scalability.

Focusing on a narrow marketplace

In the beginning, it is very useful to confine an experiment to a narrow marketplace, such as a specific geographic area or a small group. There are several reasons for this, which are as follows:

- Expansion and saturation within a targeted marketplace is much easier than within a large one.
- A narrow market is a good way to achieve a critical mass of users that will take you from a tribe of early adopters to a majority of users. Once you achieve saturation in one demographic, geographic area, or marketplace, you can use that position as leverage to scale even further.
- Data collection and testing is easier, cheaper, and more useful.

Think of a small market as a laboratory for the experiment. When proving your first hypotheses, it is often better to learn about your customers in a confined environment. Doing so on a large scale is usually unaffordable and wasteful.

Manually recruiting early adopters

Paul Graham, cofounder of the renowned startup incubator Y Combinator, probably coined the phrase, "Do things that don't scale."

In a much-cited essay bearing the same name, he said, "The most common unscalable thing founders have to do at the start is to recruit users manually." While cumbersome and slow, Graham says that nearly all startups must do this. To make his point, he relates the story of how the payment processing company stripe got started. The founders approached new users in person and used their laptops to create new stripe accounts right there on the spot.

Though certainly not scalable, manual recruitment may be necessary to acquire users. After you have gathered a group of early adopters, you can begin learning from them and evolving your product.

Another significant reason to manually acquire users is genchi genbutsu, a core principle of the Toyota Production System. Jeffrey Liker wrote about this concept in his book, *The Toyota Way*, which represents two decades of study of Toyota. He said, "You cannot be sure you really understand any part of any business problem unless you go and see for yourself firsthand."

This is why the first users and the firsthand data you collect at this stage are worth their weight in gold. Firsthand interaction will tell you how your users perceive your idea, whether they see it as useful, and whether you will want to pay money for it.

Perfecting the user experience

Steve Jobs once said, "You've gotta start with the customer experience and work backwards to the technology."

A similar sentiment was echoed by Airbnb's founders, who said, "We start with the perfect experience and then work backward." It is worth noting that the user experience does not limit itself to a user's interactions with a product—it also includes the user's experience with the company and the company's services.

Since users sit at the center of the lean mindset, it is vital to also place them at the center of product designs. Perfecting the user experience during the experimental phase accomplishes several goals:

- When you make their experience as good as possible from the very outset, they will be more willing to offer feedback and forgive any inevitable usability issues
- The emotions a product evokes are just as important as how functional it is—improving the emotional experience has as much an impact as improving features or usability
- Happier users are more likely to become loyal followers and recommend your products to others

To get the most out of your users' participation—from collecting data to building a tribe of advocates—you must do more than just monitor and respond to feedback. It is necessary to offer over-the-top concierge treatment. In other words, treat your first users like royalty.

In the early years of my old company, I used to call customers directly to see if they were happy with the product and their services. I had very little time in my schedule, but getting direct feedback from the ones who used my software told me where I was making mistakes and helped keep the customers satisfied and engaged.

Airbnb's founders also became famous for their hands-on involvement. When their product's growth in New York suffered due to low-quality listings, the founders flew to New York to personally help users fix the problem.

Chebbia said, "We went door to door with cameras taking pictures of all these apartments to put them online. I lived in their living rooms. And home by home, block by block, communities started growing. And people would visit New York and bring the idea back with them to their city."

This example illustrates not only how far your products must go in order to please your users, but also how much you can learn from engaging with them directly.

How to transition from an unscalable MVP to scalable code

On the one hand, you have the setting for your experiment, which includes your users, the marketplace, and real-world conditions. On the other hand, you have the MVP itself. Although its earliest iterations are just an experiment, it is also an actual product. From the beginning, it is necessary to plan for potential growth.

In this section, we will discuss tools and techniques that will help you test economically and scale sustainably, without being overwhelmed by the ever-present danger of technical debt:

Focusing on learning with wireframes and prototypes

As discussed earlier in Chapter 5, *A Pragmatic Approach*, wireframes and prototyping do not directly scale as actual software code, but they help avoid a lot of downstream problems by giving you something you can present to your users. It is also possible to gather preliminary feedback at these early stages by collecting data on how your users react to your product. As you move forward with design options, you can incorporate this data to determine when and how to add or modify design functionality.

Wireframe sketches and prototypical designs are ideal low-cost options for early design stages. These can come, for instance, in the form of hand-drawn sketches, photoshop files, or HTML mockups. There are also paid tools that bridge the gap between these design files and actual interactive prototypes.

Additionally, there are a number of design tools on the market that specifically assist teams with collaborative design, development, and user testing. These are three of the most popular and useful, although there are others. My team has used all three for quite some time and found them to be very useful. Employing these tools has saved us a lot of time, money, and customer goodwill by ensuring that we learned through prototyping rather than customer complaints.

Zeplin

Zeplin is aimed at bridging the gap between designers and developers.

Designers can import files from photoshop or sketch, and Zeplin can be used to generate design specs, such as font details and color palettes. It can export sized image files, CSS files, and color files for major platforms. It integrates with Slack and is very simple to use.

I have found that Zeplin is extremely useful in avoiding past pitfalls, where you hand off designs for developers to cut up and apply with the application. Often these hand-offs can be messy, in that the tested designs end up compromised in the process—either consciously or unconsciously—by the developers. Zeplin hands off all the files ready for use, which saves a great deal of time and heartache.

Zeplin is free to try out and pricing can be fairly reasonable, depending on your budget, so it is worth a look if you want to ensure that your tested designs are followed to the pixel.

InVision

InVision is a must-try toolbox for designing and testing in low or high fidelity. It allows product teams to collaborate, co-create, and communicate in real-time with each other and with users. This software suite is ideal for early-stage UI design and experimentation, since you can create interactive designs, present them to test users or stakeholders, and collect qualitative data immediately.

InVision also continues to add more tools and features on a regular basis, further shortening the gap between the drawing board and the prototype. Craft, for instance, allows you to turn sketch or photoshop designs into interactive prototypes that can be tested directly on your phone. The Inspect tool operates like Zeplin by pulling coding specs—such as font information and color palette information—from design files.

UserTesting.com

UserTesting.com offers a range of testing solutions for apps and websites. Video recording, audio recording, and analytics are available for websites, published apps, and unpublished apps. Data is turned around quickly, so you can respond quickly.

One perk of UserTesting.com's tools are that they offer video and audio recording via the users' devices. These allow you to present hard data and real human reactions to stakeholders and other team members. In some cases, when it's necessary to make a case for one design versus another, then this feature can be invaluable by giving you executable feedback from test subjects.

Focusing on scaling and sustainability

At this point in the chapter, you understand how and why it is important to acquire early adopters, operate inside a narrow marketplace, and present them with interactive designs and prototypes. However, as your experiments progress, it will become necessary to transition from unscalable prototypes into scalable code. As your MVP evolves, you will be required to make a number of technical decisions. These include the following:

- When to take coding shortcuts
- When to automate and optimize
- How to handle technical debt

From the very beginning of your experiments, these issues should have their place on the table. Understanding such technical considerations will help you deal with them as they arise, so they do not become too costly or overwhelming.

Writing perfect code versus getting the job done

At every stage, you must make choices that balance practical needs, such as budgets and release dates, against coding efficiency and stability.

We have seen how the founders of two extremely successful companies prioritize the customer experience and doing whatever it takes to push their product into the marketplace. This means, fortunately or unfortunately, that you cannot be a perfectionist when it comes to coding. When creating your MVP and working within tight constraints, you must put learning first and set aside any attachments to ideal code.

To use a phrase that I love, "Don't make perfect the enemy of good."

Perfecting an experiment should be an ongoing process achieved through customer-guided iterations. If you perfect designs, code, or features that haven't been validated, you run the risk of improving something that will be rejected by your users. To avoid burning money, focus on delivering iterations to market as quickly as possible so you can learn from the real world.

Automation and optimization

When speed to market is critical, testing and quick delivery take precedence within reason.

At a certain stage in the development lifecycle, you will need to transition from unscalable processes to scalable ones. Although such manual, quick-and-dirty business practices are more economical and even necessary in small marketplaces, they are unsustainable as you improve and grow over time.

Automation—whether in code, deployments, or monitoring—is the foundation of stable, secure, and performant apps. It can be delayed at the start of your project, so you can learn and adapt quickly, but it must be applied over time so as to minimize technical debt and avoid delivering pain to your users via a buggy and unreliable app.

How to handle technical debt

Technical debt, or the extra work that you accrue when taking coding shortcuts, is like financial debt. A little bit can sometimes be necessary but too much can kill you.

As mentioned, if you are a perfectionist, your product will risk going over budget or being delayed indefinitely. However, quick-and-dirty programming will need to be fixed at some point. While perfectionism can overwhelm you in the short run, technical debt can overwhelm you in the long run.

There are different ways of viewing technical debt. You can view it as long-term versus short-term, prudent versus reckless, or intentional versus unintentional. Practically speaking, technical debt, like financial debt, is sometimes necessary to achieve a certain goal. However, in the same way that both types of debt can be useful, they can also get out of control.

The best way to manage technical debt is by intentionally and iteratively eliminating it from the backlog as you proceed through the lifecycle of your product. Notice a pattern here around iterative practices? It is simple; good agile practices can help prevent technical debt from burying you.

Here are a few tips for dealing with technical debt:

- **Create a technical debt management plan**: A properly executed plan is the first step towards tackling technical debt. It should be engaged with consistently as part of your sprint cycles and should prioritize debt based on how much it affects your customers—from the most impactful to the least impactful.

- **Log your debt**: A backlog will help you track when, where, and why certain decisions were made. Your log should include estimates for how long shortcuts will take to fix, while remembering that every loan you take out accrues interest over time.
- **Quantify the debt financially**: Coding time translates into billable hours. Therefore, it should be clear that technical debt translates directly into financial costs. Viewing technical debt through a financial lens will help your teams and your company understand the impacts of development decision-making so that priorities can be set accordingly.
- **Execute your plan**: A technical debt management plan will not help if no one is accountable. Establish documented guidelines, responsible personnel, a repayment schedule, and ensure that your debt management plan is executed on a regular basis.

A solid technical debt management plan can help you prevent unnecessary technical debt. In cases where debt is unavoidable, a strategically executed plan will help you control that debt so that it doesn't control you.

Summary

Doing things that do not scale is about prioritizing learning and speed to market by shortening the build-measure-learn cycle.

Most of the time, doing things that do not scale is the only way to get things done. During the experimentation phase, the work involved may put you in unfamiliar territory and it may seem, superficially, to go against industry best practices. However, these early efforts quite often spell the difference between success and failure.

When you are fanatically committed to growing, you can collect data on your market, quickly pivot, and deliver an MVP that will help you learn, iterate, and improve over time.

In the next chapter, we'll take a look at how we can learn even more about our MVP via Play Store and App Store hacks.

13
Play Store and App Store Hacks

In order to continually learn from your MVP, you must be continually running tests, collecting data, and evolving your app. However, one barrier to validated learning comes in the form of the App Stores themselves.

As we will see next, the two platforms have different limitations and requirements that impact every aspect and stage of an app's release. Store listing requirements, app approval delays, analytics, and beta deployment options, for instance, all differ between the two platforms.

However, there are ways to workaround these challenges. In this chapter, we will explore the following:

- What split testing is and why it is a crucial tool for every app developer
- How to run split tests in both store listings and in apps
- How to overcome limitations and obstacles that are inevitable when performing real-world split testing
- Essential split testing techniques, as well as examples of how to run split tests in the App Store and in Google Play

Before covering these topics, let's briefly elaborate on what experiments are:

What is an experiment?

As in science, a business experiment posits a hypothesis, and then runs a test or tests to validate or invalidate that idea. In the lean methodology, MVPs are experiments that test fundamental hypotheses about value and growth—that is, whether your idea solves a problem and whether your product can grow sustainably.

Though the MVP is an experiment itself, there are many other experiments that you can run within that context. In this chapter, we will cover the obstacles to testing inside the App Stores, workarounds that allow you to split test inside your app and inside the App Stores, and, finally, we will look at how you can apply these skills with a pair of practical examples.

A/B testing as a technique for experimentation

Split tests can be viewed as experiments, like any other experiment, which begins with a hypothesis. These tests are much smaller in scale when compared to large-scale hypotheses, such as the value hypothesis upon which the entire MVP is built. However, the underlying principle is the same.

For those who do not know, a split test serves alternate versions of a web page or app, for instance, to a group of users in order to determine which version converts the highest. In a two-way split test, called an A/B test, you might test two separate landing page headlines in order to test their impact on conversion rates.

You can also test the following:

- Copywriting, such as headlines or calls-to-action
- Design elements, such as colors or button shapes
- App Store listing elements, such as screenshots or descriptions

Why perform split testing?

This will be covered in more detail as follows, but there are a number of benefits to split testing. Here are some of the biggest benefits:

- Split testing allows you to better understand your users
- Conversion rates can be improved, that is, it's a bread-and-butter optimization method
- You can improve the user experience and usability
- Important metrics, such as user retention and time-in-app, can be more deeply understood and improved

There are two types of app experiments that we will cover in this chapter: store listing tests and app tests.

Store listing tests

App Store rankings, such as search engine rankings, have an enormous impact on how many people find and try your app. If you can improve your store listing's ranking and its conversion rate, then you stand to reap significant benefits as follows:

- Improved organic discovery and more users
- Increased download rates
- Decreased cost of user acquisition

Improving your App Store ranking, or **App Store Optimization (ASO)**, has been called the new SEO, as a testament to its importance. Keeping in line with other search engines across the internet, App Store search algorithms rank based on a variety of predictable factors, such as keyword relevance and user reviews.

The app marketplaces have never published best practices that can guide developers on how they can improve their App Store rankings. However, widespread unofficial ASO improvement techniques focus on a few important areas:

- Download rates and uninstall rates
- The quality of the reviews from users
- Relevancy of the keywords in the headline and description
- Usefulness of the listing copy, the icon, screenshots, and so on

Listing tests are split tests that are designed to help you improve all of these areas, either directly or indirectly. Every time you split test elements, you will measure the result that you are trying to impact. An A/B test, for example, could compare two versions of a description, then use install rates to measure the results of that test. A test that compares review solicitation mechanisms could examine the impact on positive reviews.

App testing

Split testing the app itself is another crucial tool in your experimentation toolbox. While App Store listing tests will help you improve conversion rates, app testing helps you learn about your users, improve your product, and increase engagement rates.

When testing the app, you will perform split tests designed to improve the app experience, usability, and engagement. App tests can be performed on any number of app-related variables, including the following:

- Screen design
- User flow
- Images
- Buttons

Appropriate metrics that can help you judge your testing efforts include engagement metrics, such as time in app and retention rates or conversion rates for specific targets. A change designed to improve the conversion rates for advertising, for instance, should measure ad conversion rates. As with App Store listing tests, you should focus on metrics that measure the result you are trying to impact with any given test.

Why do you care?

App testing is not just icing on the cake, since such experiments can make or break an app. Testing has become a critical facet of the lean developer's *modus operandi*, so it pays to understand what makes testing so valuable.

The competition is intense

Apps need a way to stand out in a saturated, competitive marketplace. According to Statista, Google Play grew from 1 million apps in July 2013 to 2.8 million in March, 2017. Between June 2013 and January 2017, the App Store count grew from 900,000 to 2.2 million.

This ocean of apps poses two concerns—not only do developers need to stay visible in the ocean of apps, they need to engage their users' attention and keep it.

Although people spend dozens of hours per month using apps, they are quick to abandon apps that bore them. According to 2016 data from Localytics, which was widely publicized on major tech blogs, nearly one in four users will abandon an app after only one use. A number of causes can lie behind app abandonment rates, from users' busy schedules to usability issues.

Though not all of these causes can be influenced, there is one reason that developers use experimentation to stay competitive.

Experiments work

As with engagement metrics, conversion rates are impacted by a number of factors, including:

- **Traffic source**: The exact number changes depending on where you get your information, but studies usually show that between 40-50% or more users find apps by searching in the App Store. Think with Google reports that one in four users find their apps through a search.
- **The app listing itself**: As mentioned, every element of an App Store listing can impact conversion rates, from the icon to the description to the screenshots.
- **The industry**: Not all industries have the same average conversion rates. Music apps, according to data published by splitmetrics, have the highest App Store conversion rates, while games have the lowest.

- **App pricing**: Free apps are governed by different averages than paid apps. In general, free apps have higher download rates, but they also have higher abandonment rates.

The best way to impact any of these factors is by performing experiments. Split testing can improve App Store conversion rates by 20% or more.

Decreased conversion rates, in turn, decrease the cost of user acquisition, while in-app split tests help you improve engagement metrics, which often has a direct impact on your revenue model.

Although the app marketplaces pose their own difficulties, these are not insurmountable. Next, we will look at some of these obstacles and how to overcome them so you can make the most of your tests.

Why running experiments with Google Play or App Store is hard

Once your MVP becomes listed on the App Stores, it becomes harder to split test. Your app becomes bound by the rules of each App Store. Then, when you want to update, you must wait for the App Store's approval. Additionally, certain limitations inhibit your ability to run tests or collect accurate data.

Obstacles to testing with store listings

Each of the two major platforms behaves differently and each has its own set of listing requirements. Generally, Google Play is easier for testing, since re-listing takes less time, the requirements are less strict, and it offers simple split testing options for the store listing. However, the App Store's significant audience—and that audience's purchasing power—is reason enough to code for iOS.

Here are a few of the major platform differences that make testing all the more difficult.

Different app listing requirements

When listing your app, you must learn to operate in two separate ecosystems. Not only do you have to code each app differently, you need to learn the ropes for maximizing visibility in each marketplace.

Here are three examples and different requirements for each App Store as of the writing of this book:

- **App titles**: On Google Play, titles are limited to 50 characters, while on the App Store they are limited to 30.
- **App descriptions**: Apple does not have a short description. But it does have a "Subtitle". Subtitle is limited to 30 characters. If the differences between the two platforms with description feels too complicted, we swap this item for Promotional text. Apple's promotional text is limited to 170 characters. Google terms this field "Release notes" and it is lmited to 500 characters.
- **App categories**: The App Store allows you to choose a primary and secondary category, but special cases allow you to add more categories, thus increasing potential visibility. Google Play, on the other hand, only allows one mutual category for both apps and games. Google allows for an application type along with the category.

These are just a few of the differences that you must take into account when running App Store optimization tests. The other differences between the two stores include the following:

- The number of screenshots allowed
- The length of promo videos allowed
- Whether social media actions are allowed
- Whether promo graphics are allowed

No standard way to measure results

Each store offers separate metrics with which to measure the results of your experiments:

- **Apple**: You can view sales and trends through iTunes Connect, which gives you access to data and reports on downloads and sales. App Analytics is an analytics package that tracks many standard metrics, such as engagement, monetization, and marketing.
- **Google**: From the Google Developer console, you can track user acquisition with the option to narrow your focus on specific acquisition channels, locations, and time periods. Google Analytics for mobile or Firebase Analytics, similar to Apple's analytics package, allows you to track monetization, engagement, and marketing efforts.

Since these precise numbers differ, you will not be able to measure results in parallel, even if these experiments are conducted simultaneously. It is worth mentioning that Apple and Google are both continually improving their tools to make testing easier, so some specific features may have changed by the time of publication.

Limited infrastructure for A/B testing

Once your app is listed, you have limited options when it comes to split testing in the store itself. Apple, in general, has a reputation for enforcing stricter standards across its App Store, from screenshots to keywords to bugs. Therefore, it is not surprising that they offer no support for split testing.

Google Play allows you to split test store listings. With this program, you can create two types of experiments:

- **Global**: Global tests allow you to test graphics, screenshots, the promo video, and the icon. These tests only affect your app's default language, so the ones using other languages will still be shown their default localized versions.
- **Localized**: When you perform a localized test, you can test all of the preceding variables, plus descriptions in as many as five languages.

These experiments are created and run from the Google Developer console, where you can choose targeting information, attributes, variants, and more.

Why it is difficult to run parallel experiments

It may be clear by now why running experiments side by side is no easy task:

- Different store listing requirements means that each listing must be different
- Different coding requirements makes parallel app creation difficult
- Different A/B testing capabilities in each App Store means you cannot run the same listing tests simultaneously
- Different metrics means you will be measuring slightly different results
- Different turnaround times for each store means your updates will have different timelines

Another challenge is that since testing conditions fluctuate with time, it is difficult to maintain strong controls and reliable results when testing serially. For instance, user behavior and market temperament could vary enough between two time periods to alter the results of two otherwise identical tests. Though effective testing clearly has its share of roadblocks, there are ways to overcome these challenges, as we will see next.

Hacks to workaround the challenges

Though none of the following methods are ideal, they will allow you to learn from your customers, validate your hypotheses, and create continual improvements to your MVP. Each of the upcoming sections will cover some essential techniques for working around the platform limitations that have been discussed so far.

Store listing hacks

As mentioned, Google Play allows you to split test core elements of the listing itself, while Apple does not. If, however, you want to expand your testing options and perform more complex multivariate testing, you will need to explore other options.

How do users find apps in the first place?

Knowing where users come from and how they discover your apps can be very useful, both for testing and for your business. Not only can you learn about how various traffic sources compare in terms of quantity and quality, you can also perform tests outside the App Store, which can then offer more information about your customers.

Before examining the experiments themselves, it pays to briefly examine the major discovery portals and traffic sources:

- **App Store search**: As mentioned previously, think with Google research discovered that at least 40% of users find new apps by searching within the App store itself, making it one of your most important traffic sources. For this reason, App Store indexing and optimization should be top priorities.
- **Traditional search**: The same study also reported that 27% of users discovered apps through search engines, making search another critical traffic source.
- **App packs**: App packs are grids that appear above, within, or below standard Google search results when the search engine determines that a person is searching for an app. The apps that appear in App packs are chosen by the search engine, not the App Store rankings. However, since the search algorithms rely on many of the same factors, the results are strongly correlated.

- **Deep linking**: Deep linking, or URIs that open up apps, can be triggered from a variety of places, including search ads and other digital ads. In the event that an app is not installed, users will be directed to install the app, which can then complete the action initiated by the original link.

As mentioned, Google will allow you to perform in-store listing tests. Since certain traffic sources, such as in-store searches and app packs, send users directly to these listings, Android developers should certainly take advantage of this option.

Use microtesting to collect data

Although you cannot test listings in Apple's App Store—and although there are limitations to tests you can run inside Google Play—you can still use external landing pages to test essential content such as screenshots, headlines, icons, and descriptions.

To perform this technique, which has been called microtesting by some, you simply experiment with a landing page that mimics the App Store listing itself. Create a test that mirrors the appearance of the App Store as closely as possible and when users click on the install button, direct them to the actual store listing.

After the testing period has finished, use the highest-converting landing page to recreate your App Store listing.

To track and analyze results, you should utilize a split testing platform. Some are free and some are paid, but given the benefits they provide, paid platforms can be well worth the investment. A few of the most popular include the following:

- **Google Analytics**: This is an essential testing solution that is included as part of Google Analytics, making it easy to use and work into any existing GA workflow
- **Optimizely**: This is one of the world's most popular split testing options, offering features that extend far beyond a straight landing page test
- **Unbounce**: This is another extremely popular landing page platform, with an easy-to-use landing page builder
- **Kissmetrics**: This is one of the world's most robust split testing and analytics platforms; Kissmetrics is ideal for deep customer research

A little research will help you determine which price point meets your budget and which features meet your needs. For the teams that plan to engage in expansive tracking, such as marketing tests and app tests, it is worth looking at platforms that are more in-depth. Kissmetrics, for example, offers analytics for both apps and websites, so you can manage, view, and review more of your analytics from a single place.

Running app tests

In the same way that you can use split testing to experiment with multiple versions of web page elements, you can run tests that collect data on in-app elements, including design elements and workflow changes. This approach is the practical application of the build-measure-learn cycle you measure data, learn from it, and build new iterations.

When working with preproduction versions, you can run tests in parallel. Testing two versions of the app simultaneously doubles the amount of information you can collect.

The following are the ways in which you can run parallel tests on both platforms:

- **Google Alpha Deployments**: Before releasing your app to production, you can perform open and closed alpha and beta tests with users who have Google Accounts or G Suite accounts. Since you can only run one open and one closed at the same time, Google recommends testing a closed alpha alongside an open beta.
- **Apple TestFlight**: This operates similarly to Google Alpha Deployments, allowing you to create open or closed beta tests. You can segment multiple builds among up to 2,000 open beta testers, which gives you plenty of room to receive feedback on different versions of your app.
- **Third party applications**: There are a number of services that help streamline beta deployment and distribution. Install, DeployGate, and Fabric, which was acquired by Google in early 2017, are platforms that make this stage of prototyping easier and more efficient.

With the right approach to deployment, and a creative approach to split testing your listing, it is possible to hack your way past some of the obstacles posed by the two app marketplaces. Next, we will apply some of the skills and tools we have examined so far by looking at example experiments in the App Store and in Google Play.

Summary

An experimental, scientific approach is the foundation of the Lean method.

Experimentation and split testing are fundamental tools in every developer's toolkit, but running tests in the marketplace can be tricky and messy. The techniques covered in this chapter can help you circumvent real-world limitations and obstacles, improve learning, and accelerate growth. The examples provided can give you ideas on how to run your own experiments in either the App Store or in Google Play.

With the right tools, the right techniques, and a creative approach to testing, you can continue to learn and experiment, even after you have launched your product in an app marketplace.

Now it is time to look at how we can use split tests to find out what works best in our apps as we seek to create apps that our customers will love.

14
A/B Testing Your App

All successful app developers learn from the feedback they get from their users. They investigate it and determine if they need to improve, to remove, or to add features in order to better support of the user's workflow. In this chapter, we will investigate what tools we can use to get feedback from our users if we cannot ask them in person. Multiple iterations of testing and optimizing are required to build an app that solves your customer's problem. Split testing (or A/B testing) is an ongoing process that can help you find the workflow, which will lead to the highest conversions. Using split testing, you can, for example, find the best registration flow for your app. In `Chapter 10`, *There is an API For That!*, we have seen some good suggestions of what you can do to improve the onboarding process. Now you can also run some experiments and measure what works best for your app. It can also give you feedback about other topics, such as user retainment, engagement, or in-app purchases. We will see why obtaining statistics matters and what we could learn from them.

Pragmatic as we are, we will investigate what tools we can use for this purpose. We will have a quick look on how Firebase, remote config and analytics, could work for us. Split testing is a methodology that you can use any time, even when your app is already in the store. Finally, we will see what we can do for split testing our App or Play Store listing.

Specifically, in this chapter, we will cover the following topics:

- See why statistics matter
- Learn what actionable metrics are
- Check out what split testing is and how it can help us to improve our apps
- Investigate what tools we can use for testing
- Figure out how to use Firebase Remote Config and Firebase Analytics

Why do statistics matter?

Without statistics, you will have little to no feedback. You will be blind to all insights you could otherwise have obtained from your users and their behavior. Do not release your app without any implementation required for obtaining analytical data:

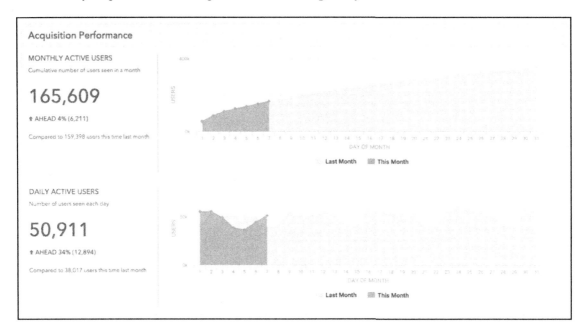

In general, statistics could inform us about the following:

- User acquisition performance
- User behavior and conversion
- User demographics
- User behavior by segment or cohort
- Financial insights

So, the right statistics tell us something about app usage. It gives an answer to questions such as: How well is the app doing and what exactly does "doing well" mean? Is this about the number of downloads? The number of active users? The number of daily new users? It is important not just to have statistics, but to have actionable metrics. It is easy to gather a lot of data. It is more difficult to determine what numbers really matter. Do not get drowned in numbers. Determine what your business objectives are so you know what to measure. It is important to have concrete numbers so you can instantly act upon them by doing the right things.

About actionable metrics

In `Chapter 10`, *There is an API For That!*, we already had a preview on the concept of conversions and metrics. Gathering statistics about your mobile app usage matters, as it often is the only way to get feedback from your users. If we want to learn something about this feedback, it is important to realize that the quality of the statics you obtain is more important than the quantity. While it may be tempting to gather as much data as possible, the opposite is actually true. Focus on what really matters. Actionable metrics is what we want. Ash Maurya writes about this in his books *Running Lean and Scaling Lean*. He claims user growth is more important than your total user base, and he certainly has a point there.

Acquisition and engagement are important metric categories. Acquisition numbers tell you something about your app's downloads, the number of new users, and the number of active users. Engagement is about how often your users are opening your app (and keep using it), retention, and churn rates (the users that have abandoned your app). It is interesting to learn how many of the users that have downloaded your app will stick with your app? And will they still be using your app after 1 week or 1 month? The other important metrics are customer lifetime value and key funnel behavior, but let's start with acquisition and engagement first.

Acquisition

Before users will download your app, they need to be aware of its existence. You need to promote it on social media, on your website, or in some other way. How else would one know that it exists and that your app is really awesome? Getting new users every day is important, as your number of active users will drop otherwise. No matter how cool your app is, it will not work for some people. That does not have to be an issue. As long as the numbers for acquisition is higher than the churn rate, your app will grow.

Engagement

User engagement metrics are all about your app's stickiness. People spend more and more time on mobile devices, which of course is a good thing for your app. But people also have little more than the attention span of a goldfish so average churn rates (app users that no longer use your app) are often higher for mobile apps.

You might wonder how much time a user spends on the app during a session or during a certain period. A session is any kind of interaction until the attention of the user gets interrupted by something else, such as an incoming phone call. To improve your app's retention rate, you should often remind users about the app or you should provide them with a good reason to visit the app on a regular basis. Email and push notifications can be used to get the user's attention again, thus maintaining app awareness.

The retention rate is about the number of users that remain active after a certain period of time, let's say, after 2 months or more. The churn rate is about the users that no longer use your app after the same period of time. To grow, the retention rate needs to be higher than the churn rate. To do so, your app constantly needs to deliver value by providing relevant content, incentives, and new or improved features. In short, you continuously need to give your users reason to come back to your app.

Daily or weekly active users are the most valuable ones as they will be the easiest ones to convert later. The higher the engagement rate, the more valuable the app is to your users. They could become an ambassador of your app by making referrals, or contribute to your app's monetization by clicking on advertisements or by making in-app purchases (revenue).

Conversions and pirate metrics

Pirate metrics, as we have seen in `Chapter 10`, *There is an API For That!*, are about the conversion of your app users. Here the conversion steps are shown from acquisition to revenue:

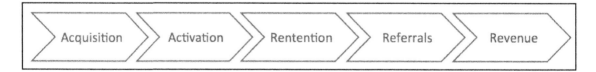

For our app, in particular, it comes down to these steps: **Awareness**, **Visit and search store**, **Download app**, **Open app**, **Activation (Register)**, and finally **Retention**. To keep things simple, for now, the ad income or in-app purchase (revenue) is not displayed here:

With each step, you lose a number of users. That is a completely normal phenomenon, but you need to make sure that you will not lose too many of them on the way. Let's say 1,000 people learn about the existence of your app by reading about it on a website or on Twitter. 800 of them click on the link to view the app in the store.

They see the app's icon, some screenshots, a description, and some feedback from other users. About 300 users think, "Hmm, this is not for me". So, only 500 users will download the app. 100 of them forget about it while downloading (on their way home, something else is asking for their attention: A call? A whatsapp message?). Eventually, 400 users will open the app. They see an onboarding story with a clear call to action. The app asks them to register using Facebook or Twitter. Probably 200 of them will do this. The remainder of the users have the intention to do this later (but they probably will forget about it). 200 users start exploring the app and, if they are not often reminded about the app, and if the app does not give them sufficient reasons to return to it, they will forget about it within a couple of days. After 1 week only 50 users are still using the app, and after 1 month only 25 of them are still active.

Is this a negative scenario? Not at all. It is a very realistic one for a lot of apps. If you want to make a difference between a failing and a successful app, then you need to think of this. Also, we did not even discuss the monetization part yet. In Chapter 17, *Monetization and Pricing Strategy*, we will have a look at that part specifically.

Fortunately, we have tools to improve the conversion rate. It is important to learn what the exact conversion percentages are. If, of all the users that have downloaded the app, only a small percentage sign up, then you will know you have work to do. There probably is something in your onboarding process that is preventing people from signing up. In that particular case, you need to find out if the on-boarding barrier is too high and what you can do to change this. Another example is the conversion number for in-app purchases. It also is an interesting pattern if you notice that they visit that part of your app where they can make such a purchase without ever converting to customers (actually buying something). There is something that needs to be changed there. Perhaps the added value for the products are unclear or maybe the pricing level is just too high.

Get to know your audience

But what is it that you need to change? If you have a small number of beta users, you can just text them to ask. There are also tools available to include some sort of survey, but most people consider them as annoying. It might help if you offer them specific incentives (a free purchase, for example). They could be digital incentives, such as the well-known badges (gamification) or real-life incentives. If you are interested in the latter, checkout Kiip at `http://www.kiip.me/developers` for some examples. They have a great SDK that you can add to your app. For example, it enables you to offer a free cup of coffee to your user if he has fully completed his profile.

If you want to know who your app users are, you need to have additional information about them, such as their locations and what they expect from your app. It is also interesting to know something about their age, gender, the types of devices they use, and at what moments or in what situations they use your app. Knowing your audience well is vital in order to be able to create an app that fully meets the user's expectations. And, in the end, it also leads to better monetization of your app. In fact, this is why Facebook ads have way better conversions than Google ads. Facebook knows much more about their audience and about each individual, so advertisements can be targeted more specifically, thus making the ad **Click Through Rate** (**CTR**) higher. We will learn more about this in `Chapter 14`, *Growing Traction and Improving Retention*, about traction and retention. First, let's see what we need to do to learn more about our app's audience:

Split testing can help us to improve our apps

A/B testing, also known as split testing, in its most basic form comes down to two different implementations shown at random to different kinds of people. A small number, say 5%, are shown the new feature, A, which could be something like a new feature or a new view, and another 5% will see feature B. The remainder of the users will not see the new feature yet. The feature that will prove to be most popular (by conversion or otherwise, depending on the objectives) will be fully implemented and offered to the complete audience of your app.

In case you want to find out what works best for signing up users, you can set up a split test like this:

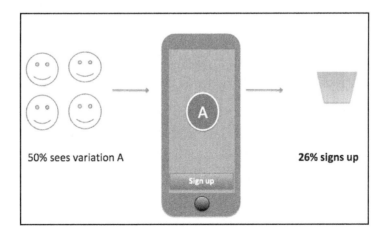

So 50% of your test audience sees variation A, showing a button that says **Sign up**, which will lead 26% of the visiting users to sign up. The other 74% might think "Hmm, this is not for me", or decide to sign-up later: something they probably will forget about. What happens with the other 50% of the test audience? They will see variation B. It displays a **Get started!** button. If we look at this variant, we see that 63% of the audience decides to sign up:

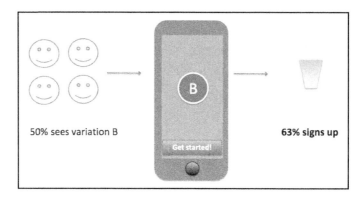

In theory, this proves that variation B is the one that should be implemented as it leads to the highest conversions. The reality is somewhat different. If we have little to no knowledge of our audience the preceding conclusion may be true, but if we do know a little more about our audience we might not accept the results on face value and might consider other questions. Is the audience that sees variation A comparable to the audience that sees variation B? There may be specific customer segments that specifically prefer one feature above another.

We will never find out if we will just do random tests. As stated earlier, we can increase our success on our app monetization only if we know what our audience is and what they want. Step 1 is getting to know our audience (by gathering user data) and step 2 is to take this knowledge into account when doing A/B tests. What if we could choose our target audience and see what works best for them? There are tools available that could help us to do a little bit more sophisticated split testing. We will look at them in the next section.

Keep the differences between variations subtle

The difference between A and B in our example is very subtle, and that is for a reason. If the difference between the two variations is too big, you will not know what it is that you are testing:

The preceding is a brilliant example of what not to do. If your onboarding split test shows that variant A leads to a 61% conversion and variant B leads to a 66% conversion rate, then what does the outcome prove? Not only is the difference in conversion percentages not very convincing, it also is not clear what has led to a slightly better conversion. Was it the background color that did the trick? Or the text (call to action)? Or maybe was it the color of the **Sign up** button? We will never know. This test has too many parameters.

Think of what the objective of the test is. What is your hypothesis and how can you prove it using a split test? Test one element at a time, so you know what change was responsible for the improved conversion. Run multiple split tests, as a single test will typically not provide sufficient information to fully understand what works best. Remember, it is not important what you think that your users will do. It is important what your users do. And you better find out as early as possible.

The other things that you should take into account are events that may influence your tests. Running a test around holidays or particular events may have a different outcome. Also, conversion rates may be different on different days of the week. For these reasons, always make sure you are running tests for at least a couple of weeks.

Tools for split testing and getting actionable metrics

From a technical perspective, it is pretty easy to do web split-testing experiments. Mobile-optimizing experiments, on the other hand, are more difficult to accomplish. The Play Store or the App Store are the most important reasons for this. A web browser always is connected, but apps live on a device which is not always connected.

Although mobile-app split testing is not as mature yet as for website A/B testing, there are many tools available that can help you test your users. Once you have decided what metrics you want to measure, you can pick the tool that is most convenient for that purpose:

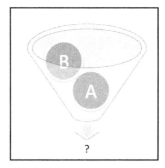

Among others, you can use some of the following tools:

- **Firebase:** This comes with many options, such as remote configurations and analytics. Firebase is a good candidate for split testing your app if you combine these two features. Remote configurations allow to make instant updates to the appearance of your app. Perhaps you are using Firebase already for data storage, real-time data sharing or for onboarding purposes.
- **Taplytics:** This is a split-testing tool that you can use to make changes that do not require an update in the Play Store or App Store. Without even changing code, you can have multiple fast-test iterations, which makes it one of the most suitable solutions for mobile split-testing purposes.

- **Fabric**: The Fabric SDK comes with many handy tools, about onboarding. It is a platform that makes it easy to install and maintain SDKs, including, for example, Optimizely. In addition to a Fabric account, you also need to set up an Optimizely account. Optimizely can help to easily integrate split testing into apps. It is a well-known testing tool and is available for both iOS and Android. Just as is the case with Firebase and Taplytics, there are no App Store or Play Store updates required to run A/B tests.

The other interesting tools are SplitForce, Flurry Analytics, Amazing A/B testing, Arise, Switchboard, Leanplum, and Apptimize. They all support both iOS and Android. Customer segments are supported by most of them. This functionality allows you to run tests for a particular type of audience. Depending on your objectives, you need to pick the tools that suit your needs best. As an example, we will take a look at Firebase remote config and Firebase analytics specifically to see how this works.

Using Firebase for split testing

You can use Firebase for split testing your Android or iOS app. Tutorials on how to set things up for Firebase and remote configurations specifically can be found at `https://firebase.google.com/docs/remote-config/`.

For this example, we will be looking at an Android implementation. Download the sample project from `https://github.com/mikerworks/packt-lean-firebase-split-testing`. The Android Kotlin app that you will find there is to demonstrate how you can run split tests for the onboarding flow of an app. It uses Firebase remote configurations and Firebase analytics.

The project has been setup using the Firebase option of the **Tools** menu of Android Studio. The Firebase assistant can help you to configure your project for `Analytics` and `Remote Config`:

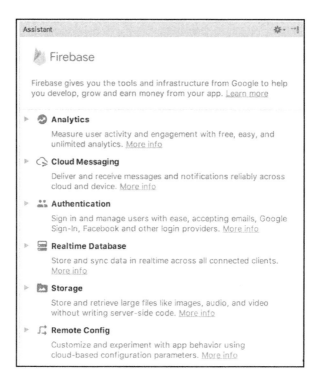

For the sample project, it has been set up already. In the `build.gradle` file within the `app` folder, you will find these dependencies for Firebase:

```
dependencies {
  ...
    implementation "org.jetbrains.kotlin:kotlin-stdlib-jre7:$kotlin_version"
    implementation 'com.android.support:appcompat-v7:25.4.0'
    implementation 'com.android.support.constraint:constraint-layout:1.0.2'
    implementation 'com.google.firebase:firebase-config:11.6.0'
}
apply plugin: 'com.google.gms.google-services'
```

The `google-services.json` file in the project should be replaced by your own file. You can download it from Firebase as soon as you have configured your app. (Choose settings in the project overview.) You can use the Firebase assistant to do so or you can go to the developers console of Firebase at `https://console.firebase.google.com`:

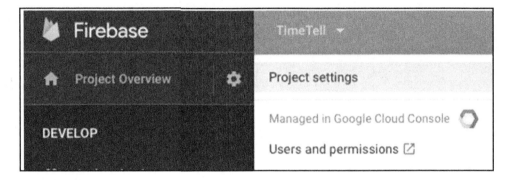

If you do not have a Firebase account yet, you need to create one first. In the console, you can add and configure your project:

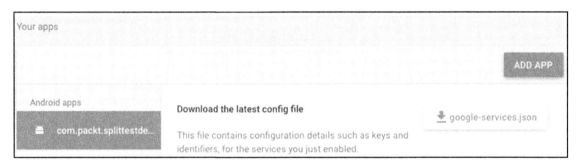

In the project overview, you can go to the **Grow** section and choose the **Remote config** option. If you choose the A/B testing on the right, you can determine what variants you want to split test:

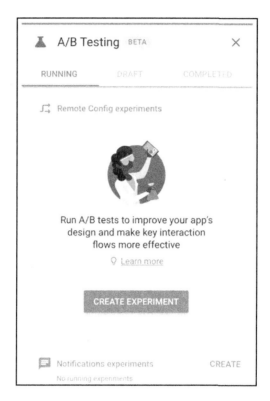

Let's say the example project is an app that has already been published. And let's say we want to test a new onboarding experience. By clicking on the **Create experiment** button, we can test what works best. We want to figure out how which variant leads to the highest conversion for sign-ups.

There are two variants: Variant A and Variant B. The Control group will see the app as is; they will not see any variations:

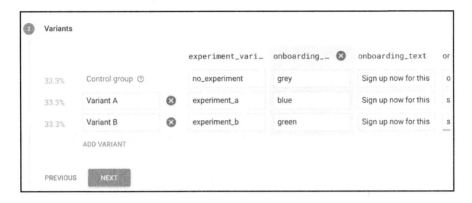

You can define one or more parameters for the experiment. Each variant has its own values for these parameters. Things that we could test are for example: the background color of the **Sign up** button (Blue or green), the sign up text or the background image (strawberries or oranges). As you can see, you can set up multiple parameters, but it is best practice to limit them to two or three.

You can define a user segment for your split test. In this example, we will just target 5% of the user base to keep it simple. More sophisticated segmentation options are also available. For example, you can target a specific country or users in the age group of 18 to 36. You can create very specific segments if you have obtained a lot of information about your users.

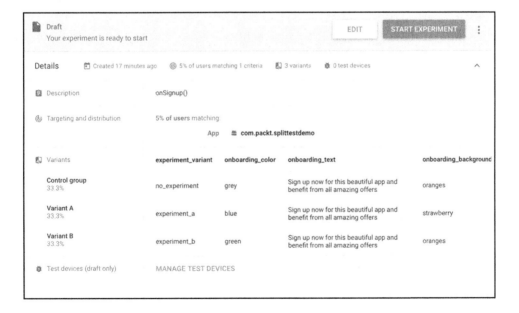

The app can read any of these values that you define here. The default ones can be found in the project in the `remote_config_defaults.xml` file (in the `res/xml` folder). We need them to let the app function properly in case the remote config values cannot be retrieved (because there is no internet connection, for example).

In the **MainActivity** app, you can see how it is done. The Firebase remote configuration and analytics are initialized here. The developer's mode is enabled for the debug variant. This will ensure that there is no caching of data, which allows us to test the variants first.

We are also telling the `firebaseRemoteConfig` instance that it should use the variables for the `remote_config_defaults.xml` file as a fall-back option:

```
val firebaseRemoteConfig = FirebaseRemoteConfig.getInstance()
var firebaseAnalytics: FirebaseAnalytics? = null
override fun onCreate(savedInstanceState: Bundle?) {
  ...
    val configSettings = FirebaseRemoteConfigSettings.Builder()
            .setDeveloperModeEnabled(BuildConfig.DEBUG)
            .build()
    firebaseAnalytics = FirebaseAnalytics.getInstance(this)
    firebaseRemoteConfig.setConfigSettings(configSettings)
    firebaseRemoteConfig.setDefaults(R.xml.remote_config_defaults)
    val token = FirebaseInstanceId.getInstance().getToken()
    Log.i(javaClass.simpleName, "token = ${token}")
    val cacheExpiration = 1L
    Log.i(javaClass.simpleName,"fetch")
firebaseRemoteConfig.fetch(cacheExpiration).addOnCompleteListener(this)
}
```

Finally, we are logging the device token. Later, we need this token to test a specific variant on our test device. At the end of this code snippet, we fetch the data and listen for the results.

If all the parameters and values have been retrieved, we tell the `firebaseRemoteConfig` object to apply these values. The call to the `applyRemoteConfiguration` method ensures that the UI will be updated:

```
override fun onComplete(task: Task<Void>) {
    if (task.isSuccessful){
        Log.i(javaClass.simpleName, "complete success")
        firebaseRemoteConfig.activateFetched()
    }
    else{
        Log.i(javaClass.simpleName, "complete no success")
    }
```

```
    applyRemoteConfiguration()
}
```

Here, we set all the colors and texts that are applicable to the current variant:

```
private fun applyRemoteConfiguration(){
    val variant = firebaseRemoteConfig.getString("experiment_variant")
    Log.i(javaClass.simpleName, "experiment = ${variant}")
    firebaseAnalytics?.setUserProperty("Experiment", variant)
    val onboardingColor = firebaseRemoteConfig.getString("onboarding_color")
    Log.i(javaClass.simpleName, "onboarding color= ${onboardingColor}")
    if (onboardingColor=="blue") {
findViewById(R.id.sign_up_button).setBackgroundColor(Color.parseColor("#000
0ff"))
    }
    else{
findViewById(R.id.sign_up_button).setBackgroundColor(Color.parseColor("#00f
f00"))
    }
    val onboardingText = firebaseRemoteConfig.getString("onboarding_text")
    Log.i(javaClass.simpleName, "onboarding text= ${onboardingText}")
    (findViewById(R.id.sign_up_text) as TextView).text = onboardingText
    val onboardingBackground =
firebaseRemoteConfig.getString("onboarding_background")
    Log.i(javaClass.simpleName, "onboarding bg= ${onboardingBackground}")
    if (onboardingBackground=="strawberry") {
(findViewById(R.id.image).setBackgroundResource(R.drawable.strawberry))
    }
    else{
        (findViewById(R.id.image).setBackgroundResource(R.drawable.oranges))
    }
}
```

This will result in displaying variant A or variant B for the onboarding flow. Since we want to measure the differences in conversion between these two variants, we set a user property for the `fireBaseAnalytics` object, and if the user clicks on the sign up button, we log the event like this:

```
private fun onSignup(){
    logEvent("signUp")
    Log.i(javaClass.simpleName, "sign up button clicked")
}
private fun logEvent(eventName: String){
    firebaseAnalytics?.logEvent(eventName, Bundle())
}
```

With this approach, we can measure the number of clicks on the sign up button and we can see the results in the Firebase analytics dashboard console for each variant.

First, we need to test both variants. If you run the app for the first time and everything goes well, you will find something like this in the log output (filter on: token):

```
11-10 11:22:09.856 27547-27547/com.packt.splittestdemo I/MainActivity:
token = cG-QulinNq0:APA91bH2lOQThh57qNseb3PDoBRDy-mPXvE_vezn1nNFBiDrWd0a...
```

Copy the token value and go back to the Firebase console. There you can set up a test device. Paste the token at the field **Instance ID token** and choose **Variant A** or **Variant B**:

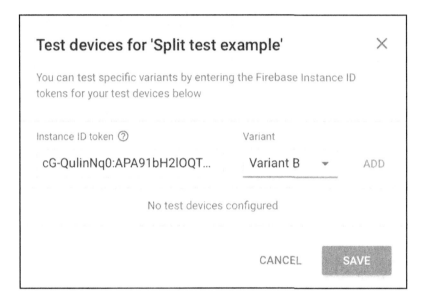

If you choose Variant A and run the app now, it will look like the screenshot shown on the left. It has a background filled with strawberries and it has a blue **SIGN UP** button. However, if you choose Variant B at the Firebase console and run the app again, it will suddenly show oranges in the background and it has a green **SIGN UP** button. Variant B is shown on the right:

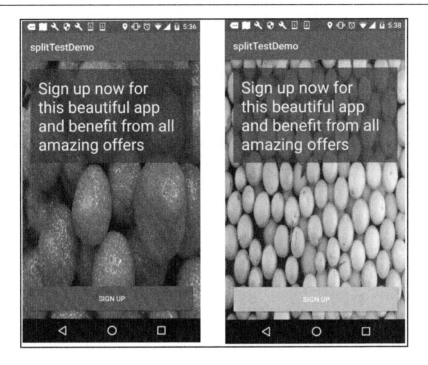

Will this onboarding screen with the blue **Call to Action** button and a background of strawberries be the winner? Or will we see the highest conversion (sign up) for the onboarding view that uses a green button and a background of oranges? Only time will tell what the outcome will be.

If we run this split test live for a couple of weeks, we will know which of the two results provide the highest conversion. The winning variant will be the one that we are going to roll out for all users.

This was just a brief example. There are many other options available to be discovered that are not covered in this chapter, as it is just an introduction to split testing. However, you have an idea of the possibilities now.

To learn more about Firebase split testing specifically, have a look at:

`https://developer.android.com/distribute/best-practices/develop/in-app-a-b-testing.html` or `https://techcrunch.com/2017/10/31/google-firebase-gets-predictions-crashlytics-integration-and-a-new-ab-testing-service/` or `https://firebase.google.com/docs/remote-config/use-config-ios`.

Summary

In this chapter, we have seen why statistics matter and which statistics matter. We have learned about split testing and what the do's and don'ts are. We have some idea of what tools are available for it and what we need to do to set up a split test of our own apps. We learned something about metrics and about the importance of acquisition and retention.

In the next chapter, we will learn more about retention and how we can further improve it. We are going to improve traction and examine some practical approaches to accomplish that for our app. Let's get started.

15
Growing Traction and Improving Retention

In this chapter, you will learn about traction, the proof that somebody wants to use your product and, in most cases, is willing to pay for it, resulting in a profitable business in the end. Now that we have obtained some actionable metrics, as we have learned in the previous chapter, we will see how to grow traction. Without sufficient retention (returning users to your app) or too much churn (users abandoning your app), the moment of truth will be gone quickly and we will lose traction. Let's investigate how we can increase the retention rate. Also, we will see what we can do the keep the churn rate low.

Specifically, in this chapter we will cover the following topics:

- Learning about the definition of traction
- Finding out how we can grow traction and when "growth hacking" comes into play
- Seeing how we can improve retention
- Learning how to stay in touch with your app users
- Seeing what it takes to implement a notification mechanism to remind users

Traction

So, what is traction? Basically, it is about upcoming patterns that indicate a scaling and repeatable business. Traction is an evidence of a sufficiently large market demand and more specifically about adoption and engagement. If you do well, traction is the confirmation of the hypotheses that you have about your product or service. Traction is about making actual progress and it is important in each phase of your app. It is about the first few early adopters that sign up when you just got started, and eventually it also is about the users that make (in-app) purchases. How well is your app doing converting people into users and users into customers?

Even emerging app clones (or copycats) are a sign of traction. It proves, along with your grown user base, that the problem that your app is solving really matters and that the problem is worth solving.

Things as profitability (revenues), the number of registered and active users (retention), engagement, traffic, and even partnerships are all things that you can use to measure traction. Be aware that isolated information is no real proof for traction. For example, you can run some campaigns to grow your user base but if the **Customer Acquisition Cost (CAC)** is higher than the **Average Revenue Per User (ARPU)** then it makes no sense to look only at the revenue to determine traction. You need to make sure that the **Lifetime Customer Value (LTV)** will be higher than the cost of onboarding new users. You need to lower the cost or you need to increase the LTV. To do the latter you can, for example, consider offering subscriptions. Other than one-time in-app purchases, it will lead to recurring revenue.

Working on the scalability of your apps, business will help to get and improve traction. However, to understand how this will work for your app, you will often need to do stuff that does not (yet) scale, as we have seen in `Chapter 11`, *Onboarding and Registration*. You first have to learn what works and what does not. The "concierge service" has been mentioned earlier and it is something that definitely does not scale. However, it could help you obtain a lot of useful insights. Other things that you can do include cold canvassing and networking in general. Since these strategies are things that business-oriented people love to do, but most developers will hate, we will examine what else there is that we can do to grow traction.

There are a couple of things that you can do to improve awareness for your app and to find your early adopters. If people see your app listed on any of the following sites mentioned and decide to download your app, then you will see the first signs of traction.

In addition to writing posts about your app on Facebook, LinkedIn, and Twitter, here are some places to get started:

- **Product hunt**: `https://www.producthunt.com`
- **Betali.st**: `http://Betali.st`
- **Start-up list**: `http://startupli.st`
- **Reddit startups**: `https://www.reddit.com/r/startups`

These are the places where your (potential) early adopters are, people who are curious to learn about new apps and services. Since they love giving feedback about new products, these are exactly the people what you are looking for.

Of course, you should have a blog about your app (if not, start one right now), way before the first (beta) version of your app is launched. It is important to build an audience first before putting any effort into developing an app. Make sure that you have a clear call to action for the readers of your blog. Make it as convenient as possible to sign up for your email newsletter and send those newsletters on a regular basis to your subscribers. Once your app is out, continue your blogging and do some experiments (split testing for your email) to see what leads to the best conversion (from reading to opening your app, landing page and downloading, and using your app).

Freemium or premium only?

Some say that the only relevant traction is price traction. If your app is completely free the demand for your app can be infinite. However, that alone is not really important if there is no revenue. Asking money for your app right from the beginning is the ultimate way to measure traction. The earlier you generate revenue, the faster you validate the app concept. If you think this approach won't work, think again and have a look at the various crowdfunding sites on the net. Of course, you need to have an awesome story about your app. You need to tell them what is so great about your app, but you already have a great story, right?

No business will survive without any income. In fact, a free app does not exist. The money has to come from somewhere. Offering in-app purchases is one way to monetize your app, but only a small amount of users (2% or less) will really do so. The other 98% will continue to use your app without ever paying for it. The freemium models work because hosting is inexpensive and because you can scale your app without too much effort. However, you still need to pay attention to the full 100% of the user group. You have to respond to their reviews and you have to keep posting on social media. That can be very time-consuming. The income from 2% of your users should cover the cost for that.

It can be difficult to decide what features should come with the paid variant of the app. You need to have a clear understanding of how valuable each part of your app is for your users. Also, you can decide to offer a premium app only. If you charge directly from the start for your app, you will raise the barrier, but your sales numbers will be a real proof of traction. In Chapter 17, *Monetization and Pricing Strategy*, about monetization, we will have a closer look at price strategies.

There are, of course, others ways to monetize your app. You can think of showing advertisements. Also, you can also think of a solution that utilizes the web and mobile channels. Do not think of your app as the product any longer, but think of your app as a channel for your service. So, you offer your app for free, but, on the web you ask your users for money for subscribing to your service. That approach works very well for business-oriented solutions in particular. The revenues will be higher, probably because the perceived value of an app alone is likely to be lower. It is just a matter of perception but perception is important when it comes to marketing. It may also have to do with the fact that, often, people are less willing to pay for an app running on a smaller device. This is a bit silly but nevertheless, it is true. Perhaps we can focus on developing apps for large TVs only? I am just kidding of course.

From the perspective of a developer, it makes no sense at all. Developers know that it takes the same amount of work and that the size of a device does not matter here. Anyway, the perceived value and the channels you use do matter. They will have an impact on the amount of traction and how it will be determined.

Without clear objectives, you cannot measure traction or any other kind of success. The more abstract your goals are, the more difficult it will be to perceive the outcome clearly. To make the outcome measurable (actionable metrics), you need to define clear goals. Clear goals come with numbers, such as how many new signups (1,000?) do we want to have in a particular amount of time (1 month?), or how many emails do we have to send to grow the conversion of our users by 25%?

Improving retention

Mobile app retention and engagement are metrics that can be an indication of your app's success. High app retention and engagement ratios often are a reason for your app's success. Retention says something about how often your users relaunch your app within a particular amount of time. Engagement is an indicator of activity. It says something about what they are doing while using your app, and how long and how often they are doing this within a particular session. Probably, the most important one of these two is retention. If you understand what makes your app sticky for your users, then you will be able to improve the retention rate.

You should always wonder: what's in it for them? And you should give your users some good reasons to come back to the app regularly. Social apps have the best retention rates. People come back because they want to be kept up to date on the regular stream of information. This is known as the **fear of missing out** (**FoMo**). It is a skill that Facebook has mastered completely. Unfortunately, unlike Facebook, most apps are not used on a daily basis.

Churn is a phenomenon that is more or less the opposite of retention. There will always be churn, but you can try to keep it as low as possible. Today, numbers show that if an app is not started once a week there is a chance that 60% of people will forget about it. You need to keep your app relevant. You have to regularly offer fresh content and new features. It is needless to say that you have to inform the user about these updates. You can send them push notifications for example. That is a very common approach to catch the attention of users and send them back to your app!

An onboarding experience with a low barrier, offering fresh and relevant content and features, personalization (social sign up strategies could help here), incentification, and sending push notifications are all features that can greatly contribute to better retention and engagement values.

Incentification is closely related to gamification. Both come with rewards if the user has come to a particular achievement in your app. While gamification is more about digital incentives, such as badges (as available at Foursquare and Stack Overflow, for example), incentification is about real-world, non-digital rewards, such as a free cup of coffee at the nearest coffee shop. If you want to learn more about the concept of incentification, you can check out `http://kiip.me`.

There are many ways to improve retention, resulting in better traction. For now, we will just examine how to stay in touch with our users by enabling push notifications. You need to give people a reason to keep coming back and you often need to remind people of the existence of your app. If you do not want your app to be forgotten, abandoned, and eventually deleted, you should kindly remind them of the app.

There are many ways to improve retention, resulting in better traction. For now, we will just examine how to stay in touch with our users, by enabling push notifications. You need to give people a reason to keep coming back and you often need to remind people of the existence of your app. If you do not want your app to be forgotten, abandoned and eventually deleted, you should kindly remind them of the app.

Please do not spam your users. Do not send too many messages and try, through segmentation, to send relevant information only. If your user stays away for too long and if you have something interesting to share with them you can send them a friendly reminder. It is an excellent candidate for a concierge service if you want to learn what type of reminders work best. Find out what type of messages works best and see what customer segments will show the best conversions. Once you have learned that then you can do the automation later. If you already have a large user base you can also perform an A/B test to see what works best. There are many services available that can help you with both the segmenting of your customers and running split tests.

Also, think about the frequency of your reminders. Is one week of abstinence a good time to send out a reminder? Or is two weeks better? It is important to tell a story and to build an experience. Stating what is in it for them should come with a clear call to action, such as "Check out our new feature X" or "Look at what your friend Y has posted".

Push notifications can help to increase retention rates. Numbers show that, on average, users who have opted-in to receive push notifications results in 25% higher retention rates. That seems to make sense. By the way, push notifications for iOS apps are always opt-in. Only if users state that they do want to receive push notifications, they will receive them. Android has an opt-out mechanism. Users install an app and they will receive push notifications unless they choose to opt-out.

Notifications

There are three ways of communicating with your app users using notification messages and badges:

- Local notifications
- Push notifications
- In-app notifications

Local notifications

Local notifications are like services, running on the user's device. The app does not need to be active to receive a local notification related to your app. They also do not need internet access or a server. Instead, they are scheduled for a particular date and time, like an alarm. They are initialized by your app.

What you can do is schedule a local notification to remind the user about the app but cancel it as soon as the user launches your app. It is a great instrument to remind your user about your app's existence:

You can use local notifications to increase your app's retention rate. You can schedule a notification when your app is closed or loses focus but cancel them when your app becomes active again. If you set the fire date to one or two weeks from now and users forget about your app, they will receive a friendly reminder. If, however, they use the app within this particular time frame, then the notification will be canceled and the user will not be bothered with any reminder notifications.

Push notifications

Push notifications involve a server (and with that an internet connection) that initiates the action. Such notifications are a great instrument for promotional actions, and can inform the user about the availability of new content and new features in the app. Further, it depends on the nature of the app to decide what notifications will be relevant. For a dating app, it would be nice to be notified about a new app. In this case, displaying a badge on the icon of the app indicating the number of new matches and messages also would be very helpful. For a news app, it would be great to receive a notification each time a new and important message comes in. You can create user segments based on interest or based on their geographical location, for example, to notify your user only about local news events.

In-app notifications

Finally, you can use in-app notifications to indicate that there are new events. You can display a badge at those places, where it is relevant. This could be a tab or a menu item. You can also use app notifications to stimulate particular behavior while your app is being used. Think, for example, of a reminder notification such as "Rate this app 5 stars!" Some methods can be quite clever, like a dialog that is only shown if the user has used the app five times (engagement) and the app has not crashed.

Only then will the dialog ask for a 5-star rating! It is important to provide convenience and lower the barrier to rate the app for your users that are enthusiastic about your app. For users who might be less happy with your app, you can keep the barrier as is. This will help you get better App/Play Store ratings.

There are components that do exactly this. One of them is iRate for iOS. With only a few lines of code, you can implement a 'Rate us' or 'Give us 5 stars' popup in your app. You can configure when and under what conditions it will be shown:

For each type of notification, it is important to not be annoying. Do not ask too much from the user too often. You should only notify a user if there is something relevant to mention. A push notification for no particular reason, just to let the user come back to the app may convert well once. However, if this happens too often, it will become annoying and your users might uninstall the app instead.

Services for push notifications

To distribute your push notifications to your Android and iOS devices, you need to have a push notification server that will distribute messages to the correct devices. Although you can build this yourself, it is more convenient to use one of the ready-made solutions that are available for this purpose. The benefits of existing solutions, besides a big-time saver, will be their scalability, multi-platform support, and segmentation options, making it easier to determine which message goes to what user.

Some examples of such solutions are Urban Airship, Azure Push Notification Hub, Amazon Push, Hosted Parse Servers solutions, as found at back4app.com for example, and Firebase push notification services. They all have different pricing plans and they support different OSs.

As an example, here is a schematic view of Azure Push notification hubs. It can deliver push notifications to iOS and Android (And Windows Phone if you still really want to do so):

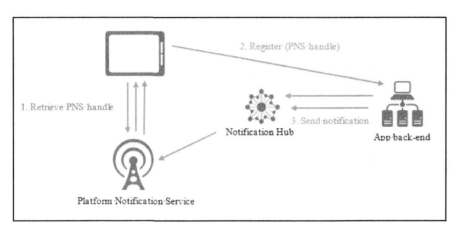

If you want to deliver push notifications to operating systems other than Android or iOS, or if you want to deliver push notifications outside the western world, it is good to carefully examine the different options. Let's say you want to deliver your app to the Chinese market as well. In that case, it is good to know that Amazon supports Baidu Push notifications, since this is not supported by all services. Amazon has a single hub for sending notifications to any device no matter if it is running on Amazon, iOS, Baidu, Android or Windows.

Push notifications for Android are delivered through the **Google Cloud Messaging (GCM)** protocol. Apple uses **Apple Push Notification Service (APNS)** for iOS. Configuring push notifications for iOS is a little bit more complicated as it requires some hassle with certificates. However, if you are an iOS developer using certificates and distribution profiles, then you will not be scared of it.

Back4App is a party that is offering Parse server hosting including support for push notifications (Android and iOS). You can easily target all users or specific users (segments):

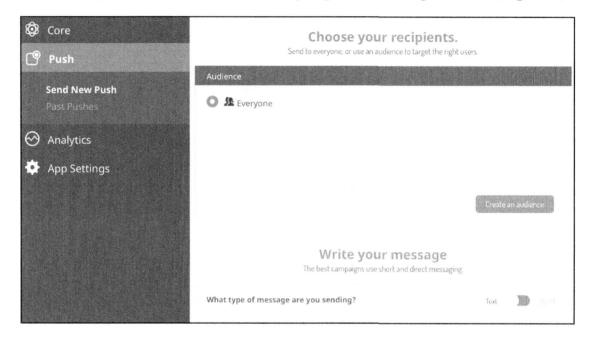

As you can see, most services offer support for Android and iOS and a couple of other platforms. Scalability, supported platforms, pricing plans, and ease of integration are all things to consider when choosing a push notification service provider:

	Amazon	Apple (APNS)	Baidu	Google (GCM)	Microsoft
Amazon	Supported	Supported	Supported	Supported	Supported
Azure	Supported	Supported	Not sure	Supported	Supported
Firebase		Supported		Supported	?
Urban Airship	Supported	Supported		Supported	Supported
Parse Server		Supported		Supported	

Implementation

The approach for both platforms is more or less the same. If the user launches the app, the device and app will be registered for receiving push notifications. It will result in a token (or an optional registration ID for Android) that you can use later to send a notification to this particular device and for this particular app. The main difference between Android and iOS is that iOS uses an opt-in strategy for receiving notifications, while Android uses an opt-out strategy.

An iPhone user will see a question pop up which asks if he wants to allow the app to receive push notifications (opt-in). This is something the OS does for us when we register as shown as follows:

For Android, we will just register the device and the app and we will receive push notifications, which the user won't notice until he receives his first notification. On Android, you can turn receiving push notifications off (opt out) using the Settings app.

So, here is an Android Java example of such registrations in your App class. The GCM_PROJECT_NUMBER refers to the project number in the Google developer console, but we will come to that later:

```
private GoogleCloudMessaging gcm;
...
String regid =
gcm.register(FlavorConstants.PushConfiguration.GoogleConfiguration.
 GCM_PROJECT_NUMBER);
Log.i(getClass().toString(), "Obtained RegId from GCM : " + regid);
```

Additionally, here is how it is done for iOS (Swift 3.x, iOS 10) in the AppDelegate class. For iOS, you also need to configure a couple of things in the developer's portal, which we will see later:

```
func registerForPushNotifications(){
        print ("PN - register for PN")
        let center = UNUserNotificationCenter.current()
        center.delegate = self
        center.requestAuthorization(options:[.badge, .alert, .sound]) {
(granted, error) in
            if error == nil {
                print ("PN - No error")
            }
            else{
                print ("PN - Error ")
            }
            if (!granted){
                print ("PN - Not granted")
```

```
        }
        else{
            print ("PN - granted")
        }
        guard granted else { return }
        self.getNotificationSettings()
    }
}
func getNotificationSettings() {
    UNUserNotificationCenter.current().getNotificationSettings {
(settings) in
        print("Notification settings: \(settings)")
        guard settings.authorizationStatus == .authorized else { return
}
        UIApplication.shared.registerForRemoteNotifications()
    }
}

 func application(_ application: UIApplication,
didRegisterForRemoteNotificationsWithDeviceToken deviceToken: Data)
    {
        let installation = PFInstallation.current()
        installation?.setDeviceTokenFrom(deviceToken)
        installation?.saveInBackground()
        PFPush.subscribeToChannel(inBackground: "global") { (result, error)
in
            print("PN - subscribed to global")
        }
    }
```

Setup

To set up GCM for your Android app, you have to go to your Google Developer Console, which you can find at https://console.developers.google.com/.

There you can configure your app and obtain a server key.

To set up **Apple push notifications** (**APNS**), you need to go the Apple Developer's portal and find your app at the identifiers/app ID's section (assuming that you have already created an app id for your app):

Application Services:		
Service	Development	Distribution
App Groups	○ Disabled	○ Disabled
Associated Domains	○ Disabled	○ Disabled
Data Protection	○ Disabled	○ Disabled
Game Center	● Enabled	● Enabled
HealthKit	○ Disabled	○ Disabled
HomeKit	○ Disabled	○ Disabled
Wireless Accessory Configuration	○ Disabled	○ Disabled
Apple Pay	○ Disabled	○ Disabled
iCloud	○ Disabled	○ Disabled
In-App Purchase	● Enabled	● Enabled
Inter-App Audio	○ Disabled	○ Disabled
Wallet	○ Disabled	○ Disabled
Push Notifications	● Enabled	● Configurable

Click on the **Edit** button and scroll down to the **Push Notifications** section. Click on the **Download** button to download the certificate or click on the **Create Certificate** button depending on your needs.

Follow the instructions. Use the `keychain` app to create a CSR file (certificate signing request). Doing this from the building machine is preferable.

Upload the request file (CSR) to the Apple Developer's portal:

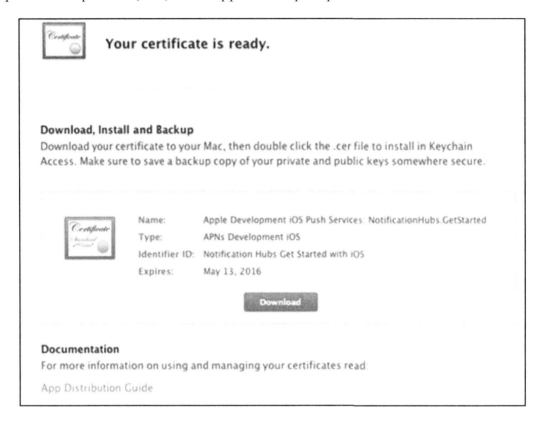

Download the certificate (that will contain both the private and public part) and double-click to install. In the `keychain` app, find the APNS certificate and choose **Export** from the **Context** menu.

Provide a password for the file and save it. You now have a file with a P12 extension that you can later upload to your notification service, for example, to Azure Push Notification hubs.

The following example shows the section in Notification hubs, where you can upload this certificate file in sandbox mode (development only). This approach is more or less the same for other services. They all require you to upload this file to make the magic happen:

The following is an example of all the push services you can configure here:

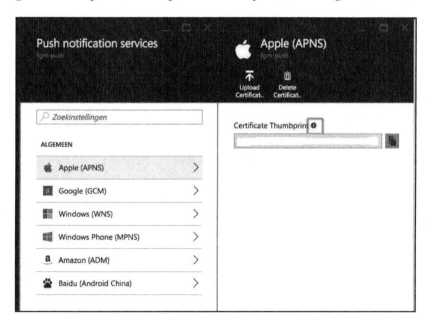

After deciding which notification service to use, find some good references (books or tutorials on the subject) as, in particular, iOS push notification configuration can be a bit tricky.

Handling an incoming notification

If a notification comes in, it will be shown in the **Messenger** section, something that the OS will provide for us. In addition, we can define what to do with it. In Android, we can implement a `PushHandler` class that consumes the notification and defines specific actions for it using the `NotificationCompat` builder. Here is an Android Java example:

```java
public class PushHandler extends NotificationsHandler {

    Context ctx;

    @Override
    public void onReceive(Context context, Bundle bundle) {
        ctx = context;
        String nhMessage = bundle.getString("message");
        Parcelable parselableObject = bundle.getParcelable("parcel");
        consumeNotification(nhMessage,parselableObject);
    }

    private void consumeNotification(String msg, Parcelable
parselableObject) {

        Log.i(this.getClass().toString(), "Consume notification");
        Log.i(this.getClass().toString(), "Notification msg = "+msg);

        if (parselableObject != null) {
            Log.i(this.getClass().toString(), "Consume has parcel");
        }

        displayNotificationMessage(ctx, "Message", msg,msg);
    }

    public static void displayNotificationMessage(Context context, String
title, String contentText,
        String tickerText){
displayNotificationMessage(context,title,contentText,tickerText,null);
    }

    public static void displayNotificationMessage(Context context, String
title, String contentText, String tickerText, Parcelable parselableObject){

...

        NotificationCompat.Builder builder = new
NotificationCompat.Builder(context);
        Uri soundUri =
RingtoneManager.getDefaultUri(RingtoneManager.TYPE_NOTIFICATION);
```

```
Bundle extras = new Bundle();
extras.putParcelable("parcel", parcelableObject);

Notification notification = builder.setContentTitle(title)
        .setContentText(contentText)
        .setTicker(tickerText)
        .setSmallIcon(R.mipmap.appicon)
        .setContentIntent(pendingIntent)
        .setPriority(Notification.PRIORITY_HIGH)
        .setSound(soundUri)
        .setVibrate(new long[]{0, 500})
        .setExtras(extras)
        .build();

    NotificationManager notificationManager = (NotificationManager)
context.getSystemService(Context.NOTIFICATION_SERVICE);
    notificationManager.notify(0, notification);
}
```

For iOS, you can do the same thing. This is the event handling in the `AppDelegate` class, and it is a Swift 4/3.x, iOS 11 example (for previous versions of iOS, it works in a different way), and it uses the Parse Server to get the push notifications delivered.

Here, we can determine as well what should happen when a push notification arrives (to some extent). The completion handler determines if a notification or badge is shown and if a sound will be played:

```
    func application(_ application: UIApplication,
didFailToRegisterForRemoteNotificationsWithError error: Error) {
        print("Failed to register: \(error)")
    }
    func userNotificationCenter(_ center: UNUserNotificationCenter,
willPresent notification: UNNotification, withCompletionHandler
completionHandler: @escaping (UNNotificationPresentationOptions) -> Void) {
        print ("PN - willPresent")
        let userInfo = notification.request.content.userInfo as
NSDictionary
        let body = notification.request.content.body
        for (key, value) in userInfo {
            print("userInfo: \(key) -> value = \(value)")
        }
        if ... {
                print ("PN - completion handler silent")
                completionHandler([])
        }
        else{
                print ("PN - completion handler alert badge sound")
```

```
                    completionHandler([.alert,.badge, .sound])
            }
        }
        ...
    }
    func userNotificationCenter(_ center: UNUserNotificationCenter,
  didReceive response: UNNotificationResponse, withCompletionHandler
  completionHandler: @escaping () -> Void) {
        print ("PN - Did receive")
        ...
        completionHandler()
    }
```

Sending a notification

To send a notification, you can use the web interface of the service or you can use the features that the service provides if you want to send a message programmatically.

The following is a cloud code example for the Parse Server (Back4App). It sends a message to all devices that are listening to a particular channel. You can send a push notification to all users or you can set up channels for customer segmentation. You can set the number of the badge on the icon (iOS only), the title, and the message:

```
 Parse.Push.send({ channels: "channel or channels", data: { title: "title",
sound: 'default',  badge: 2, alert: "message", extraParam: "something" } },
    {    success: function () {    response.success("ok");    },
        error: function (error) { response.success("nok: " + error); },
        useMasterKey: true
    }); // push send
```

No matter which service you are using, the basic payload is always the same. Also, note that you can send custom parameters with it:

```
data: { title: "title", sound: 'default',  badge: 2, alert: "message",
extraParam: "something" }
```

So far, for a high-level perspective on push notifications, you now have an idea what it takes to implement it. To continue on this subject, examine the tutorials that Google and Apple provide about it.

Summary

In this chapter, you learned what the definition of traction is and why it is important. We have seen that engagement and retention are important elements too. We have seen that there are different types of notifications and what the benefits are of each type. You can remind your user about specific events in your app. This will increase the retention rate. Notifications can also help you to improve the awareness for your app, for example, by asking for a user rating for your app. Finally, we have seen what notification services exist to deliver push notifications and what it takes to actually implement a push notification mechanism for your Android and iOS apps.

In the next chapter, we will investigate scalability. In the beginning, you often do things that do not scale, but once you have established sufficient amount of traction, it is time to think about a scalability strategy. This is particularly important when your app uses a backend.

16
Scaling Strategies

In this chapter, you will learn what determines your app's scalability and what you need to do for it to scale well. You will also learn when scaling will become important and what elements will influence your scaling strategy. When you just get started, the scale is not important at all. In fact, we did tell you earlier to do things that do not scale. So, what made us change our mind? Nothing really. It is still important to prove your hypotheses and, until that is done, it would be a waste of time to make your app scale. However, what is important is that you should think about the scalability of your app and what your strategy will be in case your app becomes very popular and starts to grow quickly. Now, it is perfectly fine that your app backend can handle only one hundred simultaneous connections. But your app backend also needs to be capable of handling thousands of simultaneous requests, if not more. Not being able to scale things quickly leads to downtime, which leads to sad users, which in turn leads to a large churn percentage. People walk away and, instead of steady growth, your short moment of fame will be gone. This would be even a bigger waste. So, we need a plan and this chapter will help you to define this plan.

Specifically, in the chapter, we will cover the following topics:

- Learn why it is important to make your app able to scale
- Determine when and how to scale your app and how analytics can help
- Find out what you need to do to have a scalable backend

Make it scalable but do not scale it right away

In the real world, the definition of scalability may vary from culture to culture, but for your app it is important that it is responsive and functional in the most common circumstances.

If you foresee any issues at a given moment in time, it is time to scale up; but the key element here is that being able to scale up quickly is more important. Make sure that you can do the right things when there is momentum!

So, you made an app and it has been shown on a site such as Product Hunt or Betalist. You have some enthusiastic early adopters for an audience. As an early-stage startup company, you should not care too much about how well your app scales, but you should have an idea on how to make it scale if your audience suddenly becomes larger than expected.

Scalability is not just about the backend solution for your app. It is also about to what extent it is possible to automate the services for your app and how easy it will be to serve any amount of app users. Only when your app services can be near 100% automated, will you have a really scalable solution. Anything that requires your personal, or other people's attention, prevents your app from being fully scalable. The more support your app requires, the less scalable it will be.

The scalability of your app could also be limited by the nature of your app and its targeted audience. A game app: Flappy Bird, for example, can by definition be very scalable. It has no backend and the game is distributed by the App Store or Play Store. For things such as leaderboards, you can use the Google or Apple services. You can trust that these services are scalable. A social app will be harder to scale because it requires that you have a (complex) backend solution. Although it is distributed via the stores, your users need to be able to download and upload streams of data that not just involve text, but also images and video. Your server should be capable of handling that load.

All of it needs to be stored somewhere and it needs to be delivered quickly. Also, moderation, although it can be automated to a large extent, becomes more important when user-generated content comes in. Moderation requires manual intervention that will have an effect on the scalability of the app. Other apps, such as Uber, come with other (non-technical) challenges. They need to deal with all kinds of regulations that also require manual interaction. Anything that requires manual interaction can threaten the scalability of your solution. Once your hypotheses are proven and your app starts to grow, it is important to automate as many components of your app as possible.

If you need more staff, you can hire more people, of course. However, automation is better. In this chapter, we will focus in particular on the technical scalability of an app. When the distribution of the app itself is taken care of by the Play Store or App Store, there is no need to have a strategy. The stores can distribute these apps as often as you want without the need to worry about scaling. Well, this is why they charge 30% (for paid apps), right? Discussing the scalability of your app is relevant if your app will use some kind of backend. For example, you might use a backend to share stories, images, videos, or whatever.

Let's say that you have created a first MVP for your app. The MVP itself is not an app yet. It is just there for validation. Imagine that through a website or email, you obtain user input that requires some kind of processing. As we have seen in previous chapters, it is perfectly fine to have a concierge service. You will be doing the process partly or completely manually. True, that does not scale, but why would you automate the process if you do not know yet if it is going to work out?

If your MVP does work as expected, it will result in a few happy customers. You have proven your hypotheses and you can start to automate the process. You actually built an app and created the backend for it. You stored all data (texts, images, and video) on a single server. If this went well, there will be more happy customers. And then, your app gets featured in the App Store or a very influential early adopter writes a blog about your app and it goes Boom! Suddenly a lot of people start using your app and smoke is coming out of your server(s). You quickly need to come up with a solution before things start to slow down or before they stop working. You need to prevent people from becoming disappointed or your momentum will be gone. You can add a couple of extra servers and think of some smart load-balancing solution, but, on the other hand, you could save yourself a lot of trouble if you start to utilize cloud services, running on, for example, Amazon or Azure from the beginning.

If you think it won't go that fast, then consider this: If you do not expect your app to go Boom! then why bother building it in the first place? Even pet projects can suddenly become very popular!

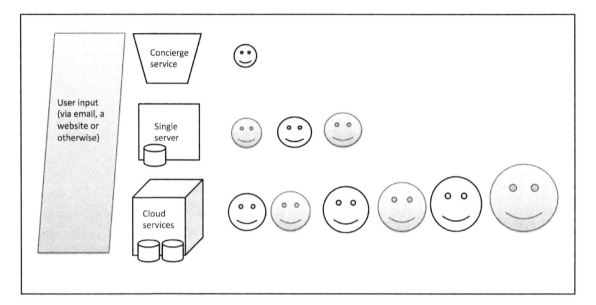

A scalable backend

Depending on your particular situation, a mobile backend solution may have to deal with these situations:

- Database and load balancing the database tier
- Web server and load balancing
- Reducing the amount of data that goes 'over the line' (low bandwidth support)
- Storage of media (images, video, and audio)
- Content delivery (video streaming)

Cloud storage space is pretty affordable nowadays and, with most solutions, you just need to click a few buttons to scale up (and spend a little bit more money). So, why not use cloud services right from the start? If you have the skills and the time, you can build your own solution and run it on the (scalable) cloud using an Infrastructure-as-a-Service (IaaS) solution such as AWS or Azure. If you do not have the skills or time, you can also choose to use a Mobile Backend as a Service (MBaaS). The latter will be less flexible and it will be more costly, but no matter which one you choose, both services will be scalable without too much effort on your side.

Cloud-based storage and processing

Run your app backend solution and store your data in the cloud, for example at:

- Amazon (Amazon Web Services and Amazon Storage Service, S3 for example)
- Google (App Engine, Cloud Storage, Cloud Datastore, and Cloud SQL)
- Azure (Virtual server, databases, storage, and content delivery)
- Heroku

Most of these solutions offer at least these components:

- Virtual servers
- Databases
- Storage of media (images and video)
- Content delivery (video)

Things that will have an influence on what service to use are pricing, specific needs, database support, database type (NoSQL versus SQL), and the programming language that is most convenient for you or your team. Also, the ease of use and the pricing for push notification services are important to evaluate. The programming languages that you can use vary from cloud solution to cloud solution. Google App Engine is a better choice for Java developers, and .NET believers better deploy their solution in the Azure Cloud.

Most cloud solutions offer multiple programming environments. If you want to do Java on Heroku, or Node.js on AWS or Azure, then you can do so. All solutions support Java, PHP, Python, and Ruby programming languages. Azure and Amazon both support .NET but Azure will probably be the preferred choice here. Go is supported by all of them, except Amazon:

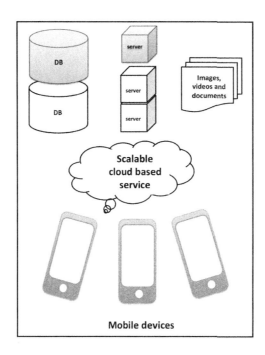

If you prefer to go for a ready-made backend solution, such as Firebase and Parse server, please check out `Chapter 8`, *Cloud Solutions for App Experiments*. An MBaaS is convenient and to a particular extent just as scalable, but convenience comes with a price. You start with a freemium plan, but when you need to scale up to a premium plan, it is often more expensive than developing your own cloud solution. Another pitfall can be that it could lead to a vendor lock-in more than would be the case otherwise. However, if you need an extra database or an extra server for storage or to process data, it is easy to scale things up, but the same applies to IaaS.

Seen from a client perspective

Let's look at an example. From the perspective of a client (here, an Android app) the architectural picture could look as shown in the following figure. From some endpoint, the API is being consumed. This will result in receiving data that will be handled by the Retrofit client (HTTP client for Android) in this example. It consumes data in the **JavaScript Object Notation (JSON)** format and eventually changes this data into objects using a JSON converter, such as Gson library, a library capable of doing object mapping on JSON data. Often an SDK is available from the party offering the service, which will make it faster and easier to consume data from the endpoint or to send data to it. The Parser Server SDKs, for example, will take care of object mapping and data synchronization from and to the Parse server. As you can see here, it does not really matter to your Android or iOS app what the structure of the backend will look like and where it is hosted. For the client side, all that matters is the interface, which, in this example, is a REST API delivering JSON data on request:

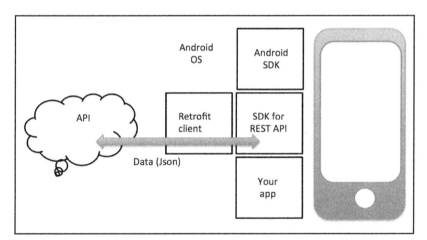

Things are not always as ideal as in this preceding image. If you are developing an app that is getting its data from an endpoint that originally was intended to use with a website or another non-mobile solution, you might need to create a middleware solution first. Mobile scalability also means that you need to deal with low bandwidth circumstances. It is important to limit the amount of data in a single transaction as much as possible. Anything that is not instantly needed to be displayed in your app should not be in there. Your app should download thumbnails instead of downloading images or videos; it should have a paging mechanism (**Load More** options) and the data should be optimized for use on a device that may have a low bandwidth connection.

The following picture nicely demonstrates the difference between a non-optimized and an optimized situation for mobile usage:

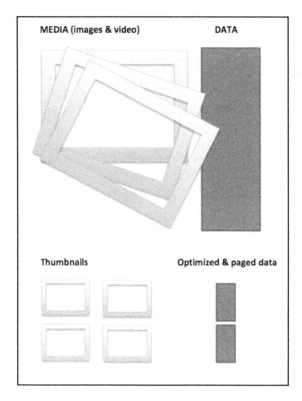

Instead of loading the whole dataset in JSON with large and descriptive names, you should load the smallest amount of data possible and persist it on the device for caching purposes. Even with low-bandwidth conditions, and even if you do not have an internet connection, your app will remain responsive and usable. For further optimization, your app should retrieve thumbnails first. It makes no sense to download hi-res images if your user only sees a small picture of it. Also, your (middleware) solution should allow your app to retrieve the app in chunks. Have a look at the Facebook app for example. It only loads a part of the stream, and when you scroll down (some apps have a **Load More** button for this at the bottom of the list), it loads another section of the data. If you are building things from scratch and you go for a mobile-first strategy, then this paging mechanism is something you need right away. If the current API is intended for non-mobile use, you should consider creating a middleware solution first to optimize the data stream.

A well scalable app comes with an improved user experience and better reliability, and will be easier to leverage particular events. Think of holidays or particular happenings that, depending on the type of app, could all heavily influence the amount of traffic involved with your app. A scalable app backend should be easy to scale up, allowing you to deliver what is needed during peak hours/day. It should also allow you to scale down at other moments to avoid wasting resources when they are not utilized.

You should know when you need to scale up or to scale down

If you are using analytics the right way, you will know when to up or to downscale your solution. Seasonality and also the nature of your app can help to make some forecasts here. At what time of the day or during what specific events will your app be used the most, or when will your users be using the app less? For example, if your app is an alarm clock, people will use it less during the holiday season. Also, if your app is related to the Olympic Games you can expect a peak usage during that event. During holidays, people often spend more money in the App Store, resulting in additional downloads and app usage. Finally, campaigns, certainly when you are offering your app at a lower price, will have a heavy impact on your app's usage rates. Other events are much harder to predict. What if your app gets featured and grows 150% a day? You better be prepared for it.

The number of users says something about the number of simultaneous users. That last number is what is really important for scaling your app backend. You can have ten million users that are using your app regularly or you can have ten million users that are using your app every day. One is quite different from the other. Metrics can tell you something about the average time spent in the app in a particular time frame. If you have an international app, it is important to segment this by time zone. Your users may use your app all day long but (maybe) not while they are sleeping.

Anyhow, it is important to realize that it is okay if your app does not scale yet or if it only supports a small number of (concurrent) users as long as it can be scaled up relatively easily. Do not scale because your app needs to be scalable. You need to be prepared to do the right things when necessary, but also do not put too much effort in it. Perfectionism has killed many great projects. Do not let that happen to you.

A real horror story about an app backend that did not scale

Low bandwidth can create a poor user experience even with caching and keeping data consumption to a minimum, but some things are outside your control. On the other hand, a totally overloaded backend is something that you have control over to a certain level. Your users judge the total app experience. This is why the whole architecture matters.

Here is an example to illustrate this point. A while ago, I was working on an Android SecondScreen app for a well-known international TV show. A **Non Disclosure Agreement (NDA)** prevents me to tell you which one, but it does not really matter to the story. Anyhow, the show was broadcasted on television. The people watching the show at home were able to give their votes for the various candidates that appeared on the show. Due to this, it was easy to predict that there would be a lot of traffic at the time the show was broadcasted. So, when asking the third party that was developing the backend of the app about the scalability of their solution, they told me that they could guarantee that at least 100K users could use the use the app while watching the show. I was naïve not to ask them if they did some proper load testing at their end. I just assumed that they were a professional company. Unfortunately, they turned out to be not so professional.

When the show's new season started and people began to use the app for the first time, something went horribly wrong during the first broadcast. The first 30 minutes went fine and about 40K users were using the app actively by voting. Then, the app stopped working in most cases and it became very hard to vote. The reason for this was that the backend could not handle the large traffic load. Although it was not the frontend (the app) to blame instead of the backend, from the user's perspective it was the app that sucked. The poor performance generated a lot of negative reviews. Even though the next broadcast went well, it was hard to recover from the bad reviews. The damage was done.

Captain hindsight to the rescue!

Here is the retrospective on this issue. If we had a proper load test that proved what was promised, then the situation perhaps could have been avoided. Also, if we would have been able to upscale quickly, we could have avoided a lot of trouble.

Predicting the future is pretty hard unless you have a crystal ball that actually works. As far as I know, there are none. So instead, always make sure that you can respond quickly to new situations.

You need to be prepared for situations that you can, more or less, foresee. Go figure it out for yourself and do some heavy load tests. Break things before your users do it for you. If you notice any trouble, then you need to find the bottlenecks and see what the best fixes are for them.

To scale up or to refactor? That is the question

Just realize that upscaling is not always the correct answer. If your architecture is bad you can add another database or another server, but that would just be a short-term patch and you would be wasting hardware resources (and money). If a better architecture without upscaling results in a better performance, then that is what you should preferably do. In addition, you still need to make sure that you can scale up quickly.

It is a common practice to keep the app as thin as possible (although there are some exceptions). Let your servers do all the heavy work instead of a small device that otherwise could lead to battery drain and heavy CPU usage. From this perspective, scalability often applies to the backend alone.

As your app user base grows from 10 users to a population of 100, to 10K, 100K, or 1 million, scalability becomes more and more important. The best practices here are as follows:

- Keep the app as thin as possible
- Keep it simple and do not scale yet, but make it scalable
- Use cloud storage and deployment
- Consider building the interface (API) first
- It is important to obtain great insights through analytics
- Follow the market, plan your campaigns carefully
- Keep data traffic as low as possible and don't transfer data that will not be utilized
- Use autoscale options where possible

Things that influence the scalability of your solutions involve the following:

- Database
- Storage
- Average size of traffic
- Regions of your server and where (most of) your users reside
- The choice between using an MBaaS, hosting your solution yourself, and cloud-based solutions such as App Engine, Azure, or Amazon

Auto-scaling

If you choose to use Azure as a backend for your mobile app, you can use Azure's mobile services. It offers most infrastructure for you, including processing, storage, and scaling options. You can pick a pricing tier, such as free, one of the basic, or one of the premium plans. An example from the Microsoft document that shows how scaling works in Azure is provided in the following picture. The picture is taken from the classic environment and it looks a bit different in the 'new' portal; however, the way it is presented here is clearer:

Most Azure services, including the previously mentioned one, come with autoscaling. The solution will automatically scale up or down depending on traffic or by following schedules. Think, for example, of a day and night schedule, a weekend versus weekdays schedule, or a schedule for a specific period when you are running a campaign. It depends on how your app is used as to what will work best for you. If you have no clue, you can learn what the best approach will be by keeping an eye on statistics.

On Amazon, you have more or less the same options for autoscaling and AWS Mobile Services can help you to build apps faster. It comes with support for push notifications, user analytics, data storage, and synchronization options. It can automatically increase the number of instances during peak hours (or days) and decrease them when less capacity is needed, thus saving you money by reducing costs:

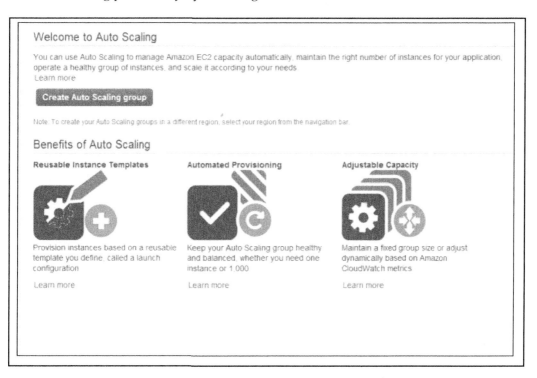

Amazon Cloud Watch enables auto-scaling, which is a monitoring service for AWS Cloud resources and applications. You can read more about it at
https://aws.amazon.com/autoscaling/.

There are some very good books available on the topic that provide you with more in-depth knowledge of any of the IaaS here. I suggest that you check them out later. In this chapter, we just had a look at what your options are and how it affects your strategy.

Another interesting read is:
`http://highscalability.com/blog/2016/1/11/a-beginners-guide-to-scaling-to-11-million-users-on-amazons.html`.

Scaling an MBaaS, such as Firebase, basically comes down to picking another price plan. Unlike Azure, Amazon, and App Engine, it does not come with autoscale options and in general, it is less suitable to support a very large number of users. This, however, should not prevent you from using Firebase, for example, as it is a great solution to get started and more importantly, it allows you to validate quickly. Additionally, if you want to migrate from MBaaS to IaaS later, you can use the time that you have saved earlier.

Summary

In this chapter, you have learned about a scaling strategy for your app and how this strategy applies in particular to your app backend. A good architecture and the ability to scale, not the scale itself, are key elements here.

By definition, storing data and processing services in the cloud is often very scalable but, depending on what you choose, could also be very costly. If you want to use data from an API that originally was not intended to be consumed on a mobile device, you might need to create a middleware solution first. This way you can ensure that your app works well even with low-bandwidth conditions. Minimizing the amount of data and paging it can help improve your app's performance.

Cloud services offer convenience but at a price. This should not be an issue as soon as your app becomes profitable. There are many ways for monetization and we are going to look at that in the next chapter. Do you need to create a premium app or will in-app purchases lead to more revenue? Let's find out!

17
Monetization and Pricing Strategy

In this chapter, we will look at how we can make revenue from our app. It is obviously one of the most important parts of the business model canvas, and also the most exciting one. It is not easy to get money for a mobile app. People are often less willing to spend money on a mobile device and apps, though games can be an exception to this tendency. Fortunately, there are plenty of other possibilities to build a profitable app business, and we will see what approaches there are to accomplish this.

We will look at multiple ways of monetizing your app. Also, we will examine what a smart pricing strategy will be if you want to sell your app, or if you want to sell a product within your app (also known as in-app purchases).

Summarized, in this chapter, we will cover the following topics:

- Looking at what monetization strategies you could apply to your app
- Learning about pricing strategy
- Finding out how to apply a pricing strategy to your listing in the App Store or Play Store
- Looking at how in-app purchases will be implemented

Monetization strategies

There are some strategies that you can use to make money. You can sell your app, display advertisements, use in-app subscriptions, or sell user data to third parties. They all can be a bit tricky to accomplish, but making revenue is always a challenge, and you will need to figure out what works best for your app. Do not be (too) greedy. People are used to a world in which everything seems to be free. In particular, if you plan to sell user data, you need to have a good plan.

Some strategies for app monetization are as follows:

- Sell your app in the App Store or Play Store
- Provide a light and free version of your app and sell your premium app
- Show advertisements in your app
- Provide an in-app purchase product to remove ads
- Build a free app and provide premium features on the web
- Sell a product or service in the real world
- Monetize your (user) data
- Use your app to create value by promoting one of your other products or services

Selling or upselling your app

Sell your app in the App Store or Play Store. This is the most obvious way of monetizating your app. This works well only if people are very much aware of your app's existence and great reputation, or if the provided added value of your app is very clear. In the early days of the App Store, this problem was solved by publishing two apps: a light, free version and a chargeable premium version. Today, it has become more common to apply the *freemium model* by using in-app purchases (Apple's term). Google uses the term "In-app Billing" for Android devices. The idea is the same, though. Users download the app for free, but they need to pay to unlock specific premium content or functionality. Because of their addictive nature, this model works very well for games, although it can be applied to more serious apps as well. It is a great way to both promote your app and to upsell premium features.

Once users are hooked onto your app and decide they want to continue to use the app, they can make a purchase to benefit from its premium features. You have to keep in mind that only a small number of your users will be converted into paying customers. On an average, the conversion from a freemium to a premium user is 1% to 5% at the most. This should not be a problem. The expenses for some apps are often near zero (games), but it matters for apps with a backend that needs to be hosted, and for apps that require storage of large files (videos). Think, for example, of a social app where every user can upload or stream a video.

In general, the cost for cloud storage is not expensive at all, but a lot of users will obviously require a lot of storage space. In short, if 1% to 5% of your users can cover the expense made for 100% of your (premium and freemium) users, you are safe:

Selling a product or service in the real world

Selling your app in a store is convenient, as the whole payment process will be handled for you by Apple or Google. However, it is a pretty expensive process. They will charge you 30% for it. So, if you sell your app for a dollar, you will get 70 cents, right? It is actually even worse. Depending on the country, the **value added tax** (**VAT**) and income tax will make your actual revenue even less. So, at a 21% rate for VAT and 30% for income tax, it will look more like this:

Product price	$	1,00
VAT 21%	$	-0,21
		0,79
Store fee 30%	$	-0,24
Net revenue		0,55

Unless you move to a city such as Dubai, for example, paying taxes is not something that can be completely avoided, but what you can do is avoid the 30% store fee. That (probably) will only work if you are not selling anything digital (content, features, game levels, or inventory). You need to sell a physical product or a service in real life.

For example, think of a parking app. The app takes away the hassle of getting a parking ticket and coming back before the time expires, and so on. In exchange for this service, you will pay an additional fee (25 euro cents here in the Netherlands; Parkmobile app, 2016) each time you park using the app. All payments are arranged by credit card, and Apple or Google have nothing to do with it.

Offering your app for free and selling your service

If you consider your app to be only one of the many channels that your service is utilizing, then it would be a good idea to offer your app for free and charge for your service; for example, on your website. This will have two benefits. Firstly, it will influence the user's price perception in a positive way (as he or she will spend money on a website instead of on the app). Secondly, you do not need to pay 30% to Apple or Google. This, of course, means you need to handle the payment yourself, or find a **payment service provider** (**PSP**) to do this for you. However, it certainly will increase your revenue, which is, of course, a good thing.

If your app is an app that is using a backend and is suitable for use with SaaS, such as CMS, you can offer the premium features of your app on the website (larger screen, more bandwidth). Let them use your app for free, but charge for access to the website:

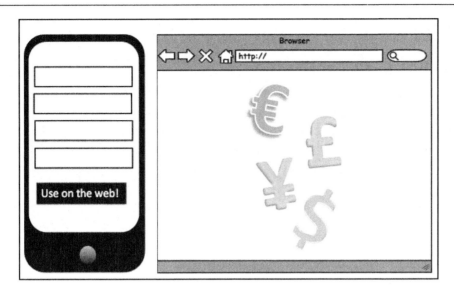

Advertisements

Displaying advertisements is the most well-known way of app monetization. Advertisements are annoying to users, but they are necessary to get revenue when your app is free. Making money from in-app advertisements only makes sense if your user base is large enough. The story goes that it was Flappy Bird's only way to create revenue, and apparently that went very well. The developer made 50K a day from it. It is a business model that is often combined with in-app purchases. Users can remove the advertisement by paying a small fee. This can be a one-time fee, or a subscription for a month or year.

Ok, so you want to add some advertisements to your app. For both iOS and Android, you can choose from a number of mobile advertising networks, each offering an SDK for the platform you are using. The network will serve the advertisements. All you need to do is to add the SDK and a few lines of code.

A network may offer multiple advertisement formats and campaign types. The most common ones are listed here:

Mobile ad formats:

- **Banner** (appears at the bottom or top of the screen)
- **Interstitial** (full screen)
- **Native** (integrates smoothly with the content of your app)

Campaign types:

- **Cost per action/acquisition (CPA)**: The advertiser pays for a particular action (contact, sign-up, submit)
- **Cost per click (CPC)**: The advertiser pays for each click on an advertisement
- **Cost per impression (CPI)**: The advertiser pays for each impression
- **Cost per mille (CPM)**: The advertiser pays for each 1000 (estimated) impressions:

Some popular mobile ad networks are as follows:

- AdMob (acquired by Google)
- Inmobi
- TapJoy
- Flurry
- Kiip
- MoPub
- RevPub
- Smaato

And there are many others! Be careful when and how you display advertisements in your app. Interstitials (using native Facebook ads, for example), covering almost the whole screen, are the most annoying ones to the user. For your user, the best way to display advertisements will be via banners shown at the bottom of the screen. However, that is not necessarily the best spot for you. Maybe the conversion for full-screen advertisements will be much better. It depends on the nature of your app, and it also could vary from Android to iOS. Perhaps, you can run a split test to find out what works best for your situation.

If you want to provide an option to remove the advertisements, you should consider putting a button with a clear call to action near the advertisement. What about a **Remove ads** button just above your bottom ad banner? That way, you create an income through advertisements and an income from people willing to get rid of them by paying, let's say, $0.99:

Monetizing your data

If you have a large number of users, you can think of a way to sell data to third parties as a way of making money from your app. You have to be careful with this strategy, as your users are probably not going to like this option. Always make sure that the data that you are selling is anonymous, and again try not be too greedy. Don't sell user data to send your users spam messages later.

If you have a large user base where each user has a rich profile, then you can create segments from those profiles. In Chapter 11, *Onboarding and Registration*, we have reviewed the process of continuous onboarding. Building a large user base combined with rich user profiles increases the value of your company and your app, even if you are not selling data to third parties immediately; it gives you the option to sell it later. The more you know about your users, the more valuable they will be. For example, you can create a dataset of middle-aged housewives who frequently travel on particular days within a certain area, or you can create a dataset of young people who love to listen to metal music. All segmentations you can think of can be of interest, as long as they result in a dataset that is large enough.

If you are going for a buyout strategy, a large number of users might be more important than the app's profitability. Also, if your app helps to promote or to sell another product or service, digitally or physically, it is providing value. The revenue will come from selling a product and service. Your app, again, will be just a channel that is supporting your sales strategy.

Pricing strategy

Let's assume that you want to sell your app, or that you want to add in-app purchases. What will your strategy look like? When are you going to charge money? Right from the start, enabling the user to download the app in the first place? Or will you offer a trial period, allowing the user to evaluate your app first? Or will it be an app with premium features that can be unlocked with an in-app purchase? The answers to these questions will depend on the nature of your app, the region of your users, and the nature of the device operating system.

Price perception

Price perception is an important element here. Everybody knows about the psychological effect of the 99 cents approach. We know that $0.99 is just one cent away from $1.00. Still, it looks cheaper. Apps and games also apply some interesting tricks based on the pricing psychology. One of them is the effect of price points; given three products, including a cheap product offering minimal value and a ridiculously high-priced product makes the product in the middle look like the best deal, even when its price is higher than the amount the user originally intended to spend. We will see a sample of this later.

For games, interesting items to sell are additional lives, coins, or levels. The following is an example of the products available for the 8-ball pool game app, taking the price points theory to the maximum and do you want a stack, pile, wallet, stash, heap, or a vault of coins:

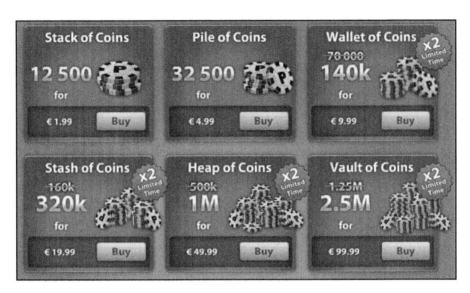

For games selling coins, this strategy works pretty well. At the start of the game, when the player is still discovering things and not addicted to it yet (Remember Candy Crush?), there are plenty of coins or credits to spend. Often, the player can unlock/gain new credits in the game; but often, the bottom of the virtual treasury is seen too early. If that is the case then, for the impatient players, there are virtual coins to the rescue. Typically, only 1% to 3% of the players will actually make a purchase. That is still enough to make a game very profitable.

For apps that are not games, it is more important to think about which features should be premium versus freemium. You need to determine what features, in the perception of your user, provide additional value. If it is anything other than removing ads, then which premium features should your app offer, and which features still need to be available for free? You can run some experiments to find the answer to this question: What are your users willing to pay for as premium features?

Although not specific for mobile apps, there is an interesting e-book to read about pricing, titled *Don't Just Roll the Dice*. To understand product pricing, this book helps you to understand some (but not too much) economics. You can find an example and the free PDF download available at `download.red-gate.com/ebooks/DJRTD_eBook.pdf`. Alternatively, you can do a search for it on Google.

You can also look at this SlideShare:

`http://www.slideshare.net/omohout/lean-pricing-startups`

Android or iOS first?

As a start-up company, you need to decide on which platform you are going to develop first. If it is important to reach an audience as large as possible, then Android would probably be your first pick, unless you know that the percentage of iOS users amongst your targeted audience is higher. However, if monetization by selling your app or selling in-app products is the most important thing to you, then iOS probably would be a better first pick. The reason for this is that iOS users are more willing to spend money on apps than Android users. On the other hand, displaying advertisements seems to work better for the latter. The **click-through rates** (**CTR**) are, on average, better for the Android platform.

In-app purchase product types

For iOS, there are four types of in-app purchase products. The iOS in-app purchase product types are:

- Consumable
- Non-consumable
- Non-renewing subscription
- Auto-renewing subscription:

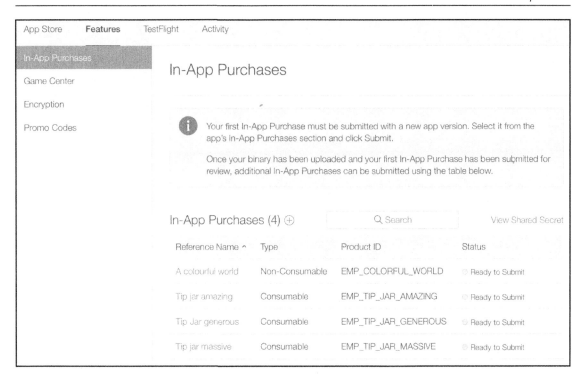

Consumable products are consumed in the process; for example, an extra life in a game. Non-consumable products can be bought once, and unlock features permanently. A subscription unlocks features or a functionality for a particular amount of time; for example, to access particular (premium) content. There are also two types of subscriptions available: a non-renewing subscription, and an auto-renewing subscription.

You can set up products of each type in iTunes Connect. For each product, you can choose a product ID, a reference name (for internal reference), a display name, a description name, and a price tier. You can also sell your app or products at certain price points. The first tier refers to a price of $0.99; for example, it looks like shown later. These are the products of the Empurror app, the sample that we are going to have a closer look at later on in this chapter.

For more information, see `https://developer.apple.com/in-app-purchase/`.

In-app billing

In-app billing products for Android can also be a consumable, non-consumable, or a subscription type. From a high-level perspective, there are no large differences.

You can implement In-app billing only in applications that you publish through Google Play. You can specify two product types for your In-app billing application: managed in-app products, and subscriptions. Google Play handles and tracks ownership for in-app products and subscriptions for your application on a per-user basis.

If you are using the In-app Billing API, you can also consume managed items within your application. You would typically implement consumption for items that can be purchased multiple times, such as in-game currency, fuel, or magic spells. Once purchased, a managed item cannot be purchased again until you consume the item.

A subscription is a product type offered in In-app Billing that lets you sell content, services, or features to users from inside your app, with recurring monthly or annual billing. You can sell subscriptions to almost any type of digital content, from any type of app or game.

To initiate a purchase, your application sends a billing request for a specific in-app product. Google Play then handles all of the checkout details for the transaction, including requesting and validating the form of payment and processing the financial transaction.

When the checkout process is complete, Google Play sends your application the purchase details, such as the order number, the order date and time, and the price paid. At no point does your application have to handle any financial transactions; that role belongs to Google Play.

For more information, see `https://developer.android.com/google/play/ billing/billing_overview.html`.

See how in-app purchases can be implemented

Since in-app purchases (iOS) often show higher conversions than those for in-app billing (Android), we will have a look at in-app purchases, in particular, using the case of the Empurror app.

The case of the Empurror

The Empurror is a little SpriteKit game for iOS that I have worked on previously. It is a very simple game about a cat (the Empurror) and many kittens, jumping off a roof. In this game, our hero (the player) needs to catch them all in order to succeed:

The game comes with three in-app purchases, all donations, not adding any special features to the game, other than a view of the Empurror saying thank you. Oh yeah, and you can rub his belly to make him purr.

Anyway, the in-app purchase view looks as follows. The game offers three products: a generous donation (cat food), a massive donation (a nice-looking fish), and an amazing donation (a huge turkey). We have added these three types of donations to do some experimenting on pricing.

The first focus is on the middle one, the massive donation. We tried to make it look like the best deal. Give that cat a fish if you like the game! The amazing donation just seems, well, a little bit too amazing and is obviously overpriced. Paying 99 cents only? Your name is not Scrooge, is it? Well then, go for the "Massive donation".

This is basically what we were trying to do here. Of course, this pricing strategy works best with real digital incentives, but you get the picture:

If we had developed an app that offered in-app purchases, then our products for removal could follow the same strategy: a fair deal in the middle, a minor one on the left, and an expensive one on the right, just to make the middle one look great:

- Remove ads for 1 week for $ 0.99
- Remove ads for 1 month for $ 1.99
- Remove ads for 1 year for $19.99

If you use the app for at least a year, the best savings will be the third one. However, when the options are presented as we have done it, most people will be encouraged to choose the middle option. This works for most apps, but there is no reason for not getting feedback on this strategy. Measure and figure out what product leads to the best conversion. There are analytical tools that will help you do this. See Chapter 13, *Play Store and App Store Hacks*, and Chapter 14, *A/B Testing Your App*, for more information.

Now, have a look at the code to see what needs to be done to implement this payment model. The following code is for iOS in Objective-C, but it is not hard to convert it to Swift (4) if you want to. Also, for Android, things work a little bit different, but the main idea remains the same for all cases.

You will define a number of products for your app at iTunes Connect (or Google Developer Console) that you need to download when the user navigates to your in-app purchase view. Notice the import of StoreKit and the SKProductsRequestDelegate here:

```
@interface PurchaseViewController : UIViewController
<SKProductsRequestDelegate, SKPaymentTransactionObserver>
...
#import "PurchaseViewController.h"
#import <StoreKit/StoreKit.h>
...

/*
 4 In-App Purchases
*/
#define kProductTipGenerous @"EMP_TIP_JAR_GENEROUS"
#define kProductTipMassive @"EMP_TIP_JAR_MASSIVE"
#define kProductTipAmazing @"EMP_TIP_JAR_AMAZING"
@implementation PurchaseViewController
...
```

When the view appears, we add an event to measure conversion (we use Flurry here), and load the products from the store, that is, if we are allowed to do so:

```
@synthesize scene;

- (void)viewDidLoad {
    [super viewDidLoad];
    [Flurry logEvent:analyticsPurchaseViewShown];
...
    [self loadProductsFromStore];
}

-(void)loadProductsFromStore{
    if([SKPaymentQueue canMakePayments]){
        NSLog(@"User can make payments");
SKProductsRequest *productsRequest = [[SKProductsRequest alloc]
initWithProductIdentifiers:[NSSet setWithObjects:
kProductColorfulWorld,
        kProductTipGenerous,
        kProductTipMassive,
        ProductTipAmazing, nil]];
        productsRequest.delegate = self;
```

```
                [productsRequest start];
        }
        else {
            NSLog( @"User cannot make payments,
                    perhaps due to parental controls");
        }
    }
```

Once we have received a response, we can show them to the user, or, as is the case here, enable the corresponding buttons allowing the user to make a purchase. For each product, a product identifier, a name, and a price will be returned:

```
- (void)productsRequest:(SKProductsRequest *)request
didReceiveResponse:(SKProductsResponse *)response{
    if (self.view == nil){
        return;
    }
    SKProduct *validProduct = nil;
    int count = (int)[response.products count];
    products = response.products;
    if(count > 0){
        validProduct = [response.products objectAtIndex:0];
        NSLog(@"Products Available!");
        ...
        for (SKProduct* product in products){
            [self enableProductPurchaseOption:product];
        }
    }
    else if(!validProduct){
        NSLog(@"No products available");
    }
}

-(void)enableProductPurchaseOption:(SKProduct*)product{
 if ([product.productIdentifier
      isEqualToString:kProductTipGenerous]){
        [nameGenerous setEnabled:YES];
        [priceGenerous setEnabled:YES];
        [nameGenerous setTitle: @"Generous donation"
      forState:UIControlStateNormal];
        [priceGenerous setTitle: product.price.stringValue
forState:(UIControlStateNormal)];
        }
 ...
if ([product.productIdentifier isEqualToString:kProductTipAmazing]){
        [nameAmazing setEnabled:YES];
        [priceAmazing setEnabled:YES];
        [nameAmazing setTitle: @"Amazing donation"
```

```
        forState:UIControlStateNormal];
    [priceAmazing setTitle: product.price.stringValue
        forState: (UIControlStateNormal)];
  }
}
```

If the user clicks on an any of the buttons (massive donation!), the purchase transaction will be started. There are a couple of transaction states for which a callback will be generated.

If the payment succeeded (SKPaymentTransactionStatePurchased), we need to let the app know to act upon it by calling the EnablePurchaseProduct method. If the payment failed (SKPaymentTransactionStateFailed), or if another event occurred, we can act upon that as well if needed:

```
-(void)purchase:(SKProduct *)product{
    if (products==nil || products.count==0){
        return;
    }
    SKPayment *payment = [SKPayment paymentWithProduct:product];
    [[SKPaymentQueue defaultQueue] addTransactionObserver:self];
    [[SKPaymentQueue defaultQueue] addPayment:payment];
}

- (void)paymentQueue:(SKPaymentQueue *)queue updatedTransactions:(NSArray
*)transactions{
    for(SKPaymentTransaction *transaction in transactions){
        switch(transaction.transactionState){
            case SKPaymentTransactionStatePurchasing:
                NSLog(@"Transaction state -> Purchasing");
                //called when the user is in the process of
        purchasing.
                break;
            case SKPaymentTransactionStatePurchased:
                //this is called when the user has successfully
        purchased the package
                [self enablePurchaseProduct:
        transaction.payment.productIdentifier];
                [[SKPaymentQueue defaultQueue]
        finishTransaction:transaction];
                NSLog(@"Transaction state -> Purchased");
                break;
            case SKPaymentTransactionStateRestored:
                NSLog(@"Transaction state -> Restored");
                [self enablePurchaseProduct:
        transaction.payment.productIdentifier];
                [[SKPaymentQueue defaultQueue]
        finishTransaction:transaction];
```

```
                break;
            case SKPaymentTransactionStateFailed:
                if(transaction.error.code ==
        SKErrorPaymentCancelled){
                    NSLog(@"Transaction state -> Cancelled");
                }
                [[SKPaymentQueue defaultQueue]
        finishTransaction:transaction];
                break;
            default:
                break;
        }
    }
}
```

If a user has made a purchase previously that is non-consumable or otherwise still valid (think of a subscription), then a restore option needs to be made available. Think of a user who gets a new device, or who has reinstalled the app. According to Apple guidelines (Google has something similar), the app needs to be able to restore the previous purchase, and it will probably not accept your app if it does not have such an option.

The app calls the restore method (because the user clicks on a restore button, or something like that), which triggers the restoreCompletedTransactions method:

```
- (void)restore{
    [[SKPaymentQueue defaultQueue] restoreCompletedTransactions];
}
```

This is where the SKPaymentTransactionStateRestored state comes from. The app should act upon this just as is the case when a purchase succeeds. In addition to this, you can provide some extra feedback to the user about the fact that premium features, or other purchases, have been restored.

Finally, the transaction is finished and the paymentQueueRestoreCompletedTransactionsFinished method is triggered. This method is probably even more suitable to respond to a restored or a succeeded state:

```
- (void) paymentQueueRestoreCompletedTransactionsFinished: (SKPaymentQueue
*)queue
{
    NSLog(@"received restored transactions: %lu", (unsigned
    long)queue.transactions.count);

    for(SKPaymentTransaction *transaction in queue.transactions){
        if(transaction.transactionState ==
        SKPaymentTransactionStateRestored){
```

```
//called when the user successfully restores a purchase
NSLog(@"Transaction state -> Restored");
[self enablePurchaseProduct:
 transaction.payment.productIdentifier];
[[SKPaymentQueue defaultQueue]
 finishTransaction:transaction];
break;
        }
...
    }
}
```

Applying a pricing strategy to your store listing

Although in-app purchases on average have higher conversion rates, you can also charge for your app right away. If you sell your app in the App Store, then the most important question is what price tier to pick for it. You can try to figure out what is being charged for similar apps in the App Store. Check App Annie, for example, to see how other apps are doing. Use your browser to visit https://www.appannie.com/apps/ios/top to learn more. Charging for an app upfront works well only for those apps that a lot of people are aware of, when it has a good reputation, and when it is totally clear what the app is offering. Often, there are comparable apps offered for free by competitors, so the added value that your app offers must be obvious to the user.

If your app is related to a well-known brand, or when you are operating in a niche market, then charging before the user can download the app could work as well. Otherwise, you should seriously consider the freemium model and make money from in-app purchases instead.

Here is an example of the top paid iOS apps as shown at App Annie (US market, Q3, 2016). It is no surprise that there are a lot of Minecraft clone apps in the store. A million copies of Minecraft Pocket edition have been sold for almost $7 each!

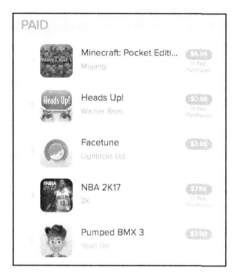

Of course, the best way to find the right price point for your app is to run some tests. Start with a high price for your app, and lower it later if needed:

If you want to test if a lower price point increases the number of purchases, and if you want to test at what price point the revenue from your app is optimal, you should consider offering a special discount for a limited period. If you have found that price point, you may apply it to your app permanently. The number of sales is not the most important factor here. Instead, find the price point that results in the largest revenue. For example, let's say that if you charge $3.99 for your app, you can sell 10 copies a month. If you lower the price by one dollar to $2.99, you can sell three times as much. What happens if you sell your app at the minimum price of $0.99? Wow, you sell 60 copies instead of 10:

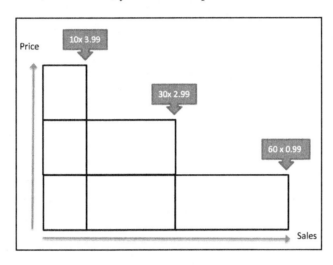

But when you do the math to find out what your revenue is, you will find that the price point of $2.99 is the one that you should pick:

10 x $3.99 = $39.90

30 x $2.99 = $87.70

60 x $0.99 = $59.40

Summary

In this chapter, we have seen multiple ways of monetizing your app. A large number of users is nice to have, but a large number of customers is more welcome. After all, you have a business to run, right?

We have seen the differences between selling your app and the freemium model, where you offer your app for free and where you make money from selling premium features. If you do this, your app will become more valuable to the user after a certain amount of time. Because of this, a small percentage of users will convert to paying customers. Your app probably will be more profitable with the in-app-purchases strategy.

We had a look at pricing strategies, and we saw a sample of how to implement in-app purchases in an iOS app. You need to test which strategy will work best for your app. You can run some A/B tests, and you will have to listen to the feedback you get from your users. You need to find out what the premium elements of your app are, according to your users. You can have a look at the reviews for your app and, if needed, reply to the comments they give.

When you have a look at the reviews in the App Store (or Play Store) then, in particular, the negative reviews are interesting. Do not be offended with what people write about your app. Apparently, they thought it was worthwhile to give you this feedback. If you respond, not just as a comment to their review, but also by releasing a new version that solves the issue that they are experiencing, you can turn an angry user into a happy one!

You will have to make the feedback loop smaller by releasing early and often. What you need is a Continuous Delivery strategy, and that is exactly what you will read about in the next chapter!

18
Continuous Deployment

In this chapter, we will see how we can organize a workflow in which we automate the process of testing and delivering your app. You can do this for both the ad hoc and the public releases of your app. To make the build-measure-feedback loop really work for you, you need to release early and often.

You can install Jenkins or TeamCity on a build server or another dedicated machine to make a new build of your app each time a new feature becomes available. Basically it comes down to that, but there are many interesting strategies to consider. For example, what is your branching strategy (Git workflow)? Do you want to run unit or UI-tests on the build server? How can you support variants (Android) or targets (iOS) for your app? Let's find out in this chapter.

We will have a look at various tools that can help us with the ad hoc distribution of the app. Some of them can also help you with the deployment of your app to the Play Store or to the App Store.

Specifically, in this chapter we will cover the following topics:

- Learning the benefits of an automated workflow
- Seeing what Continuous Integration, Continuous Delivery, and Continuous Deployment are about
- Figuring out how a good branching strategy can help you to get things done
- Learning about **TeamCity** and **Jenkins**
- Having a look at build variants or build targets to support different versions of an app

- Examining how **Gradle** can help us create different build flavors and types
- Seeing how we can distribute the app using **Fastlane**, **Fabric**, or **HockeyApp**

Continuous Deployment = Continuous Integration and Delivery

Why are Continuous Integration and Continuous Delivery important in the first place? There are number of answers to this question. One of them is that you need feedback as early as possible. Since you also want to ensure a certain quality level, there may be some friction here. Distributing and testing your app will take a large amount of time, however, you also need to release early and often.

A build server can help you to accomplish this goal, because a build server can, among other things, verify if your code compiles and if your tests still succeed. In addition, it can distribute the app to beta testers or to the App or Play Store. At a specific time, or each time a new feature has been implemented, the build server will be triggered to perform these and other tasks.

Having a smart-branch strategy is required if you want to set up a Continuous Deployment environment. It can also save you a lot of trouble. Here is an example of such an environment:

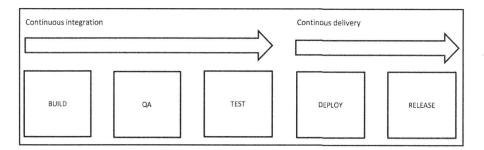

Continuous Integration

Typically, this event will be triggered when changes have been committed and pushed to a repository. The build server obtains the source from a specific repository and branch. It tries to build the code and it performs automated quality checks using **SonarQube**, for example, (QA).

SonarQube is a great tool to measure code quality. It is an automated solution so it cannot fully replace code reviews, however, it is capable of finding issues that may be or may not become an issue for the quality or performance of your app.

SonarQube will take care of:

- Architecture and design
- Coding rules
- Duplications
- Unit tests
- Code complexity
- Finding potential bugs

You can define custom rules or use the default ones that exist for more than 20 programming languages, including Java (soon Kotlin will be also be fully supported), that you are probably using for your Android app. It can also check Objective-C code and Swift. You can find SonarQube here: `http://www.sonarqube.org`. If the QA check succeeds, then the build server can also run the unit tests and even UI-tests.

You can configure the build server to make a daily build at a specific time or to start each time a new pull request is made. The best practice is to create a daily build from the development branch or each time you want to have an ad hoc release for your testers. For each new pull request, you can create a new build (with each new commit) for the specific feature branch. You will find more about branching strategies in the 'Repository and Git workflow' paragraph later.

The purpose of Continuous Integration is to review code and to test code as often as possible by running automated tests (unit and UI tests). The idea is that if anything during this flow fails, you will be notified as early as possible. This enables you to make changes before your app is distributed. The app is distributed only if all steps succeed. If the build breaks, members of your team (often developers) will be notified through email, Slack, or any other communication channel that you use.

Continuous Delivery

In this workflow, the built and tested code is made available as an ad hoc distribution to testers (or beta users). They can review the app and apply some manual tests to it. They can perform some functionality tests in particular, as a lot of tests, but not everything can be automated.

The build server can distribute an ad hoc version of your app by using Fabric, HockeyApp, The alpha/beta Play Store, or iTunes Beta (previously known as TestFlight). The deployment of your app needs to be as smooth as possible. A tool such as Fastlane can help you distribute an ad hoc version and can also you help you to publish your app in the Play Store or App Store.

Repository and Git workflow

The build server needs to retrieve the code from a repository. It is always a smart idea to use a repository, even when you work alone. Two well-known Git-based repositories are GitHub and Bitbucket (also known as Stash). Both come with a free and a paid plan. GitHub offers private repositories only in the paid plan (see `https://github.com`). A private repository is accessible for your team members only. A public repository is available to anyone. Bitbucket offers private repositories in the free plan, so let's create a Bitbucket account at `https://bitbucket.org`.

A common Git workflow is shown as follows. For the development of each new feature, a feature branch will be created. Once completed, and code reviewed via a pull request, the feature branch can be merged into the development branch.

Using a smart branching strategy, at least two important things can be accomplished:

- Only versions of the app that are fully tested and are accepted can be released
- Hotfixes can be applied quickly, without disturbing the continuous integration workflow

This makes sense even when you are the only developer:

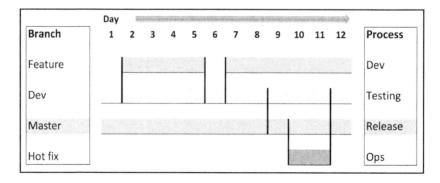

On the dev (or on the feature) branch, unit and UI tests can be run. If all tests are successful, the dev branch can be merged into the master branch and made ready for release. If, however, something seems to be broken while the app is live, you can use feature branching on the master branch to apply a hotfix, without disturbing the development of new features.

This, of course, is just a simplified example, and you may want to do things differently depending on your needs. To learn more about the Git workflow, check the website at `https://www.atlassian.com/git/tutorials/comparing-workflows` or `https://git-scm.com/book/en/v2/Git-Branching-Branching-Workflows`.

Automated tests

The build server can run the unit tests and even UI tests for your app. For UI tests, think of tools such as Espresso (Android) or Xcode UI testing (iOS). If you are looking for tools that support both platforms you can check out Appium, for example, (available for Android and iOS).

When it comes to testing, there are different approaches to consider. One of these approaches is **Test-driven Development** (**TDD**). If the functionality and all the requirements are known, we can define our tests before developing our app. Of course, all tests will fail initially, but that is actually a good thing because it will set an outline of what needs to be done and create focus to get things right. During the implementation of the features, your tests are going to succeed.

Espresso is suitable for writing concise and reliable Android UI tests. A test typically contains clicks, text input, and checks. To learn more about Espresso or Appium, see `https://google.github.io/android-testing-support-library/docs/espresso/` and `http://appium.io`.

Unit tests are often run for the feature branch, while integration and UI tests are often run for the development branch. After you pass all of your tests, your app can be deployed and released to an audience of beta or end users.

An example of a continuous workflow for an Android app

A picture of the ad hoc distribution of an Android app could look as follows. For Continuous Integration, in the picture shown next, TeamCity is used to retrieve the app source code from a repository, created at Bitbucket:

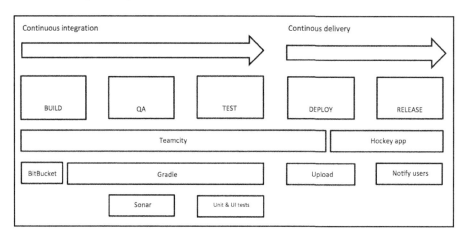

In the preceding diagram, we used **TeamCity** to instruct **Gradle** to build and sign the app and create a **Sonar** report to measure the quality of the code. Also, we ran unit tests and ran UI tests (using **Espresso**). Once configured, **TeamCity** will take care of all these steps. If they all succeed, then another step will upload the signed app (APK file) to **HockeyApp**, which, in turn, notifies users about a new version being available. If you prefer you can also use Jenkins as a build server, or use Fabric Beta instead of HockeyApp. We will discuss the highlights of CI/CD only. There are some interesting books available for both build servers. Have a look at `https://www.packtpub.com/` for more information.

Building variants

It is not unlikely that you will need to deliver more than one version of your app. In fact, it could be a smart thing to deliver your app under multiple names, each with a different look and feel. It is great for targeting more than one audience. Another example is that of delivering a light and paid (or free and pro) version of an app. Although a flavor often is used to customize the look and feel, there is no reason why you could not use it for enabling or disabling features.

In addition to a particular flavor, you might need to create build types with different configurations. Think of an app that is communicating against a backend. You probably want to test your app with a different endpoint than the one you use for your app in production. This allows you to safely test your app without the need to worry that it will mess up your production data:

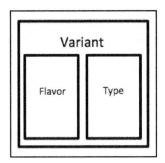

The **build flavor** term is reserved for customization, where the build type is for configuration purposes. The combination of a flavor and build type is called a **build variant**; well, at least it is like that for Android and Android Studio. If you have a light and full version of your app and you need to have at least one configuration to use as a test endpoint and one for production, then there will be four variants in total, for example like this:

Android Studio		
Variant	Flavor	Type
LightTest	Light	Test
LightProd	Light	Prod
FullTest	Full	Test
FullProd	Full	Prod

As we will see later, it is not difficult to accomplish this using Gradle. We can use multiple Gradle tasks to build each variant.

Can we do the same for our iOS app? Yes, we can, but in a slightly different way. Xcode allows you to define multiple schemes, define a build target, which you can compare with a build flavor for Android and a build configuration, which indeed, has the same purpose as the build variant:

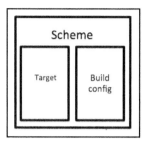

In Xcode, you will have four different schemes (two targets x two build configurations):

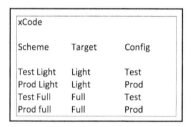

If we use a build server, we can use the Xcode command-line tools to determine which scheme we want to use for which build.

The Gradle way

For Android, we can use Gradle to:

- Determine which resources to use and for which build flavor
- Determine which configuration parameters to use for each build type
- Build the app for each variant
- Sign the app

Download or clone the sample project from
https://github.com/mikerworks/packt-lean-mobile-app-development.

Or, more specifically check out
`https://github.com/mikerworks/packt-lean-android-build-variants`.

When we look at the `build.gradle` file (inside the `app` folder) of the sample Android app, it has a couple of sections that define how to deal with different product flavors. Although it is sufficient to just define the flavors and keep the debug and release build types for your project, the sections in the example project might prove useful to examine.

The sample project has a blue and green version, with a test and a production endpoint. Each configuration has a different application ID and config fields.

productFlavors

In the `productFlavors` section, you can find the different flavors:

```
productFlavors {
    flavorBlueTest {
        applicationId = "com.coolapp.flavorblue.test"
        buildConfigField "String", "api_endpoint ",
"\"https://testapi.coolapp.com/\""
    }
    flavorBlueProd{
        applicationId = "com.coolapp.flavorblue"
        buildConfigField "String", " api_endpoint ",
"\"https:/api.coolapp.com /\""
    }
    flavorGreenTest{
        applicationId = "com.coolapp.flavorgreen.test"
        buildConfigField "String", " api_endpoint ",
"\"test.api.coolapp.com /\""
    }
    flavorGreenProd{
        applicationId = "com.coolapp.flavorgreen"
        buildConfigField "String", " api_endpoint ", "\"api.coolapp.com
/\""
    }
}
```

sourceSets

In the `productFlavors` section, you can see which sources and resources each flavor refers to:

```
sourceSets {
    flavorBlueTest {
        java.srcDirs = ['src/blue/java']
        res.srcDirs = ['src/blue /res']
    }
    flavorBlueProd{
        java.srcDirs = ['src/blue/java']
        res.srcDirs = ['src/blue/res']
    }
    flavorGreenTest{
        java.srcDirs = ['src/green/java']
        res.srcDirs = ['src/green/res']
    }
    flavorGreenProd {
        java.srcDirs = ['src/green/java']
        res.srcDirs = ['src/green/res']
    }
}
```

The `java.srcDirs` and `res.srcDirs` objects determine which folder is being referred to for a particular flavor (or flavors).

In this project, resources such as text (`values.xml`) and colors (`colors.xml`) are defined under the `/src/main/res` folder:

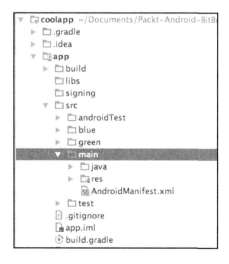

As you can see, there are, besides the main folder, two other folders: blue and green. Under the blue/res and green/res folders, you will find the files and values that override the default resources.

For example, the main folder has this content for the color.xml file:

```
<?xml version="1.0" encoding="utf-8"?>
 <resources>
     <color name="colorPrimary">#3F51B5</color>
     <color name="colorPrimaryDark">#303F9F</color>
     <color name="colorAccent">#FF4081</color>
     <color name="colorBackground">#888888</color>
 </resources>
```

For example, you can see that, for the green flavor, the same resource file exists but this time with a different value for colorBackground (a nice green one):

```
<?xml version="1.0" encoding="utf-8"?>
 <resources>
     <color name="colorPrimary">#3F51B5</color>
     <color name="colorPrimaryDark">#303F9F</color>
     <color name="colorAccent">#FF4081</color>
     <color name="colorBackground">#00dd22</color>
 </resources>
```

The same applies to the values.xml resource file, containing the texts for the app.

buildTypes

In the productFlavors section, you can see the mapping between the signing configuration for the release of a particular flavor and the entry in the signingConfigs section, which we examine after the buildTypes section:

```
buildTypes {

    release {
        productFlavors.flavorBlueTest.signingConfig
signingConfigs.flavorBlueTest
        productFlavors.flavorBlueProd.signingConfig
signingConfigs.flavorBlueProd

        productFlavors.flavorGreenTest.signingConfig
signingConfigs.flavorGreenTest
        productFlavors.flavorGreenProd.signingConfig
signingConfigs.flavorGreenProd
```

```
    }

    debug {
        testCoverageEnabled = true
    }
}
```

signingConfigs

In the `productFlavors` section, you see that we can use different signing using a different key store for each flavor:

```
signingConfigs {
    flavorBlueTest{
        storeFile file('../app/signing/coolapp_flavorBlue.jks')
        storePassword 'secretFlavorBlue'
        keyAlias 'secretFlavorBlue'
        keyPassword 'secretFlavorBlue'
    }
    flavorBlueProd {
        storeFile file('../app/signing/coolapp_flavorBlue.jks')
        storePassword 'secretFlavorBlue'
        keyAlias 'secretFlavorBlue'
        keyPassword 'secretFlavorBlue'
    }
    flavorGreenTest{
        storeFile file('../app/signing/coolapp_flavorGreen.jks')
        storePassword 'secretFlavorGreen'
        keyAlias 'secretFlavorGreen'
        keyPassword 'secretFlavorGreen'
    }
    flavorGreenProd {
        storeFile file('../app/signing/coolapp_flavorGreen.jks')
        storePassword 'secretFlavorGreen'
        keyAlias 'secretFlavorGreen'
        keyPassword 'secretFlavorGreen'
    }
}
```

For the sake of simplicity, you will see all properties, such as `storeFile`, `storePassword`, `keyAlias`, and `keyPassword` here, which all refer to the equally named properties of the key store. It is a good practice to put these values in a separate signing file.

In Android Studio, it will look like this if you open the **Build Variants** panel:

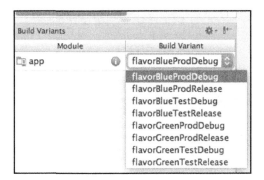

Now, all you need to do is tell Gradle to build a particular variant, like this:

```
./gradlew assemblectFlavorGreenTestRelease
./gradlew assemblectFlavorGreenProdRelease
./gradlew assemblectFlavorBlueTestRelease
./gradlew assemblectFlavorBlueProdRelease
```

Open a Terminal window to build each variant locally. Next, we will look at TeamCity and see how we can use it to build all variants automatically.

Using TeamCity as build agent

A build server, such as TeamCity or Jenkins, can be used to automate these processes. We will use TeamCity in our examples and you can download it for free at `https://www.jetbrains.com/teamcity/download/`. If you prefer Jenkins, you can get it at `https://jenkins.io`.

Download, install, and configure TeamCity on a server or, if just for testing purposes, on your development machine. After installing TeamCity, you can start the build server. On OS X, open a Terminal window, locate the `bin` folder of the `teamcity` folder (for example, `/Users/mike/Dev/teamcity/bin`), and type the following command:

```
m010:bin mike$ sh runall.sh start
```

Start a browser and point it to `http://localhost:8111`. Wait until the setup of TeamCity has completed and then create a new project, shown as follows:

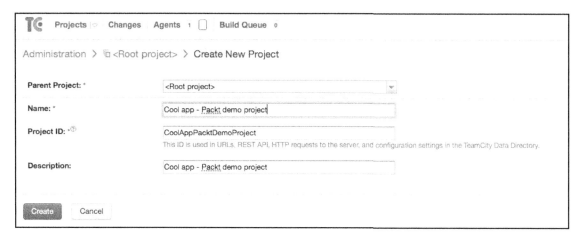

Now that we know how to use Gradle to build different variants, the picture shown next cannot be too challenging. We have a light and a full version. We want to have two built for each version: one that is consuming the data from the test endpoint and another one that is obtaining data from a production endpoint. This will result in four APK files in total:

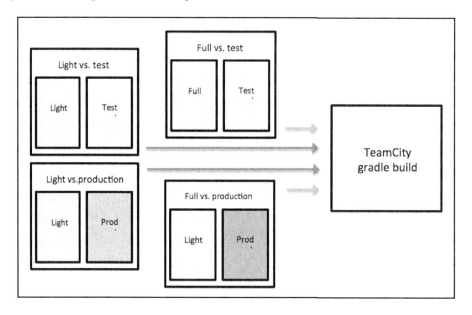

Now we will create some build steps to create four APK files using Gradle, just like we did locally. First, we need to tell where TeamCity should get the repository from for this particular project. For this project we will use the same repository and branch for all flavors, but for more complex projects this may be different for flavors and it should be different for build types. This is because it makes sense to run your ad hoc tests on a development branch and to run your final tests on a production branch.

Define **VCS Root** for your project and choose **Git** as the type of VCS. Give it a name and choose the following URL as **Fetch URL**:

`https://github.com/mikerworks/packt-lean-android-build-variants.git`.

> You do not need to enter credentials here (**Anonymous** for **Authentication method**) as this Bitbucket repository has public access.

Now you are ready to create your first build step. Choose **Command Line** for **Runner type**, so you can enter the same thing for the build script content as you did on your local machine:

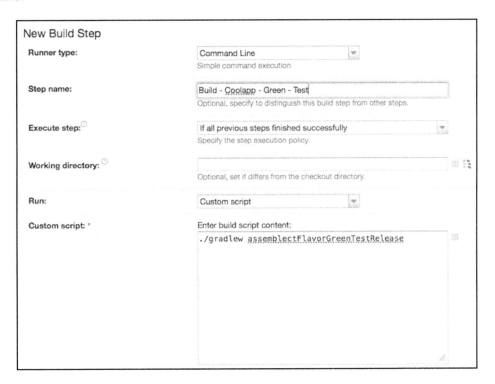

For the **Custom script** field, enter `./gradlew assembleFlavorGreenTestRelease`.

You can define additional build steps in TeamCity, for example, to run unit tests, UI tests, SonarCube QA check, and basically anything else that you can automate from a command line.

Automated deploy and delivery

Your app needs to be distributed once it is built, signed, and tested. There are multiple ways to do this:

- Self-hosted website
- HockeyApp or Fabric beta
- Play Store alpha/beta or iTunes beta/TestFlight

Self hosted

You can upload the signed APK and make it available on your own website. For Android, it will be sufficient just to host the APK (although you need to do some additional configuration for IIS). For iOS, you can distribute your IPA file using an **Over the Air (OTA)** manifest. If you choose this option, you still need to register UDIDs and create a corresponding ad hoc provision profile.

From a high-level perspective, this approach looks like this:

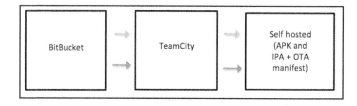

You also have to notify your users about a new version being available on your website.

HockeyApp or Fabric beta

There are many SaaS solutions available to distribute and to notify your users of new ad hoc releases. One of them is HockeyApp. You can use a (**cURL**) script to upload your signed APK or IPA file to HockeyApp. HockeyApp can also notify your users of the new build, and each version can contain release notes, for example, by adding a build step running this command:

```
curl -F "status=2" -F "notify=0" -F
"ipa=@//TeamCity/buildAgent/work/<work folder>/app/build/outputs/apk/app-
release.apk" -H "X-HockeyAppToken:<your hockey app token>"
https://rink.hockeyapp.net/api/2/apps/<app id>/app_versions/upload
```

Using HockeyApp, the landscape will look like this:

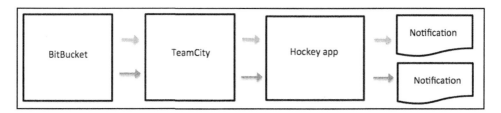

HockeyApp is a paid service, and it diminishes the provisioning profile hassle for the distribution of your iOS app. Fabric Beta is another service that you can use for ad hoc distributions. Fabric beta is a freemium service and it works pretty much in the same way.

Fastlane, alpha/beta Play Store, and iTunes beta

If you use fastlane in combination with beta Play Store or iTunes beta/Testflight distribution, then you probably can save yourself some time and headaches.

Fastlane is a tool for delivering your app to a test or production environment. Because it is using iTunes beta for ad hoc distribution of your iOS app, it no longer requires you to obtain the UDIDs of your test users up front. The downside of this approach is that initially, although it is an ad hoc beta distribution, your app needs to be (pre-)approved by Apple, thus taking a little bit more time, before a test version becomes available for your test users.

It changes the high-level picture to this one:

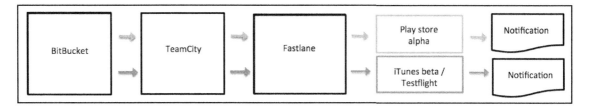

The roadmap for fastlane looks like this. It will take care of each part of your distribution flow. It was originally developed for iOS app distribution.

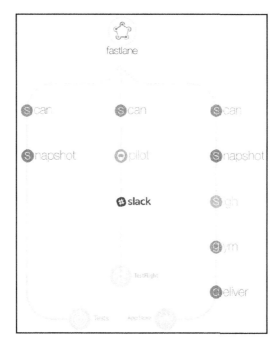

Fastlane comes with various other interesting features that will enlighten your build automation life, such as:

- Creating (localized) screenshots and uploading them
- Sending updated metadata to the App Store
- Generating and renewing push notification in profiles
- Running tests

Fastlane is also available for Android. It probably is the easiest way to automate building and releasing your apps. You can find fastlane at `https://fastlane.tools`.

It will take some time (and some pain) to correctly set up CI/CD but it is worth the investment!

DevOps

Often you are not just the developer, but also the operator. A **DevOps** culture probably is most commonly found at start-up companies; however, more and more established companies are adopting its philosophy. DevOps establishes a culture and environment where building, testing, and releasing your app will happen fast, often, and more reliably, which is exactly what we want. Basically, the idea is that the whole process will become the responsibility of the team, from development to operation (configuration, monitoring, and moderation). If something in production is broken, you create a hotfix, test it, and re-release it.

The Continuous Integration part of CI/CD is about the dev part (of DevOps) in particular. The delivery part is more about the Ops part. Together, these two cycles can correspond to the build-measure-feedback loop (from a higher perspective):

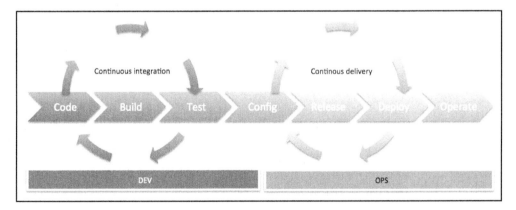

Continuous Delivery and DevOps are often used together. They have common goals, such as delivering small and quick changes with focused value to the end customer. Some of the differences between CD and DevOps are that the latter also focuses on the organization change to support great collaboration between the many functions involved. It requires good collaboration and communication skills from each of the team members. As your organization and your team(s) start to grow, this will become increasingly important.

CI/CD and DevOps make split testing and gathering feedback more easy to do. This approach will contribute significantly to the adoption of the lean start-up methodology (seen from a technical perspective). It will result in better quality, higher customer satisfaction, and more (and earlier!) releases.

Summary

We have seen what CI and CD are, along with their benefits for you. Public or ad hoc distribution can be initiated by the build server. You can use a build server, such as TeamCity or Jenkins to build and test your app.

Ad hoc releases can be distributed using HockeyApp, Fabric Beta, or the beta programs of the Play Store or App Store. Fastlane can help you with these and other tasks. By now, you probably have learned a lot already.

CI and CD are important if you want to improve and maintain the quality of your code and if you want to optimize your workflow. It allows you to gather feedback since you are able to release early and often. CI/CD and a DevOps culture can help you with the optimization of the build-measure-feedback loop.

In the next chapter we will learn why building an unfair advantage is important if you want to succeed and if you want to survive as a company.

19
Building an Unfair Advantage

It is not enough to just build a great app that your customers love. This is important, no doubt, but if you want to build a strategy that will succeed over time, you need to employ a range of tactics that will help you build and secure a market position and limit options for your competitors. In this chapter, we will look at the various techniques a savvy entrepreneur can use to build a moat around their business, thus minimizing the effects of an attack by a competitor.

In particular, we will look at the following topics:

- Intangible assets such as **intellectual property** (IP) laws and legal protections
- The benefits of the network effect and the platform effect
- Control over a vertical market or key relationships in a vertical market
- Switching costs and pricing strategies
- The benefits of good customer service and customer support
- The power of a well-developed brand name

Introduction - it's not just about your app

Will your company be profitable in ten years? An enduring competitive advantage can keep your company profitable against the inevitable onslaught of competitors, imitators, and spinoffs. Establishing such a competitive advantage, or a "moat" around your business, is vital to ensuring long-term profitability and stability.

Competitors can come from all directions, so in order to protect your business, your product, and your ideas, you will need to employ a variety of tactics to defend your fortress against would-be attackers.

Developing an idea, testing it with early adopters, and refining it are the first important steps toward enduring success. A customer-centric, innovative solution to a problem is the cornerstone to a successful business. However, after you have tested and proven your hypothesis, you need to grow that seed of an idea in the real-world marketplace, which can be brutally competitive.

Early on, after your MVP has proven real-world viability, you will need to expand and perform a "land grab" with customers that need your solution. The more your business grows, the more competitors take notice; after all, marketplace visibility helps your business expand but it is also a magnet for competition. Once your business has taken its marketplace position and marked off its territory, you need to begin defending this territory.

A competitive advantage is your best means for long-term defense. Next, we will look at the most effective strategies when it comes to building that competitive advantage, so you can keep all of the profits that you work so hard to create.

Digging your moat with intangible assets

Intangible assets typically refer to legal protections in the form of IP laws, patents, and trademarks. These are essential defense mechanisms for any product that has proven value in the marketplace. Good implementations will be stolen unless they are protected, so it is vital to look at your legal options as soon as possible.

Protecting your work with IP laws

Understanding how intellectual property laws work will help you to understand how best to protect your own work. A fringe benefit to understanding these laws is that you will also understand how to avoid stepping over an intellectual property line without knowing it:

Why you should care - Business-destroying patent trolls

A discussion about IP laws may seem far removed from the topic of lean development, especially for developers who are still in the early stages of MVP creation. However, the business world is brutal, especially when large sums of money are involved.

In the tech industry, patent demands and lawsuits are a commonplace, and it is no secret that they are frequently used as weapons against promising startups.

A 2013 paper by University of California Law Professor Robin Feldman presented data that proves why no startup should enter the marketplace without intellectual property armor. According to her survey of 200 venture capitalists:

- One out of three startups have received patent demands
- 70% of VC-backed startups have received patent demands
- 100% of venture capitalists said that "if a company had an existing patent demand against it, it could potentially be a major deterrent in deciding whether to invest"

Her survey also found that the majority of patent demands came not from product owners or creators, but from entities whose main function is the licensing or litigation of patents. This fact strongly suggests that patent litigation is being backed by competitive groups behind the scenes. Clearly, IP lawsuits and patent demands are a standard weapon in the world of business warfare.

To protect yourself against such attacks, it pays to plan ahead.

Patenting and trademarking both take research, time, and money. It is easy to make excuses and put these necessities to the side, but the longer you do, the greater the risks. Next, we will offer a brief overview of IP laws, so you can make space in your long-term business plan for legal strategizing.

How IP laws can protect your app and business

Intellectual property laws do not actually protect an idea, they only protect an implementation of that idea. Here are examples of how the major IP laws work:

- Patents protect novel, "non-obvious," unique processes. They only cover the implementation of a physical object or physical designs that emanate from that idea, not the idea itself. Software programs or specific implementations of a technology, such as a novel app feature, can be protected but the general concept cannot.
- Copyright laws protect against the expression of a creative idea, usually in a media form; Books, videos, music, and source code are examples of works that can be copyrighted. Copyrightable works are copyrighted as soon as they are created.
- Trademarks protect the representation of a good or service, such as a company name, an OS startup tone, or a logo.
- Trade secrets, such as source code or the formula for Coca-Cola, remain protected indefinitely. These secrets cannot be knowingly infringed upon, but they can be stolen.

Though these intellectual property laws are the most well-known and common defenses against infringement and theft, they are not the only ways to secure your position.

How to defend your intellectual property

The most essential step for protecting your app is the securing of patents. UI elements, unique and novel app features, and software programs themselves can all be patented. Trademarks can be used to protect specific design elements, the design layout as a whole, as well as the name and expression of your app and your company.

In the event of a patent demand, every company must decide for itself how to proceed. After all, every legal battle would come with its own risks, benefits, and drawbacks. The preceding study by Dr. Feldman found that for the majority of her survey's participants, patent demands cost over $50,000 to prepare and defend against. Every situation is unique, and each company should make its own decision in the event they are served a patent demand.

The flipside of not having a patent at all, of course, is that another company would be free to copy, steal, and patent your technology for themselves. The very first step, therefore, is to ensure that you are protecting your intellectual property every step of the way.

Next, we will examine another side of the legal arena: how to use the law as a weapon instead of a defense.

Going on the legal offensive

Though this may be an unpleasant discussion for some, it is important to reiterate that the business world is a different ballgame from app experimentation and development. Although a lean approach will help you develop relevant products that customers need and want, you must arm yourself for fierce competition as you make your way into the marketplace. Legal tactics, however, are one method to isolating, securing, and monopolizing certain sectors of your market.

Peter Thiel, billionaire founder of PayPal, argues that "*when you start a company you always want to aim for monopoly and you want to always avoid competition.*" The more money you waste engaging and out-competing your rivals, the less money you can spend on innovation and growth.

While we are not advocating stealing intellectual property, patent trolling, or bullying smaller companies out of existence, you can certainly develop legal mechanisms that bar competitors from your territory and free up company resources for other things.

Here are a few examples of how companies have used legal blockades to widen their economic moats:

- A mortgage broker training company, for whom I created software years ago, promoted state laws that required broker certification in each state, the very service his company offered. This was a smart strategy that yielded very positive results.
- As mentioned previously, in the "shark tank" world of business, it is technically legal to appropriate certain design elements or features that remain unprotected by patents or trademarks.

- Amazon, a monopoly that has decisively shaken up the retail industry in the United States and beyond, has a history of using legal offensive maneuvers. Like many tech companies, it has used patents to maintain its competitive advantage and it has used legal loopholes to avoid collecting sales taxes in many states (and thus increase its price advantage over other businesses).

On the legal front, every move you can make will help you keep your competitors away from your castle. The law is very effective for both offense and defense, but it is only one tool among many. Next, we will look at more user-focused business strategies that will further entrench your market position, stifle competition, and maximize control over your market.

The network effect and platforms

The network effect occurs when the value of a product or service increases as the number of users increase:

The first type of network effect occurs when the users themselves add value to the product or service. The user-generated content that powers Facebook, forums, and search engines, for instance, adds value to these services, effectively transforming users into assets.

The Platform Effect, which is considered by some to be another type of network effect, refers to the amplification of value that occurs when a company is able to offer a platform - an array of services - rather than just a single product. As more business partners add services to the platform, the value increases.

Both of these effects are eminently visible in today's technology industry.

The network effect

To illustrate the first type of network effect, we will look at the world's largest social app and the world's largest online retail company, Facebook and Amazon. Both starkly illustrate how users contribute to, and amplify, the value of a product or service.

Examine how the network effect plays out with both of these companies:

- The more people that use Facebook, for instance, the more momentum and value it accrues, since it can be used to connect with more and more people. A byproduct of this effect is that the value of competing social networks is diminished, making it more difficult to switch to a competitor. This effect, known as a switching cost, is examined in more detail further.
- In Amazon's case, the more sellers it acquires on its marketplace, the bigger its inventory, the more competitive its pricing, the more it becomes known as the go-to online retail store, and the more entrenched its market position becomes.
- For both companies, word-of-mouth marketing becomes more powerful as the network effect grows, consequently decreasing the cost of user acquisition.
- The more people that use either service, the more that either service's brand image and reputation is boosted.

These are only two businesses in a sea of companies that benefit from the Network Effect. Whether designing mobile apps or social networks, it pays to think about how you can turn your users into assets so that they can enhance the value of your end product.

The platform effect

As mentioned, the platform effect, another type of network effect, also occurs as more business partners augment the original service with their own complementary products or services. WordPress and Windows offer excellent examples of how you can leverage this effect to expand the moats around your app's castle.

Both of these companies, while offering very different core products, illustrate this effect into action:

- Windows, due to its decades-old market dominance, has nearly locked down its position as the de facto operating system for PCs. In doing so, it has aligned itself with an army of PC manufacturers, software developers, and associated industries that vastly enhance Windows' original services by supplying their own complementary products and services.

- WordPress, similarly, functions as a platform of its own. This open-source content management system, officially the world's most popular, has been built for expandability. It easily allows developers to create plugins, themes, and modifications. Due in part to this platform effect, WordPress functionality has grown by leaps and bounds, further amplifying its growth and making it nearly impossible for other content management systems to infringe upon their territory.

- In the automotive industry, where I work, software companies that provide a platform that seamlessly unifies a range of products put standalone startups in a tough position to succeed.

There are countless other examples of the platform effect in action. From operating systems, to web browsers, to financial software, the list of software that benefit from the platform effect goes on and on. Some products, such as Windows or Android, are primarily platform products. Others, such as WordPress or QuickBooks, offer a core service that is made much more robust by complementary products. If your product can benefit from a network of users, or if it can be leveraged as a platform, you should make that a core part of your product design and market development plan.

Making use of vertical markets

In business, a vertical market, or a "vertical", is a specialized niche market that serves a narrow industry or customer base. A software company that develops mobile point-of-sale software specifically for restaurants would be operating within a vertical market. An app that serves as a social network for amateur photographers in New York would be another example.

Horizontal markets, unlike vertical markets, are generalized markets that sell their products to a wide range of customers. Technically speaking, all businesses operate both horizontally and vertically, though to varying degrees. The chief advantage of a horizontal market is that it offers a much larger user base than a vertical market. On the other hand, horizontal marketplaces are much more competitive and are extraordinarily difficult to penetrate.

As we will see, making use of vertical markets can give you a major competitive edge, aid horizontal expansion, and provide you with a secure economic foothold.

Why target vertical markets?

Access to and control of a vertical can mean the difference between rapid growth and a snail's pace. Though verticals have their weaknesses, such as a limited customer base and financial conditions that fluctuate with the health of that particular industry, they offer significant advantages:

- Vertical markets give you a channel where you can sell your product and build relationships with customers in a focused way
- Though some vertical markets are saturated with competition, others are not, which will make it easier for you to take a dominant market position
- Controlling a vertical, in essence, allows you to create a monopoly within that market, which guarantees income, customers, and economic relationships
- Due to the specificity of the user base and the industry, many aspects of business become much easier and more cost-effective, from marketing to user testing to user acquisition

Though you should gain access to and control a vertical, this is not to say that you should operate exclusively within that vertical. As we saw in `Chapter 11`, *Onboarding and Registration*, monopolizing a narrow market is an ideal first step towards horizontal expansion.

How successful companies exploit vertical control

Although complete control over a vertical is no easy feat, the exclusion of competition from your territory allows you to, in some respects, dictate the terms for your marketplace. The following are examples of how companies have expanded and exploited via such vertical control:

- Apple's control of its value chain demonstrates a nearly complete example of vertical control, or vertical integration. It designs and develops its own desktop and mobile hardware, the operating system that runs on that hardware, as well as a wide range of apps and software products that operate within this environment.

- One Stanford study found that vertical integration in the healthcare field, in the form of contractual obligations between hospitals and physician practices, often resulted in higher healthcare costs and hospital spending - in other words, increased profits for healthcare professionals.
- In the automotive industry, suppliers that grew quickly usually did so through OEM relationships. OEM endorsements or promotions translated into rapid market growth and a more secure market position.
- My previous company grew rapidly when it secured a relationship with an ad group that gave it access to many auto dealers. The boost was immediate, resulting in a rapid surge in business.

The ultimate form of vertical control comes in the form of vertical integration, where a company is able to control its own supply chain. For the vast majority of companies this is impossible, but the more access you have to a vertical market, the easier it is to reap economic benefits.

Switching costs

Switching costs refer to the costs that arise for a customer when they switch to a competitor's product or service. Steep switching costs can prevent users from leaving. Depending on the situation, these costs can come in a variety of forms. Here are examples of the types of switching costs that would impact a company considering new enterprise-grade software packages:

- **Direct costs**: Costs associated with researching, evaluating, and negotiating the prices of these new software packages
- **Relationship costs**: Disruption or dissatisfaction among team members who are used to the old product
- **Product-related costs**: Purchase price and training costs, as well as financial costs associated with decoupling oneself from the original product

These are just a few examples of the costs associated with a B2B product switch, but they tend to be the most common that you find.

Maintaining high switching costs for acquired customers, and lowering inbound switching costs for new customers, is an integral part of any product strategy. Although switching costs can be so high that customers are effectively trapped onboard, we will see next how this strategy can backfire.

How to use switching costs to improve user retention

In order to raise switching costs for your own product, look at the preceding list. Consider the ways in which you can deliberately increase these costs for existing customers to deter abandonment, while lowering competitors' switching costs to incentivize adoption of your product. Here are real-world examples of switching costs that you can use to brainstorm ideas for your own product or service:

- Large-enterprise software packages, such as InfusionSoft, QuickBooks, or Salesforce, involve high switching costs across the board. They require significant research and evaluation; they have steep learning curves and training costs, and can cause significant disruption to employees who are used to doing things a different way.
- Cellular phone contracts are excellent examples of how companies decrease competitors' switching costs while increasing their own. Once locked into a contract, contract cancellation fees make it financially difficult for customers to leave. To incentivize signups, however, many contracts offer significantly discounted mobile phones to new customers.
- Social apps and most other modern apps have reduced the barrier to entry significantly - they are easy to use, free, and allow immediate social interaction. The network effect, however, makes relationship switching costs so high that it can be nearly impossible to make the change. The loss of connection with friends or family, for instance, makes it difficult for many users to leave Facebook.

These are just a few examples of how switching costs are used by large businesses to keep users on board. For more ideas, examine any successful technology company in your market or a similar market and think about ways that the company keeps switching costs high for its existing user base, and then apply that same thinking to how you position your product in the market.

As mentioned, decreasing the cost of customers from switching from a competitor is one way to lower the barrier to entry for your product or service. Next, we will look at how you can use this strategy to accelerate the growth of your user base and erode your competitors' territory.

How to decrease competitors' switching costs

To make it easier for people to defect from your competitors, find ways to neutralize or reduce competitors' switching costs. Building upon the previous examples, we will look at a few ways that the aforementioned companies reduce switching costs for competitors' customers:

- QuickBooks employs many standard techniques to make signups easier and cheaper. To ease the stress and perceived costs associated with using a new product, QuickBooks naturally offers a free trial. To reduce the learning curve, it offers user-friendly videos as well as in-app tutorials and guides. Also, it makes judicious use of the platform effect; the plethora of plugins and third-party integrations make it easier for users to get up and running with services that customers may already subscribe to.

- Though the previously mentioned cellular contract cancellation fees kept many customers from switching to other providers, the 2-year contracts, the early termination fees, and the up-front investments made customers feel trapped. Underdog carriers took advantage of this sentiment by removing onboarding and offboarding barriers alike; customers could use their own phones instead of purchasing new ones, they were not required to sign contracts, and they could leave whenever they liked.

- Most social apps decrease competitors' switching costs using many of the same tactics that you can employ in your own app via the Lean methodology. Namely, successful social apps are very relevant, usable, well-designed, and high-performing. All of these factors contribute to a successful first experience of an app, which, as many developers know, can mean the difference between a new user and an uninstall.

Switching costs, as well as any other business strategies covered in this section: should be built around a product that users need and want. If the business becomes imbalanced and pours its energy into the business battleground at the expense of the product and customer, then the product itself risks becoming weak thus losing market share. This brings us to another lean-oriented strategy that will help you stay focused on your customers as well as the business arena.

Good customer support

Good customer support is often forgotten by many new businesses. This is foolish, since when your customers believe that you care about their success, then they are less likely to leave you.

Successful companies have long believed that customer service and customer satisfaction have a direct impact on customer loyalty and profits. A number of statistics back up the idea that customer service is vital to every business, both large and small:

- News of bad customer service reaches twice as many people as news of good customer service
- It is at least six times more expensive to gain a new customer than to keep an existing one
- 70% of buying experiences are based on how the customer feels they are being treated
- Gallup found that customers care more about the quality and thoroughness of customer service than the speed of that service

Startups have a lot on their plates, so it is understandable that customer service would take a backseat to other issues. However, providing good customer service is not a cliché and should not become a hollow mantra. When you consider the direct impact that customer service has on your bottom line, it is worth considering ways that you can improve customer service from the very start.

The right perspective on customer service

It is widely acknowledged that customers' treatment affects their perception of a product, a company, and a brand, which impacts loyalty. This recognition has given rise to the idea of the "customer experience," which can be designed and improved upon. What makes a perfect customer experience, however, is up for some debate.

The shift in focus toward customer satisfaction, for many businesses, has resulted in efforts to treat customers like royalty or to delight them. This pandering approach is problematic for several reasons-it is based on the statistically-backed notion that customer satisfaction matters, but the solution, "delighting" customers, has no scientific grounding.

Instead of pandering to them, stick with the lean methodology and listen to them.

Customers, whether they are app users or retail shoppers, want their problem solved. According to research published in the Harvard Business Review, over-the-top "delightful" customer service "doesn't build loyalty," while "reducing their effort-the work they must do to get their problem solved-does." Act on this knowledge, they say, and you will improve customer service, cut customer service costs, and reduce customer attrition.

A recipe for great customer service

In the early stages of your company, you may not be rolling in funds. Fortunately, technology allows many young startups to achieve 80% of the results for only 20% of the effort. Here are a few ways that you can maximize your customer service efforts without wasting money:

- Demonstrate your availability and attentiveness by responding publicly on social media and on reviews. If one person makes a comment, rest assured that others feel the same way. After all, research has shown that for one person who speaks out, there are many more who stay silent.

- Create an online knowledge base so customers can find answers quickly and easily, without needing to contact you directly. This will save time for both you and your users.

- Solve problems before customers notice that anything is wrong. Understand analytics and listen to customers so that you can discover budding pain points, solve them, and fix them as needed.

- Stay customer-focused throughout the cycle. Rather than pandering, be attentive, solve problems, and listen to them throughout.

Always remember that app users are customers, not variables or children who should be "delighted." Good customer service will have a ripple effect on the rest of your business. Even though you may not be able to measure every aspect of that effect, it can mitigate negative experiences and significantly improve the overall user experience of your brand.

How successful companies use customer service to improve profits

Top-level customer service has helped many companies receive the benefits mentioned above, including increased customer loyalty, decreased attrition, and increased lifetime values. Here are a few examples of companies that have expanded their economic moats via the customer service route:

- Amazon's central principle is the customer experience, and it has built its entire business around listening to customers. According to founder and CEO Jeff Bezos, "If you make a customer unhappy in the physical world, they might tell six friends, but online, they can each tell 6,000." Every aspect of Amazon's business model, from their return policy to their customer support staff to their product recommendation engine, is geared towards one goal: making customers happy.

- Apple's customer service training manual, which was leaked in 2012, puts the customer experience first. Instead of a sales-first approach, the *Genius Training Student Workbook* is, according to Gizmodo, "an exhaustive manual for understanding customers and making them happy," because "a happy customer is a customer who will buy things." The thoroughness of this approach makes it clear that no aspect of the customer experience should be left to chance.
- My old company sold a CMS software solution to auto dealers that had a range of add-ons to improve dealer customer outreach, acquisition, and management. We had two goals:
    - Create easy to use affordable apps
    - Always seek to make the customers happy

The result of this was a company that grew well within its market (without extensive financing) and an extremely low attrition rate. We never waited for a customer to call; we always reached out offering ways that they could maximize the use of our products so that they could make more money. We weren't Apple or Amazon, but we practiced the same principles.

Customer satisfaction is an emotion, so it is more difficult to measure than harder metrics such as conversion rates. It is also more difficult to measure the business impact of the customer experience, customer loyalty, and other customer relationship metrics. However, based on available research, as well as the behavior and customer service track records of some of the world's most successful companies, it is clear that stellar customer service can help you stick out in the minds of your customers. The last strategy we will cover in this chapter, developing a strong brand, will help you stick out in the minds of your customers as well as in the marketplace as a whole. But first we will take a quick look at some tools that will help you with customer support.

A look at some great tools to help with customer support

There are dozens of customer service tools in the market at the time of this writing. Many of them include free trials and free features. Here are just a few:

- **Zendesk** (`https://zendesk.com`): This is a robust customer support platform that offers certain free features
- **Freshdesk** (`https://freshdesk.com`): This also offers a free version that may suffice for startups and small firms

- **Salesforce desk** (https://desk.com): This is a part of the Salesforce suite, making it a good choice for companies that use Salesforce
- **Zoho desk** (https://www.zoho.com/desk/): A member of the Zoho suite of products would be a good choice for businesses that use Zoho
- **Conversocial** (https://www.conversocial.com/): This focuses on social and mobile app support

A vast majority of these tools offer free trials and even free plans that naturally have limited functionality. Most of these tools integrate a knowledge base with ticket-based support, real-time chat, and call center software.

When evaluating the various options, look for features that would be pertinent to your organization. For instance:

- Do you intend to integrate live chat support within your app?
- Would it be beneficial to integrate customer support with third-party tools, such as Zapier?
- Are you already using an existing suite, such as Salesforce, Freshworks, or Zoho?
- What type of widgets and embeddables are offered by each platform?

The answers to these questions will help you sift through the mountain of customer support options on the market, narrowing down your testing time.

Finally, do not forget to explore chat tools if you want to stay close to and get immediate feedback from your customers. Today, it is very easy to install widgets in your app that integrate with customer support software. Live chat support could become burdensome, depending on the size of your operation, though that can certainly decrease the gap between you and your customers. Such real-time interaction can improve customer satisfaction and enhance your understanding of their needs. Again, like the dedicated customer support tools listed previously, you have many options. Here are just a few award winning options:

- **ZenDesk Chat** (https://www.zopim.com/): Formerly known as Zopim, the app was recently acquired by ZenDesk into their suite of products. They offer a 14 day free trial
- **LiveHelpNow** (http://www.livehelpnow.net/): This option offers a free 30 day trial with video, customization, mobile version, and analytics
- **WebsiteAlive** (https://www.websitealive.com/): This option offers a free version for one user and has backup operators to answer for you in off hours

The power of a well-developed brand name

According to Nielsen, for customers in North and South America, brand recognition was the second-most important reason customers purchased a product. Additional research by Nielsen shows that brand recognition influences purchase decisions in both developed and developing markets, with the majority of people preferring to buy new products from brands with which they are familiar.

A brand name keeps you "top of mind" for your customers and prospects, making it harder for new competitors to get noticed. The right brand name can create positive feelings about your product and a level of loyalty that makes it hard for startups, upstarts, or existing companies to compete.

Building that brand name may take time and effort, but it is possible with a concerted effort and a strategic marketing plan.

Reasons to brand yourself

Since customers statistically make more purchases from recognized names than unrecognized names, it is clear that a brand is important. While this intangible asset may seem vague and even more difficult to measure than customer service, it is vital to any business that wants to stand out from its competition. Here are a few of the most important aims that a brand name can achieve:

- **Recognition**: When customers recognize your brand, they immediately connect that brand to everything associated with your brand.
- **Promise**: Your brand name conveys your promise to your customers. It evokes your value proposition or your unique selling proposition and tells customers what they can expect when they purchase your products or services.
- **Trust**: The more powerful a brand name, the more trusted that name becomes. Trust is one reason that customers buy from brands they recognize: past experiences and reputation work together to evoke that trust in customers.
- **Status**: Brand also conveys status, as is particularly evident in the clothing industry. When a customer is associated with a well-known brand, they are also associated with that brand's status and image.
- **Loyalty**: Over time, brand inspires loyalty in customers that helps to accomplish the same aims as other strategies mentioned in this chapter: you establish secure market territory with a loyal tribe of users, successfully keeping competitors out.

Brand equity, or the financial value of your brand, may be even more difficult to measure than the ROI on customer service improvements. However, its power remains unquestioned and it is an essential tool in your arsenal if you wish to build an economic moat around your castle.

How to build your brand

Branding is a deep topic and beyond the scope of this book. If your budget permits, consider hiring specialists to help you develop your brand more fully. However, when you cover these essentials, you can begin to build the foundation of a good brand:

- **A good name**: The best names are carefully designed to evoke certain emotional associations. The automaker Jaguar, for instance, intentionally evokes the animal of the same name. Choose a name that projects the emotions and identity of what you want to convey to your customers.
- **Visual identity**: Your logo, your color scheme, and visual designs across your presence should remain consistent with your brand identity and with each other. Keep the same scheme across, for instance, your website, your apps, and your marketing materials.
- **Messaging**: Behind every brand lies a story. That story integrates with the other elements of your brand and manifests in your business communications, from marketing to customer service.

Begin by extrapolating from the business canvas model that you created in Chapter 2, *Lean Startup Primer*, using information about your company's mission and your target audience. Find out what impressions you want to convey to your audience and the world, then work with creatives to develop the building blocks previously mentioned.

Tools to monitor your brand via social media and app stores

Brand monitoring and social media monitoring tools have been on the rise for a while now, and they come in every shape and size. Some are free, while enterprise-grade tools can cost as much as an employee. Here are a few examples:

- **Hootsuite** (`https://hootsuite.com`): This is a popular social media management platform that also monitors brand conversations

- **Mention** (`https://mention.com`): This will track keywords or sets of keywords on social media and the web to help you track when and where your brand is mentioned
- **Buzzsumo** (`https://buzzsumo.com`): This allows you to create alerts for keywords, authors, domains, and backlinks
- **SocialOomph** (`https://socialoomph.com`): This is another social media management tool that includes monitoring functions

These are just a few of the more common options at the time of this writing, though more can be expected in the coming years. Startups on a budget can consider integrating free services, such as the preceding tools, with automation services such as Zapier and IFTTT.

Building a brand on a budget

Startups on a budget can easily take advantage of today's rapidly globalizing freelance marketplace to help with any service imaginable, from market research, to virtual office support, to graphic design, to copywriting.

Google can give you more options, but here are a few to get you started:

- **Fiverr**: Fiverr (`https://fiverr.com`) is a freelance marketplace that offers services in $5 units, and most services are well under $100 each
- **Upwork**: Upwork (`https://upwork.com`) allows you to post projects and budgets, then receive bids from freelancers
- **Freelancer**: Freelancer (`https://freelancer.com`) operates like Upwork and you can create project specs and budgets, post that project, then work with freelancers closely throughout the project
- **Craigslist**: Finally, Craigslist (`https://craigslist.org`), the world's most popular classified advertising site, allows you to advertise directly and recruit your own independent contractors

Low-cost options such as these will require investment on your part, but they can be very helpful for bootstrapped startups.

The best way to review a freelancer is to first do some research on the task you need done so that you can identify best practices for the activity. Then, when you do the interview, you can ask them questions about the best practices to see how they respond. If they have no clue, then steer clear.

The next thing is to do a pilot and then review carefully for quality, timeliness, attention to detail, and so on. If you like what you see then try something bigger. If not...run.

I have employed a lot of freelancers. Those simple rules have saved me serious money. Of course, I had to lose some money first to learn my lesson.

Approach branding in the same way that you approach your MVP: build, measure, learn. You can always evolve and pivot as necessary, once you have the resources to do so.

Branding case studies

The right brand image can distinguish you from your competitors, inspire trust, and keep you at the top of your customers' minds. Some brands are done well and others are not. Fashion brands, for instance, tend to be very brand-centric, while technology companies fall all over the map. Here are a few instructive examples of how technology brands play out in the real world:

- **Apple**: Apple has a thoroughly developed brand identity that stretches from its logo and name to its product designs to the staff training manual mentioned previously. Its branding strategy is praised universally as being extraordinarily well done. Some experts even believe that Apple's marketing and branding have been the key to its success, not its products. Regardless, Apple's brand recognition is undeniable and resonates across every aspect of the customer experience, so it pays to examine how the aforementioned branding essentials are present across the Apple empire.
- **Microsoft**: Although massively successful companies make excellent objects of study, they do not always do everything right. Microsoft's brand lacks and is reminiscent of earlier decades, when brand names were more functional than fashionable. Think of General Motors, International Business Machines (IBM), or American Telephone and Telegraph Company (AT&T). Design expert Don Norman says of Microsoft, "If you make a product that everybody loves you end up with a bland product that everybody will accept but nobody truly loves." The same can be said of branding.
- **Starbucks**: Starbucks' meteoric rise to become one of the world's biggest coffee cafe chains has been attributed to its mission, offering "the richest possible sensory experience." Their brand is visible throughout their stores, from the layout to the logo, and has become indelibly etched in the minds of coffee drinkers around the world.

Technology companies may not do branding as well as clothing companies or brand-oriented luxury companies, but we can still learn from their examples. Apple, in particular, demonstrates many successful branding techniques that are found in other modern, fashionable brands, as opposed to "old-fashioned" appearing brands such as Microsoft, Hewlett-Packard, or IBM.

Finally, let's remember that you must start with vision for your brand, your product, and your user. Ask yourself a few important questions about your brand:

- How important is quality?
- How important is the user experience?
- How do you want people to feel about your product?
- What type of relationship do you want to have with your customers?

Once you have a vision and a direction for your brand, you can position yourself in the marketplace and begin to promote that brand. Marketing is a vast field and beyond the scope of this book, so it is advisable to connect with marketers within your network, read basic marketing books, or take a course on digital marketing.

Summary

In order for your app to stay competitive, especially when you expand into larger marketplaces, it is clear that it can't just be a "great app." Your business requires a thorough, well-planned strategy in order to expand and protect its position in the market.

If you want to create an app that lasts, you must consider how each of the tactics listed previously can be used to build an unfair advantage. Identify the tactics that you can apply and exploit them in full, as early as possible in the lifecycle of your product. Here is a brief summary of the tactics and strategies covered in this chapter:

- **Intangible assets**: Legal protection can be used defensively or offensively. In the cutthroat world of business, you must be prepared for any eventuality, especially if your MVP proves successful and your product begins to build momentum.
- **The network and platform effects**: Connected users and business partners are not just customers, they are assets that add value to your software as it grows. Use this to your advantage and leverage that value to aid expansion and protect your territory.

- **Make use of vertical markets**: Access to, or, better yet, control over, a vertical market allows you to establish a competition-free zone to transact business. Establish and maintain relationships in a vertical so that you can have free reign in a specific industry or marketplace.
- **Switching cost strategies**: Switching costs can inhibit new users from leaving a company, so do your best to lower competitors' switching costs while raising your own. Doing so will improve user retention and make it easier for customers to enter your territory.
- **Good customer support**: Customers take front and center in the lean methodology, so they should also take front and center in your business strategy. Good customer support will lower attrition, boost your reputation, and decrease acquisition costs.
- **The power of branding**: A strong brand equates to a strong image. It stands for something that customers can relate to and identify with, and it helps companies differentiate themselves from their competitors. Developing an effective branding strategy will keep you at the top of your customers minds, establish trust, and foster feelings of loyalty.

Although these strategies stray outside the scope of the lean methodology, the rationale for including them should be clear: in order to be successful, a business must be pragmatic. Businesses must adopt practical business strategies that will help their products survive real-world market conditions. Competition is inevitable, which is why you must do all you can to build an unfair advantage and stack the deck in your favor.

20

The Flyng Case Study

Flyng is an iOS app and it is about dating but in a (slightly) different way. Let's have a look to see what the business and technical challenges for Flyng are. So far, this book has been full of a lot of theory. By now you know what the Lean start-up methodology is and, more specifically, how you can apply the methodology to mobile application development.

We have seen many samples for iOS, Android, and web apps, and we have learned what we need to do to learn from our users at an early stage and how to gather feedback quickly, all without too much (technical) effort.

Various providers offering their services have helped us with that. Think of a mobile backend as a service (MBaaS), such as Back4App and QuickBlox, onboarding instruments, such as social sign on and phone number sign on (digits), and analytics services.

The Lean start-up methodology is neither a religion nor an end unto itself. No way! It is just a good tool for creating apps that will matter and last. Do not waste your most precious resource (time!). Instead, use Lean methods to get feedback as early as possible. See if you can prove your hypothesis as early as possible. If you were right, proceed. If your hypothesis was proven wrong then learn and adapt. It is best to fail early and build a solution (a different feature, a better feature, or another app) that adds real value and that people actually want to use.

Earlier in the book, I promised you some real-world examples, and here is one. It is the case of Flyng, a new social app on which I am working together with my teammates. Later I will introduce them to you.

In this chapter, we will cover the following topics:

- Investigate what problem Flyng solves
- Describe how the Flyng MVP was built
- See what our Flyng hypotheses are
- Review how the user feedback was measured
- Discuss how the Flyng user base is built (the chicken and the egg)

The Flyng case study summarizes most of what you have read in this book and covers what we did well and we did wrong. With that, this case study also has become a retrospective session for the team itself.

While building our Flyng MVP, we have already accomplished some great things. And, not surprisingly, we also learned that there are a couple of things we need to improve. We have been using the lean start-up methodology since we started the project, but despite that there are some things that we could have done better.

As you will read later in the chapter, one particular feature that we included was based on an assumption that we did not validate early enough. That particular feature is hardly used, but at least we discovered the problem early before we made many releases of the app. Other than that, Flyng is already a success and its user base is growing every day.

That sounds awesome, but what is Flyng?

Flyng is an app that allows you to connect with students across your personal interests. Unlike Tinder, it is not just about dating. You can explore categories such as adventure, hookup, relationship, or party. In addition to other search criteria, it allows you to specify exactly what you like while browsing. It is this feature that attracts Flyng users the most:

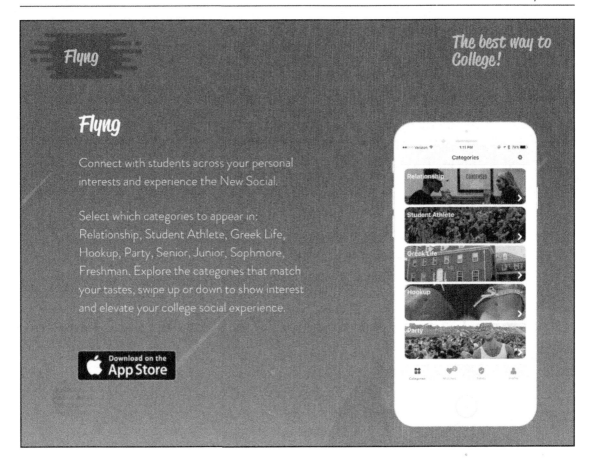

The app also comes with other interesting features, such as the safety timer (but that is just an assumption) and, in the future, some interesting games.

The team

The most important ingredient for any successful app is the team. It is the critical ingredient of a successful start-up and is something in which almost any VC is interested. Flyng, of course, has an awesome team. The Flyng team members are: Daniel Guthrie, Mitchell Trulli, and, not entirely coincidently, me (Mike).

Mitchell Trulli

Mitchell Trulli takes care of influencer marketing and branding, strategic partnerships, financing, and pitching. He has an MBA in finance (from Quinnipiac University) and dreams of working in the VC world after launching a successful start-up. He enjoys traveling and trading as well as spending his summers in Cape Cod.

Daniel Guthrie

Daniel is in charge of monitoring the growth and analytics, social media strategy, branding, and running the ambassador program.

Danny and Mitchell are extremely passionate about start-ups and working on projects in the tech space. In addition, they are also extremely interested in the college market and learning and adapting marketing strategies to it.

Mike van Drongelen

Mike is the developer for the app and its backend. For now, the app is only available on iOS, but the Android app will be coming shortly. He is also interested in UX and everything else that matters to an app. Mike is a start-up addict too, but since you are reading this book I guess you already know that rather well.

The other contributors

The team is larger than the core team. There are many other contributors and ambassadors! Take, for example, Kevin Dalvi. He helped the Flyng team with the UX and some great graphic designs.

We would also like to thank all of our beta testers and, last but certainly not least, the users of Flyng. They have made Flyng evolve to what it currently is. Without the effort of all these people, Flyng just would not exist.

The MVP

After Mitchell told me about his idea, I became quite enthusiastic and we quickly decided to create our first MVP. Looking at my own personal motivation, I can tell you that I always wanted to create a Tinder-style app and, since this solution was aiming at colleges, I was particularly interested in the concept.

Let me explain that last part a bit. My other start-up adventure, Teamspot, is an e-learning solution. It is a platform that lets companies meet students on all kinds of school levels and vice versa. It facilitates the whole organization around the setup and monitoring of internships.

I have always had a vision that learning should be fun and that it is so much more than just knowing and analyzing facts. It should also be about socializing, collaboration, and all kinds of other aspects that create a great experience. If you take away the fun, then the learning aspect will stop too. And if you are part of a start-up, you should always learn and have fun, at least once a day (maybe even twice).

That is why I am interested in Flyng. In addition, I thought it was a great opportunity to build an app the Lean way, so I could use it as a case study for this book. This is why you are reading about it now.

A distributed team

While Mitchell and Daniel are in the US, I am in the Netherlands. That is not necessarily an issue. There are some great collaboration tools available and the fact that we are in different time zones just requires a little more planning. My co-author, Adam Dennis, is in another time zone as well. And that works great too.

Mitchell says this about our distributed team:

> *"Our team utilizes Slack to communicate daily; in addition we expect a weekly or bi-weekly Skype call. Working internationally has been made quite easy with the technology at our disposal; in addition Mike has been quite flexible with our hours."*

Besides Slack, you can also use BaseCamp for your team communication. Both solutions work great for both distributed and local teams.

Flyng's USPs

You might wonder: "Why another social/dating app? What makes Flyng so different?"

When I asked Mitchell, he told me:

> *"Tinder was previously hailed as the most profitable app of Q2 2017. We see the online dating market as still being extremely young and it is only growing."*

To capitalize on the unique properties of Tinder (their swipeable profiles), and combine that with our unique spin on categories, we are able to innovate the space and attract users to our application and away from the standard Tinder or Bumble.

I believe that the ability to monitor the matches, and what categories they were matched with, is the most important part of our app. Our users will be particularly picky and will expect the entire app to revolve around these categories.

I also asked him why Flyng targets colleges in particular. Mitchell replied with:

> *"Many people do not understand why we target the college market as it has been hailed as one of the most difficult spaces to enter. We believe that our unique perspective on dating apps will allow us to stand out. In addition, our past projects have focused on the college market and we have learned extensively about how to promote and market to them."*

The theory goes that every business has a (marketing) problem and a (technical) solution component. I asked Mitchell what the problems are that Flyng wants to solve?

Flyng solves the problem of people not being able to meet exactly who they want in their local area. Flyng allows them to meet people who are partying, younger or older, or in the same social organizations as them. This will greatly increase the amount of time spent off the phone and interacting in person. Our goal is to create personal bonds between people.

Other social apps, such as Facebook and Snapchat, fail to have an effective discovery platform; they are where you communicate with people after meeting in person. Tinder and Flyng allow you to meet people online so that you can interact with them offline.

In the future, we plan to add the ability to like photos, temporary categories, location-based categories, and other features that will increase the user engagement and retention.

The big milestone we are currently trying to reach is 40K **Monthly Active Users** (**MAU**). Once we are at this point, Kevin will lead a trip with Mitchell and Daniel and pitch to VCs in our network in the greater Silicon Valley area.

Growing a user base

40K monthly active users does not sound too complicated to accomplish. But like every start-up company, Flyng started with 0 users. So how did we get our user base to grow?

Mitchell outlines what we did quite well: We initially started with marketing before launching. We wanted to create a motion behind Flyng where people were actually waiting and excited to download the app prior to its launch.

This created our initial boost of 200-500 users on the first day to provide a base for our in-depth marketing strategies. Currently, we use social media and social influencers to grow Flyng's user base. Through growth hacking tactics and partnering with like-minded organizations, we are able to increase downloads and retain users.

Our biggest challenge is growing a user base in a specific area. Our social growth strategies are scattered and don't hyperfocus downloads in a specific geographical location like people want.

Dating and matching apps are always struggling to find a good balance between male and female. Most ideally it is balanced 50/50 but with many start-ups you see that early adopters are often male for some reason. It seems important for Flyng to do this well too.

Mitchell says: We are under the assumption that boys will chase girls. To capitalize on this we are marketing mainly to females, displaying that our categories will allow them to filter out the men they do not want to be linked with, something which no other apps allow.

The business model

An impressive user base is probably very convincing, but if we want Flyng to become a sustainable business, we better think about the business model too.

A blank business model canvas is staring at us. What will the business model canvas of Flyng look like? Let's do a short iteration through all elements of the canvas.

Customer segments

Our users are college students. For now we are focusing on the Boston area. Later, we will scale up to the US and then, eventually, scale up to the world.

Our users are not necessarily our customers. If we know the sources of our revenue streams, then our customers could also be advertisers since they bring the money with them. On the other hand, the users add value to the app by spending a lot of time with it, something the advertisers love. Hmm, tricky. For now, let's add them both to the canvas.

Value propositions

What value does Flyng add? In short, it provides category and story-driven people matching aimed at one particular vertical (colleges). The focus on this is important. Because we are dedicated to this particular vertical, we are in a position to actually create value. We know what needs our users have by aiming at this particular niche. I am sure you agree that this is a good strategy, assuming you know the history of Facebook. Rather than focusing on everyone, they began with the focus on university students. Your app may be in a total different space, but starting with a relatively small audience or solving a niche problem is always a good way to start.

Customer relationships

An online product, an app or a website for that matter, makes the relationship with your customers more anonymous. Still, there are ways to have a relationship with them, such as by providing feedback on Twitter, Instagram, and to App Store comments. It is important to let your users know that they are heard.

We also look at statistical information at Fabric Answers, Crashlytics, and the insights that iTunesConnect gives us.

It is too early to look at particular customer segments, but when we scale up it will certainly make sense to do so. Users in the U.S. and, for example, Asia, might express different behaviors and/or have different needs.

Channels

Our (sales) channels are, as mentioned previously, social media and the App Store. In addition, we use push notification messages to notify users about app improvements and so on. If our user base is large enough, I expect that we will target specific segments to promote specific features.

Revenue Streams

From where does the revenue come? A buyout would be great, of course, but let's be realistic for now. So, where will we get our money? I think premium features are a good idea, but another option, according to Mitchell, could be:

Advertisements within a category, such as an ad for a beer company placed in the party category or endorsed category. For example, the party category could be sponsored by a beer company. Other categories could have sponsors as well.

In the app business, it is not difficult to reach the break-even level. As we will see later, our costs will be low. It is a totally different question as to whether Flyng will become a sustainable business. We will see what the future brings us. It is not our primary target yet. Growing the user base is the most important thing we need to do right now.

We have seen this in `Chapter 17`, *Monetization and Pricing Strategy*.

Key resources

Our key resources, without doubt, are the App Store and the services we are using, such as Back4App to host the Parse Server. Our most precious resources are human: our team, and our users.

Key activities

The key activity of Flyng basically comes down to matching people based on mutual interests and creating a perfect online experience.

By delivering that experience, Flyng is adding value. The app entertains users and brings people together, in real life, to enjoy the things they like to do most, whether it is dating, having the same hobby, or enjoying the same interests in sports.

Flyng is service oriented, so we are heavily investing in the relationship with our customers. We want them to know that they are heard and we care about their experience and the feedback they give. We use statistics to measure important KPIs, such as onboarding conversion, retention, and churning.

Partners

Flyng needs to have partners just like any other business. If we want the app to get noticed, we need the help of others. Social influencers (such as a Twitter user with many followers) are our partners. Apple and the App Store is one. Our future advertisers, and/or the organizations that will purchase ads or sponsor categories, are also our partners.

That brings us to the question, "Who are our ambassadors or who could be our ambassadors?"

This was Mitchell's answer: It is tough to have brand ambassadors for a social app that is dating based. One idea would be to have a code for each city, similar to Flyng.us/boston, and split the pay-out among the local influencers. Another would be to create a custom code for each.

Cost structure

What are the costs that are involved with our app? Hosting (Back4App) and marketing are the only expenditures if we do not take the time that we have spend working on Flyng into account.

The more interaction there is on the platform, the more calls per second will be made against the backend. The party that is hosting the Parse Server, which is Back4App in our case, offers a number of plans. Each plan comes with a maximum number of monthly requests and a maximum number of requests per second. So, the more users the app has and, more importantly, the more concurrent users the app has, the more we need to pay for hosting:

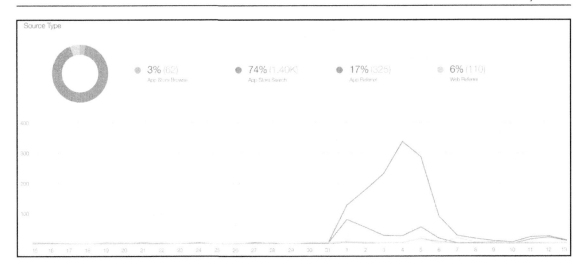

Our marketing costs depend on the platform and the frequency of our advertising. By carefully measuring our conversions, we can understand the correlation between our spending and the number of new users we secure.

When we started running campaigns, we noticed a large effect on the number of new users. We also learned that the effect lasted for only a short period of time. The preceding graph nicely illustrates this.

Unfair advantage

This element appears in the sample business model canvas, but it is included with some variants. It is probably the toughest part of BMC. I asked Mitchell: What is Flyngs unfair advantage? In other words: What prevents another app builder from copying and rolling out the Flyng concept too?

Mitchell replied saying: Since the space is already crowded with a mix of both major market players (Tinder and Bumble) and an ample amount of small players, the most important thing for Flyng is our relationship and connection with our community/consumers in the space. Our unfair advantage will be our brand perception of leading to better connections and dates, as endorsed by our users and ourselves.

Awesome! We have now gathered all the information that we need. If we fill in Flyng's BMC, it will look like this:

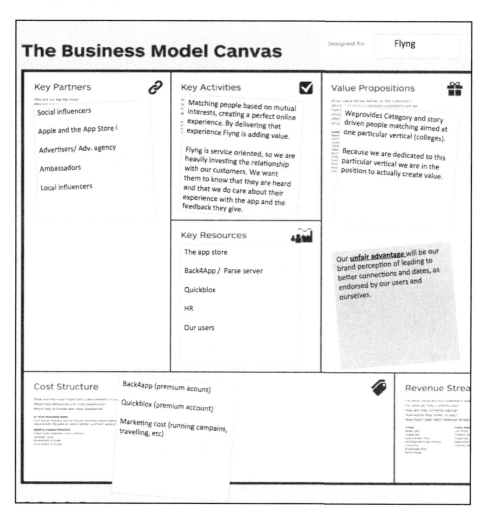

And, since space is limited in a book, here is the right part of the canvas:

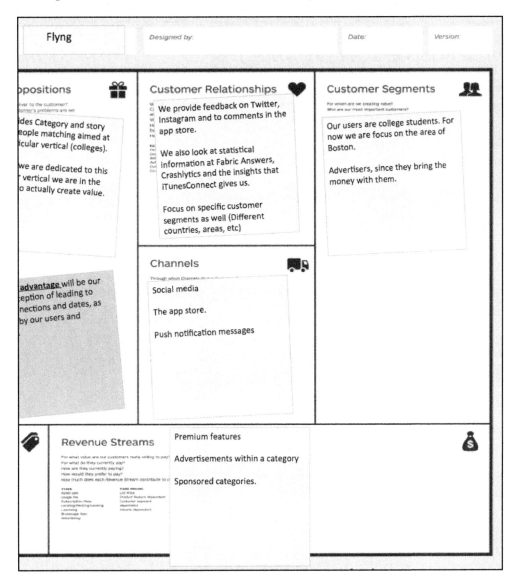

Getting feedback

So, we need evidence for our business model. What tools do we use to measure traction, retention, and other feedback? Feedback allows us to improve the app's features and prove whether our assumptions were right or wrong.

The feedback for our very first MVP came from direct interaction with our users.

If the number of users grows rapidly, we need to have some other tools to get proper feedback.

We gather our feedback from the following sources:

- iTunesConnect analytical data
- App store reviews
- Fabric answers, analytical data
- Fabric crashlytics, to measure, well, crashes
- Back4App data and statistics
- Feedback from our beta users

The information that came with this feedback has taught us a lot about what features are being used the most. Most importantly, we noticed that the category-based browsing technology was something that was most appreciated by our users.

Unvalidated assumptions

When we started to build Flyng, we had a few hypotheses that our MVP proved were right. What assumptions did we have that were totally wrong?

Mitchell said: Through our MVP launch, we were able to see that almost no users utilized our safety feature, SAM. Sadly this will prompt us to remove it in the future and perhaps spin it off into its own project.

A zombie feature

SAM is very easy to use, or, well, that is what we thought. Decide for yourself!

Say you met someone new on Flyng. Just to be safe, before you go out on your date, you use SAM to select 1 to 3 contacts from your contact book to alert if something goes wrong. You start the timer and every 45 minutes you need to check in just to let Flyng know that you are still OK. You just tap the (local) notification when it appears on your phone. If you do not respond or do not respond in time, your contacts will be notified through SMS.

Only a few people are really using the SAM feature. Apparently there are no creepy people at colleges (that is another assumption). Anyhow, we think this is a great concept, but if no one uses it then our users probably don't need it or at least they don't need it within Flyng.

The only zombie here is a great idea that risks becoming a member of the living dead:

Indeed, the feedback and statistics taught us that it is hardly used. We still need to research whether people do not think the option is useful, cannot find it, or think that it is too difficult for the assumed problem. This all needs further investigation.

For now, we can state that the hypothesis that people want to have a guardian when going on a date seems to be wrong. Just like Mitchell said, it probably needs to be removed and evolved to its own app. Of course, this idea assumes that the problem that this feature seeks to solve actually exists in a context other than Flyng.

And if not? Well, in that case this is a typical example of waste that could have been avoided by early validation. So, what could an even earlier MVP look like? Perhaps what we should have done is try to understand what problems girls (and boys?) currently face when going out a date using an online or real-world survey.

Feedback and actionable metrics

The monitoring tools that we are using give us valuable analytical insights into our app. The challenge with these insights is how to convert them into actionable metrics.

Having some numbers is great, but how can you interpret them so that they become actionable metrics? And which KPIs really matter? Traction is a word that is often used, but how do you measure it? If you think traction is a number that defines to what extent people are actually using your app, then the number of users is a useful number. Or is it the number of active users? What is the definition of active user? Or, is the number of new users the important number here?

To answer these questions, you must make things measurable and be precise. You need to have clear goals.

Let's say that by the end of the year we want to have 100K new users. That is a clear target and, as long as it is a somewhat realistic target, it is a good one. In the end, real traction is proved by actual revenue, but in the case of Flyng, that is something for later.

Using the same tools we can also measure the retention rate. How many users are still using the app after 1 week, after 1 month, or after 1 year?

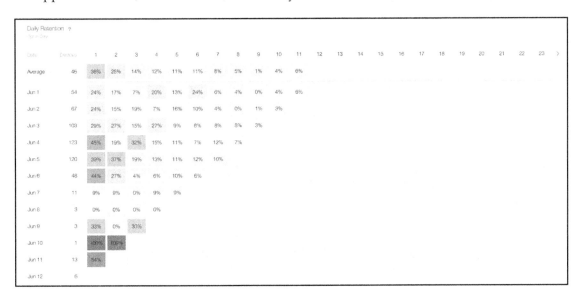

If the retention rate is low, what do we need to do to make the users stay with the app? I asked Mitchell if we could say that the currently available analytics are actionable metrics. I also wondered if we needed additional resources or tools for measuring our users.

Mitchell says: "The current analytics we have are a good representation of the early market validation we have proved. Our marketing efforts have been inconsistent; the maximum number of days in a row that we have had an ad spend has been only 7 days so far.

We often monitor the feedback we get from social media, direct messages, comments on posts, and other user interactions to let us know whether our users' apps are crashing, what features they would like to see, and so on.

The most interesting feedback we have gotten was from users who have actually used the application and met with the people with whom they interacted. They told us that the categories allowed them to plan and interact differently. For example, the ones that met in the party category were able to link up at a party."

It is interesting to hear that our best feedback comes from direct interaction with our users. It should not be a real surprise, but it is important to know that direct feedback is a better resource than analytics alone:

Split testing

What features of Flyng could be perfect candidates for split testing purposes?

Mitchell says: Testing different types of categories would be ideal for split testing purposes. For example, to test the acceptance and interaction caused from the creation of a summer-related Beach Day category, we could create it in coastal locations that we deem strategic to our research testing.

Yes, I think it is worthwhile to run a few A/B experiments, not just for the app but for the App Store listing as well. Since **App Store Optimization** (**ASO**) techniques have recently become available, including App Store split testing, I would love to try them out to see how they work and if they can help us improve our app.

Vision

You cannot have targets without a vision, so I wonder how ambitious the team is about Flyng. I asked Mitchell this: What do you think the future of Flyng will look like in, let's say, 1 year from now and in 3 years from now? Will Flyng be a sustainable business? Will it make some serious money? Will it have investors? Does it contribute in any other way business, wise or just for the society?

The dynamics of Flyng make it a great product to monetize. Category cards can be sponsored in multiple ways. First, an original category can be endorsed by a company. For example, the student athlete category could be sponsored by `http://www.thetailgateseason.com`, a company in our network. A company that appears toward the top of the page would cost a premium, while lower ones would have the best value.

There could also be limited sponsored categories. These could be interactive to further embrace the value of learning about other profiles through their category line-up. For example, say Marvel is looking to advertise a new Avengers movie. We could run a sponsored, limited-duration category that acts like a poll. Users would pick their favorite superhero and could connect with similar fans. These ads would not be seen as intrusive and would add to the user experience if implemented with time and care.

Another benefit of having categories in our social meet-up app is using them to discriminate where to place ads. With traditional apps in our space, there is only one giant category. If Bud Light only wanted to advertise to people interested in and actively partying, these apps would not be able to cater to Bud Light. With Flyng's party category, we can present the ad to users who would be interested in their product. The ad would be relevant, which would make the user and Bud Light happy.

Technical considerations

Since this book is most of all a practical approach to the Lean start-up methodology, we will have a look at the highlights of the Flyng technology as well. We cannot reveal too much, but just enough to give you an idea.

The app has been built for the iOS platform, but there are plans for an Android version too. The main reason for having an iOS-first strategy is because of the primary audience, colleges in the Boston area. If we had started the roll out in Europe, we probably would have had an Android first strategy instead.

The app is built with Swift 3.0 and will be migrated to Swift 4 in the future. It consumes data from a Parse Server, residing at Back4App. In addition, it uses QuickBlox for chat technology. The code has been structured in such a way that switching between one mBaaS and another is relatively easy.

Our technology stack includes the following:

- Xcode
- Swift 4.0
- Back4App, Parse server, PLQ, and Cloud code

- Amazon
- QuickBlox
- Twillio
- APNs, badges, messages for matches, and messages

Parse server hosted at Back4App

We have had to deal with some limitations using a Parse Server as a backend solution, but, on the other hand, it has also allowed us to develop the app rather quickly. This way we can focus on the frontend (the app) in particular.

Here is an example of a filter for the collection of matches, residing at Back4App:

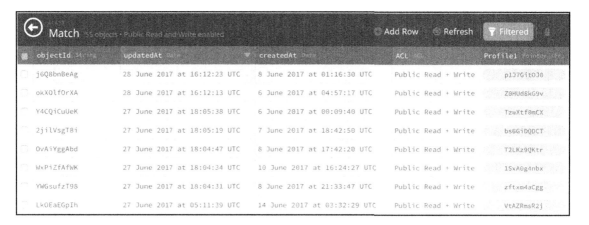

The app has been set up so that it will be easy to switch to another Parse Server or even to a custom-made backend API quickly.

Real-time data

In addition to profile and media data, we also have a need for real-time data for the app's chat functionality.

We used to use parse live queries for the chat technology, but we found that QuickBlox was a more trustable service for these kinds of things. It was a bit tough to figure how to do the authentication for a single user for two different backend solutions, but in the end it was not really so hard to accomplish.

This is a sample of the QuickBlox dashboard. The service supports many other features, but we are just using it for chat functionality:

The other dependencies

We use Twillio for sending text messages for the SAM feature. For onboarding, or the login/registration in particular, we ask the user to sign up with his/her Facebook account.

The onboarding for Flyng is tough if you do not have a Facebook account. You cannot continue until you login with a Facebook account. According to what we discussed in Chapter 11, *Onboarding and Registration,* this means that we have a bit of a high barrier to overcome for onboarding.

Without knowing anything about the app, you need to sign-up, and if you do not have a Facebook account you go no further. While I do not want to recommend this strategy for all apps, it works great for a dating app like Flyng. For apps like these, it is important to avoid fake users and to avoid incomplete data. The data obtained from Facebook helps us to personalize the app, by showing your name and avatar, right after the sign-up.

We might need to offer other social sign-on options as well. Since the app is aiming at young people, we probably have to provide ways to sign up with a Twitter, Snapchat, or Instagram account too.

It is also interesting to know that something else we did to avoid fake profiles is to use facial recognition technology. Using the iOS SDK, it is pretty easy to verify if one or multiple faces appear on an uploaded picture. When tested, we found out that it also differentiates a face from cartoons, animal pictures, and drawings. At the minimum, it prevents us from having profile avatars that show non relevant images, such as wallpapers, sunsets or even worse.

As you can see. we are using CocoaPods to add a few third-party dependencies, such as the Parse and QuickBlox SDK. As you can see, I am also using Facebook and Crashlytics as a reference:

```
target 'flyng' do
  use_frameworks!
  pod 'Fabric'
  pod 'Crashlytics'
  pod 'Cartography'
  pod 'Parse'
  pod 'ParseFacebookUtilsV4'
  pod 'ParseLiveQuery'
  pod 'JSQMessagesViewController'
  pod 'QuickBlox'
```

Queries

The data consumption relies on a few direct queries, but for the more complex requirements, cloud code solutions have been used. These cloud code solutions are JavaScript based and are closely related to the REST API functionality that is available with Parse Server.

For the sake of simplicity it is hosted at Back4App, but there is little that will prevent us hosting one or multiple Parse Servers in the future. Of course, in that case we need to handle push notifications, balancing and scaling, and other things too, but you get the picture. It allows us to be scalable if we need to scale right away.

When you look at the app's Swift code, you will notice that there are a number of methods defined for the client. They are available as protocol, which allows us to switch to another backend solution without too much effort.

Just to give you an idea, some of the available methods are shown here:

```
import UIKit
protocol RepositoryProtocol {
    func authenticate (handler: RepositoryResultDelegate, request:
AuthenticateRequest)
    ...
    func getProfile (handler: RepositoryResultDelegate, request:
GetMyProfileRequest)
    func getCategories (handler: RepositoryResultDelegate, request:
GetCategoriesRequest)
    func getCandidates (handler: RepositoryResultDelegate, request:
GetCandidatesRequest)
    func getMatchList (handler:RepositoryResultDelegate , request:
GetMatchListRequest)
    func pushMessage (handler: RepositoryResultDelegate, request:
PushRequest)
    ...
}
```

Complex operations

At first sight, it seems to be easy to figure out if there is a match between two people. But for an app, this is a complex operation. Imagine that you like a particular profile. First, we need to add that fact to your browsing history because you do not want to see profiles that you have already seen. We also will keep track of the people that you like. Later, when they like you too, this will result in a match. We want to create as many matches for our users as possible, so we need to make sure that you see the profiles of the people that did like you, first.

If you like someone, we need to run a query that informs us whether the person that you have just liked has also liked you previously. If so, a match entry will be added and we need to inform both you and your matching partner. Let's send a push notification to tell your partner and return the match that we have just created to inform you. Great, something new has happened. The badge, appearing on the app's icon (on the match tab), needs to be incremented. However, before we do this, we need to figure out how many new matches (and messages) there are, for both you and your partner. To make a long story short, this operation is a perfect candidate for a cloud-code-based solution.

The function, residing on the Parse Server, will do the heavy work for us. That makes sense, as the server has much more power, and this way we will also avoid sending too much data from the device to the server and vice versa. This is how we can keep things scalable.

From an app perspective, it is just a matter of providing the right data and consuming the result produced by the cloud function operated on the server. As an example, here is how the cloud function is called:

```
func getCandidates (handler: RepositoryResultDelegate, request:
GetCandidatesRequest){
  let params =
  [
          "myId": request.profileId,
          "fromAge": myProfile.CriteriaAgeFrom,
          "toAge" : myProfile.CriteriaAgeTo,
          "gender" : myProfile.CriteriaGender,
          "maxDistance" : myProfile.CriteriaMaxDistance,
          "category": request.categoryId,
          "skip": request.skip,
          "limit" : request.limit
    ]
    PFCloud.callFunctionInBackground("getCandidates", withParameters:
params as [NSObject : AnyObject], block: { (object, error) in
    ...
```

Push notifications

In `Chapter 15`, *Growing Traction and Improving Retention,* you will find more information about the implementation needed to show push notifications. For this case study, it is interesting to know that services such as Back4App (there are also Sashido and a couple of other ones) do not just allow you to host the Parse Server but also deal with the hassle of setting up push notifications for an app.

For our app, we use remote push notifications to show messages and to update the badge icon. We notify the user each time there is a new match or a new message. If this happens enough, the retention rate will grow just by itself. In addition, we also use local (scheduled) notifications for the SAM safety feature.

Crash reports

We test each release candidate before we ship it, but a crash can always happen in the wild despite all our testing. If so, then Crashlytics comes to the rescue. It is easy to implement and it gives you a lot of insight (including a stack trace) on crashes:

```
func application(application: UIApplication,
      didFinishLaunchingWithOptions launchOptions: [NSObject: AnyObject]?)
-> Bool {
      ...
      Fabric.with([Answers.self, Crashlytics.self])
```

In the following example, you can see how the number of crashes freely dropped to an unacceptable level. We localized the problem and released a new version. This resulted in the number of crash-free users to go up, nearly 99% or even higher. It is nearly impossible to satisfy everyone. The nature of your app and the OS it is running on can have a huge impact. For iOS, there are only a limited number of different devices and a high percentage of crash-free users certainly should be possible. Also, most devices will be using the latest version of iOS.

Note that this may be different for Android apps. You can expect that the percentage of crash-free users is lower for your Android app. This is because of the many different devices, flavors, and OS versions. There are devices with one/two/no cameras, for example. There are Android versions with Samsung or Huawei flavors, each doing things slightly differently. And it is not uncommon that you need to support Android version 4 to version 8. It is nearly impossible to test each variant. You have no other option than to focus on the top 10 popular devices and to hope it will work well on others as well:

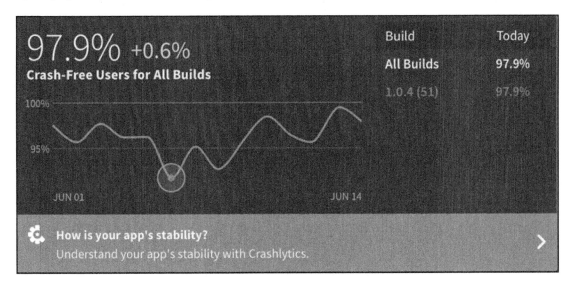

We also use Fabric to measure how the app is used, for example to measure how many people signed up within a period of time:

```
AnalyticsUtil.logEvent(AnalyticsUtil.eventSignupFacebook)

static func logEvent(event: String){
    ...
    Answers.logCustomEventWithName(event, customAttributes: nil)
}
```

Releases

We did a couple of releases and many users gave the app 5 stars. Of course, we did get a few negative reviews as well. It is these users that we are most interested in. When you think about it, the negative reviewers are valuable because when they encountered a problem, they cared enough about the app to alert us about the problem. The challenge here is to turn this angry/unsatisfied customer into an ambassador. We can always try to start that conversion by making sure we listen to the user and solve the issue he/she is experiencing. Is there really a bug in the app? Is there something unexplained or unclear in the app? Let's contact the user to have a conversation to find out!

Summary

In this chapter, we provided an extensive case study that illustrated much of what is discussed in the book. We learned about the Flyng app, covering the things that we did well and did not do well. We have seen what the earliest assumptions were and how we gather feedback. It is important to prove your hypotheses as early as possible. It is important to properly validate them. If not, then it could result in a waste of time. That is what we saw happen with the SAM feature. Maybe it just needs a small pivot to make it a success, which will require some new experiments. These are all the things that perhaps could be applied to your app as well.

As of today, Flyng is still evolving. The adventure is ongoing and we continue to build, measure, and get feedback every day. Sometimes that is tough; but given the good spirit of the team, we will continue to move forward. I have no idea where this adventure is going, but I am sure about one thing. No matter whether it succeeds or fails, we are learning a lot, thanks to a whole pile of feedback, dedication, and, well maybe, a little bit of luck.

You can do that too! Stay focused. Do not procrastinate too often. Learn every day. Fail early. Sustain. Now, it is up to you! Good luck!

Appendix

Reading list and references

- *Azure IoT Development Cookbook* by *Yatish Patil*

- *Business model generation* by *Alexander Osterwalder en Yves Pigneur*

- *Crossing the chasm* by *Geoffrey a Moore*

- *Customer development* by *Steve Blank*

- *Continuous Delivery with Docker and Jenkins* by *Rafał Leszko*

- *Continuous Integration, Delivery, and Deployment* by *Sander Rossel*

- *Do not just roll the dice* by *Neil Davidson*

- *Design patterns* by *Ralph Johnson*

- *Hooked – How to Build Habit-Forming Products* by *Nir Eyal*

- *Implementing Azure Solutions* by *Florian Klaffenbach, Jan-Henrik Damaschke, and Oliver Michalski*

- *Jenkins 2.x Continuous Integration Cookbook - Third Edition* by *Mitesh Soni and Alan Mark Berg*

- *Lean Startup* by *Eric Ries*

- *Lean UX* by *Jeff Gothelf and Josh Seiden*

- *Lean Analytics* by *Alistair Croll and Benjamin Yoskovitz*

- *Lean UX: Applying Lean Principles to Improve User Experience* by *Jeff Gothelf with Josh Seiden (and Eric Reis, Series Editor)*

- *Learning DevOps: Continuously Deliver Better Software* by *Joakim Verona, Michael Duffy, and Paul Swartout*

- *Learning Microsoft Azure Storage* by *Mohamed Waly*

- *Overcoming the Five Dysfunctions of a Team* by *Patrick Lencioni*

- *Running Lean* by *Ash Maurya*

- *Robust Cloud Integration with Azure* by *Mahindra Morar, Abhishek Kumar, Martin Abbott, Gyanendra Kumar Gautam, James Corbould, and Ashish Bhambhani*

- *Rework* by *David Heinemeier Hansson*

- *Scaling Lean* by *Ash Maurya*

- *Start with Why* by *Simon Sinek*

- *The startup owner manual* by *Steve Blank and Bob Dorf*

- *The Lean entrepreneur* by *Brant Cooper and Patrick Vlaskovits*

- *Traction* by *Justin Mares and Gabriel Weinberg*

- *The Phoenix Project* by *Gene Kim, Kevin Behr, and George Spafford*

- *The Goal: A Process of Ongoing Improvement* by *Eliyahu M. Goldratt*

- *The Five Dysfunctions of a Team* by *Patrick Lencioni*

- *The Elements of User Experience* by *Jesse James Garrett*

- *The Four Steps to the Epiphany* by *Steve Blank*

- *UX: Rocket Surgery Made* Easy by *Steve Krug*

- *UX: Don't Make Me Think* by *Steve Krug*

- *UX: Simple and Usable* by *Giles Colborne*

- *Value proposition design* by *Alex Osterwalder, Yves Pigneur, and others*

Index

A

actionable metrics
  about 205
  acquisition 205
  engagement 206
Adobe PhoneGap 123
Adobe
  URL 115
advertisement
  campaign types 262
  formats 261
Agile development 27
Agile workflow
  about 40
  kanban 41
  scrum 41
American Telephone and Telegraph Company
  (AT&T) 318
Android
  references 114
App Annie
  URL 275
app backend solution
  components 247
  data, storing 247
  executing 247
app ecosystem
  about 10
  building 11
App packs 199
App Store Optimization (ASO) 193, 338
App Store search 199
app structuring
  about 62
  data layer 64
  design patterns 62

  Mobile Backend as a Service (MBaas), using 63
app tests
  executing 201
Appcelerator 124
Appium
  URL 283
Apple Push Notification Service (APNS) 231, 235
Apple's App Store submission cycles 32
application-programming interface (API)
  about 90, 129, 132
  hypotheses, proving with IFTT 144
  iOS app, building 134
  publishing 129
  references 134
application
  automated delivery 294
  automated deploy 294
  competitive advantage 300
  factors, considerations 122
  features, exploring 158
  phone number, signing up 158
audience 114
auto-scaling
  about 254
  references 255
automated tests 283
Average Revenue Per User (ARPU) 224

B

backend
  cloud solutions, leveraging for app experiments
    91
  considerations 91
  creating 90
Betali.st
  about 225
  URL 225

Bitbucket
  URL 282
build variant 284, 285, 286
build-measure-learn feedback loop
  about 73
  build 74
  learn 75
  measure 74
buildTypes 289
Business Model Canvas (BMC)
  about 20
  channels 23
  cost structure 23
  customer relationships 22
  customer segments 22
  key activities 21
  key partners 21
  revenue stream 24
  summary 25
  value propositions 21
Buzzsumo
  URL 317

C

Canva App
  building, with Firebase 95
  URL 96
Carthage
  URL 132
chicken and egg problem
  about 57
  grab and adapt 59
  service 61
  solutions 58
Click Through Rate (CTR) 208, 266
cloud-based storage 247
CocoaPods
  URL 132
Concierge Minimum Viable Product (CMVP) 55
Content Management System (CMS) 90
Continuous Delivery 281
Continuous Integration 280
continuous onboarding 159
continuous workflow
  example, for Android app 284

conversions 206, 208
Conversocial
  URL 314
cost per action/acquisition (CPA) 262
cost per click (CPC) 262
cost per impression (CPI) 262
cost per mille (CPM) 262
Craigslist
  URL 317
cross-platform development tools
  Adobe PhoneGap 123
  Appcelerator 124
  leveraging 123
  selecting 125
  Xamarin 124
cross-platform releases 35
Customer Acquisition Cost (CAC) 224
Customer development 27
customer support
  about 310
  aims, for achieving brand name 315
  brand, building 316
  brand, building on budget 317
  branding case studies 318
  perspective 311
  power, of well-developed brand name 315
  recipe 312
  tools 313
  tools, for monitoring brand 316
  using, for profit 312

D

Deep linking 200
Definition of Done (DoD) 47
Definition of Ready (DoR) 46
design bar 32
DevOps 297
Don't Repeat Yourself (DRY) 62

E

early adopters
  acquiring 182
  manually recruiting 183
  user experience, perfecting 183
Empurror 269, 270, 273, 274

epic
  about 42
  backlog refinement 45
  daily stand-up 44
  done, definition 47
  ready, definition 46
  retrospective 48
  scrum team 43
  sprint planning 47
  sprint review 47
  sprint, planning 47
Espresso
  URL 283
experiment
  A/B testing 192
  A/B testing, limited infrastructure 198
  about 192
  app listing, requisites 196
  app testing 194, 195
  challenges, workaround 199
  limitations, for executing in Google Play or App
    Store 196
  limitations, to testing with store listings 196
  parallel experiments, executing 198
  performing 195
  results, measuring 197
  split testing, performing 193
  store listing hacks 199
  store listing tests 193

F

Fabric 280
Fabric beta 295
Fabric SDK 213
failing fast
  about 72
  build-measure-learn feedback loop 73
  build-measure-learn feedback loop, phases 74
  feedback-focused development model 74
  tech debt, eliminating 72
Fastlane
  about 280
  DevOps 297
  URL 297
  using, with beta Play Store 295

using, with iTunes beta 295
fear of missing out (FoMo) 227
Firebase dashboard 110, 111
Firebase
  about 212
  dependencies 99
  layout 99
  models 100, 103, 105, 106, 109, 110
  references 221
  signing up 96, 98
  URL 96, 163, 213, 215
  using, for split testing 213, 218, 219, 220
  using, in Android MVP app 95
Fiverr
  URL 317
Flyng, technical considerations
  Back4App, parse server hosted 340
  complex operations 343
  crash reports 345
  dependencies 341
  push notifications 344
  queries 342
  real-time data 340
  releases 346
Flyng
  about 322
  actionable metrics 336
  advantages 326, 331
  business model 327
  channels 328
  contributors 324
  cost structure 330
  customer relationships 328
  customer segments 327
  feedback metrics 336
  feedback, obtaining 334
  key activities 329
  key resources 329
  partners 330
  Revenue Streams 329
  split testing 338
  team 323, 324
  technical considerations 339
  unvalidated assumptions 334
  user base, expanding 327

value propositions 328
vision 338
zombie feature 335
Freelancer
   URL 317
Freshdesk
   URL 313
Fun with Charades
   about 80
   conundrum 85, 86
   queries 80
   scenarios 81, 82, 84, 85

G

Git workflow
   about 282
   references 283
Google Analytics
   URL 115
Google Cloud Messaging (GCM) 231
Gradle
   about 280, 284
   URL 131
   using 286

H

HockeyApp 280, 284, 295
Hootsuite
   URL 316
hybrid apps
   about 118, 121
   pros and cons 120
   versus native apps 118

I

If This Then That (IFTT)
   about 144
   channels 145
   recipes, creating 145
   triggers 145
   used, for proving hypotheses 144
in-app notifications 229
in-app purchase product types, iOS
   about 266
   auto-renewing subscription 267

consumable 267
   non-consumable 267
   non-renewing subscription 267
   reference link 267
in-app purchases
   Empurror 269, 270, 273, 274
   implementing 268
incoming notification
   handling 238, 239
InstaWeather
   URL 133
intangible assets 300
intellectual property (IP) 299
International Business Machines (IBM) 318
Internet Movie DataBase (IMDB) 134
Internet of Things (IoT) 144
InVision 186
iOS app
   building 134, 135
   data, enriching 143
   hypothesis 134
   ideas, validating through customer interviews
      135
   IMDB 136
   locations, displaying on map 138
   movie locations 135
   Uber 136
   Uber integration 140
IP laws
   app, protecting 302
   business, protecting 302
   business-destroying patent trolls 301
   intellectual property, defending 302
   legal offensive 303
   work, protecting 300

J

JavaScript Object Notation (JSON) 249
Jenkins 279
Jira
   URL 48

K

kanban 41
Kiip

URL 208

L

Lean Canvas
  about 25
  One metric that matters 26
libraries
  dynamic loading, limitations 34
Lifetime Customer Value (LTV) 224
LiveHelpNow
  URL 314
local notifications 228

M

mash-up 66
mash-up solution
  about 128
  Android 131
  API, publishing 129
  APIs, versus SDKs 130
  dependency management 130
  Duplo 130
  iOS 131
  Lego 130
  using 128
Mention
  URL 317
microtesting
  used, for collecting data 200
Minimum Loveable Product (MLP)
  about 76
  features 77
Minimum Sellable Product (MSP) 71
Minimum Viable Product (MVP)
  about 14, 29, 53, 67, 68, 79, 90, 325
  applying, to enterprise 70
  benefits 68
  building 69
  components, gathering 70
  defining 69
  distributed team 325
  fail fast-validate 72
  Flyng, advantages 326
Mobile Backend as a Service (MBaaS) 54, 63, 89
mobile marketplace app 24

Mobile Virtual Network Operators (MVNO) 59
Model View Controller (MVC) pattern 62
Model View Presenter (MVP) 62
Model-View-ViewModel (MVVM) 62
monetization strategies
  app advertisements 261
  app, offering for free 260
  app, selling 258
  app, upselling 258
  data, selling 263
  of app 258
  product, selling in real world 259
  services, selling 260
Monthly Active Users (MAU) 17, 326
movie locations
  references 135

N

native apps
  about 118
  benefits 119
  pros and cons 118
  versus hybrid apps 118
network effect 304, 305
Non Disclosure Agreement (NDA) 252
notification
  in-app notifications 229
  local notifications 228
  push notifications 229
  push notifications, services 230, 232
  sending 240
  used, for communication with app 228

O

onboarding app
  about 160
  implementation 162, 164, 166, 174, 176, 177
  signing up 161
onboarding patterns
  continuous onboarding 155
  introduction approach 155
  joy ride approach 155
  social sign up 155
onboarding
  about 152

summarizing 153
URL 156
One Metric That Matters (OMTM) 26
Over the Air (OTA) 294

P

Parse
  about 92
  services, available as MBaaS 93
  strategic considerations 92
  technical considerations 95
payment service provider (PSP) 260
pirate metrics 206, 208
Pirate metrics (AARRR)
  about 154
  barrier, lowering 155
  social network, using for single sign on 156
platform effect 304, 305
price perception 264
pricing strategy
  about 264
  applying, to store listing 275, 277
  in-app billing products, for Android 268
  in-app purchase product types, for iOS 266
  platform, selecting 266
  price perception 264
  reference link 266
product
  services, selling in real world 259
productFlavors 287
Proof of Concept (PoC) 66, 89
push notifications
  about 229
  implementation 233
  services 230, 232
  setup 234, 235, 236, 237

R

refactoring
  need for 253
Repository 282
Representational State Transfer (REST) 91

S

Salesforce desk
  URL 314
scalability 244
scaling down
  need for 251
scaling up
  need for 251, 253
scaling
  about 187
  backend 246
  from client perspective 249, 251
  issues, troubleshooting 252
  overloaded backend 252
Scrum
  about 41
  URL 48
self hosted website 294
services
  Azure 94
  BaasBox 94
  Back4App 93
  backendless 94
  CloudBoost.io 94
  Firebase 94
  Parse server 94
  PubNub 94
  QuickBlox 94
  remoteStorage 94
  SashiDo 93
shortcuts
  availability, investigating 65
signingConfigs 290, 291
small-scale laboratory
  establishing 182
  narrow marketplace, focusing 182
  user experience, perfecting 183
SocialOomph
  URL 317
Software as a Service (SaaS) 89
Software Development Kit (SDK) 90, 130
Sonar 284
SonarQube
  about 280

URL 281
sourceSets 288, 289
split testing
   actionable metrics, obtaining 212
   Firebase, using 213, 218, 219, 220
   tools, using 212
   used, for improving apps 209
   variations, differentiating 211
Start-up list
   about 225
   reference link 225
startup methodology 11
statistics
   importance 204, 205
sustainability 187

T

taplytics 212
TeamCity
   about 279, 284
   using, as build agent 291, 292, 293
technical capabilities 116
technical considerations
   automation 188
   coding shortcuts, initiating 187
   optimization 188
   technical debt, handling 188
technical requisites 116
Test-driven Development (TDD) 283
things that do not scale
   data collection 180
   failure controlling 181
   products, developing 181
   reasons 180
   scenarios 180
   testing 180
time-boxed programming
   about 54
   concierge service 55
   features 56
   features, releasing 56
tools, cross-platform development
   ionic 125
   libgdx 125
   Mobile Angular 125

Progress Telerik platform 125
Sencha Ext JS 125
unity 125
tools
   using 48, 50
traction
   about 224
   freemium 225
   premium 225
   retention, improving 226
Traditional search 199
Trello
   URL 49

U

Uber
   reference 140
   references 136
Unique Selling Points (USP) 59
unique value proposition (UVP) 130
unscalable MVP
   learning, with prototypes 185
   learning, with wireframes 185
   transitioning, to scalable code 184
   Zeplin 186
Upwork
   URL 317
users
   app ratings, maintaining 36
   app, using 15, 18
   information, obtaining 208
   obtaining, to download app 35
UserTesting.com 186
UX testing methods 75

V

vertical markets
   switching costs 308
   switching costs, decreasing of competitor 310
   switching costs, using to improve user retention
      309
   targeting 307
   using 306
   vertical control, exploiting 307

W

WebsiteAlive
  URL 314

X

Xamarin 124

Y

Yahoo's Flurry Pulse

URL 115

Z

ZenDesk Chat
  URL 314
Zendesk
  URL 313
Zeplin 186
Zoho desk
  URL 314

Printed in Great Britain
by Amazon

22481328R00209